Palgrave Studies in European Union Politics

Following on the sustained success of the acclaimed European Union Series, which essentially publishes research-based textbooks, Palgrave Studies in European Union Politics publishes cutting edge research-driven monographs. The remit of the series is broadly defined, both in terms of subject and academic discipline. All topics of significance concerning the nature and operation of the European Union potentially fall within the scope of the series. The series is multidisciplinary to reflect the growing importance of the EU as a political, economic and social phenomenon. To submit a proposal, please contact Senior Editor Ambra Finotello ambra.finotello@palgrave.com.

This series is indexed by Scopus.

Cristina Fasone · Adriano Dirri · Ylenia Guerra
Editors

EU Rule of Law Procedures at the Test Bench

Managing Dissensus in the European Constitutional Landscape

palgrave
macmillan

Editors
Cristina Fasone
Department of Political Science
Luiss University
Rome, Italy

Adriano Dirri
Department of Political Science
Luiss University
Rome, Italy

Ylenia Guerra
Department of Political Science
Luiss University
Rome, Italy

ISSN 2662-5873 ISSN 2662-5881 (electronic)
Palgrave Studies in European Union Politics
ISBN 978-3-031-60007-4 ISBN 978-3-031-60008-1 (eBook)
https://doi.org/10.1007/978-3-031-60008-1

Cover illustration: Magic Lens/Shutterstock

This Palgrave Macmillan imprint is published by the registered company Springer Nature Switzerland AG
The registered company address is: Gewerbestrasse 11, 6330 Cham, Switzerland

Foreword: Fuzzy Borders

Certain things about shared political values are so evident that dissensus on them is out of the question; dissensus, in its strongest meaning of the rejection of what is shared, places dissenters beyond the pale. But other things concerning the same values may neither be clear nor require consensus. And, in between these two, the boundary line may be fuzzy.

The rule of law is uncontestably fundamental to democracy in the European Union and its member states ever since the 1950s, so much is certain and clear. From its inception, pluralist liberal democracy under the rule of law was, more than just the accepted standard, the very criterion of like-mindedness of the countries that participated in the process of European integration. In this respect, it was an ideological rival of communism East of the Iron Curtain. Moreover, this criterion was the reason to refuse any formal arrangement of association or cooperation with the fascist regimes in Spain and Portugal (Janse 2018).

At the same time, it was quite clear that the constitutional shape of the institutions of democracy under the rule of law differed quite a bit between the original partners. The new Constitutions of Italy and Germany of 1947 and 1949, and constitutional reforms in France in the 1950s, as compared to the old nineteenth-century Constitutions of the Benelux countries, confirmed the fact that systems of government, electoral systems, vertical and horizontal conceptions of division of powers, and the shape of the administration could differ considerably, without questioning the very nature of the member states as politically pluralist democracies under the rule of law.

This state of affairs has not changed. From the Treaty of Maastricht onwards to the Lisbon Treaty, the pluralist democratic foundations and rule of law have been canonized in what is now Article 2 of the Treaty on European Union. Liberty, democracy, fundamental rights, the rule of law and pluralism are foundations both of the member states and of the Union. On this, there can be no uncertainty, ambivalence or ambiguity. Equally, there is no doubt that reasonable differences can legitimately exist as to how these principles are to be given shape in constitutional and politico-institutional arrangements.

Rejection of the underlying political values—dissensus in a strong sense—is impossible, as that would undermine the very foundations of the Union; rational disagreement on their implications for the, often 'path-dependent', institutional design and practical application in the member states is part of the pluralist nature of the Union.

It is easy to agree on this. It is less easy to make out when rational disagreement on the implications of the foundational values for institutional design and political practice turns into dissensus on the foundational values themselves.[1] Clearly the borders between the one and the other are fuzzy.

This difficulty of distinguishing with exactitude between allegiance to the foundational value of the rule of law, deciding when it is transgressed, and when it is rejected, spills over in the issue of how to deal with the infringement, the transgression and rejection of the rule of law, which is the central theme of this very important book.

The matter is further complicated by the boundaries of European integration as a political and legal project, which for us lawyers raises the question of the scope of European law, and of its demarcation from matters that are left to the legal and political orders of member states. For one thing, this issue is decisive for the competence of the Union, which hinges on the concrete conferral of powers on the Union.

There is a striking consensus among legal scholars that the scope of Article 2 of the Treaty on European Union is quite different from that of the scope of EU law in the ordinary sense in all other legal contexts. The ordinary scope of EU law hinges on the question of whether a matter is

[1] See in particular Parts II and III of this book.

the object of a competence found in the EU treaties, or is regulated on the basis of a norm that is ultimately based on the treaties, or otherwise touches on such powers or rules. This kind of demarcation is absent in Article 2 TEU, because it concerns the broad political values on which both the Union and the member state legal orders are based. It does not separate the legal orders, but emphasizes the commonality in values that transcend specific powers and normative scopes. Article 2 sums up the values on which the Union is founded and which are common to the Member States. From the Union perspective, these values are not restricted to the Union's specific competences or the operation of Union law; from the Member State perspective, these values do not target the specific operation or realization of the Union and its laws in the Member States. They are foundational values which are at the basis of the exercise of all public authority both by the Union and by the Member States.

Article 2, therefore, necessarily refers not solely to the activity of the Union within the Member State, nor solely to Member State activity concerning the implementation of Union law or the Union's specific competence. This wide scope of the values spills over into the scope of the mechanisms for compliance with and enforcement of Article 2 values, notably the value and principle of the rule of law. Generally, the specific enforcement mechanism of the EU Treaty, Article 7, has been considered the only provision conferring a power on the Union over matters which relate to Member State activity which can be outside the scope of EU law in the ordinary, narrower sense. As this activity concerns values which are also the values of the Member State concerned, we are in a situation that is doubly sensitive: on the one hand, this is due to the constitutional nature of the Member State activity and on the other hand, due to the Union acting with regard to Member State activity which can be completely outside the scope of Union law in the strict sense. This sensitivity may explain the quite 'political' nature of the Article 7 procedure, where it is the European Council and Council that hold the most decisive powers.

In the classic 'legal' instruments for the respect and enforcement of the founding values, such as the preliminary reference and infringement proceedings, the decisional power lies with the Court of Justice. In its case law, one can see how the Court tends to tie the scope of its review powers to the scope of EU law in the ordinary sense, for instance when it comes to the independence of the national courts, which are viewed in as far as they are Union courts under Article 19 TEU. Somewhat similarly, in infringement proceedings regarding the foundational value of the rule of law, there has mainly been an emphasis on elements of a 'thinner' or more formal understanding of the concept of the rule of law (a *locus classicus* is Tamanaha 2004, Chapter 7). But this, of course, cannot be said of the infringement proceedings that were started on the *lex Tusk* for reason of its infringement of the principle of democracy—of which we will have to wait and see whether and how the Court will get the chance to delimit its justiciability (see in particular Piccirilli, Cecchetti (Chapter 4), and Cecchetti (Chapter 5) in this Volume).

The importance of competition law and state aid law would traditionally be understood to be at the core of the market economy. As is argued in this book, when looked at more closely, they are also at the service of democracy and the rule of law (see Cseres in this Volume). This highlights the links between on the one hand what may at first sight seem strictly technical economic market control as an instrument of economic integration, and on the other hand the broader impact of the economic constitution of the Union and the member states on their political constitution. This has also become evident in the sphere of fiscal and other economic governance mechanisms (see Capati and Christiansen, Fasone and Simoncini, Hegedus and Christiansen, and Lupo in this Volume). The fuzzy borders between EU law in the strict sense and national constitutional competence become perhaps most acute in the area of soft law and voluntary Union *cum* member state instruments, which have recently become topical in the context of the recovery and resilience facility, and in particular through their being subjected to 'rule of law conditionality'.

Most, if not all, of the contributions to this volume implicitly or explicitly are confronted with the fuzzy boundaries of Union and member state law as regards the founding principles of Article 2 TEU of which the rule of law is the one that is focused on in this volume.

This book provides a unique analysis of all available instruments of rule of law enforcement and maps out the issues of the border areas of the rule of law as a shared value of Union and member states, conceptually, legally and politically. It thus provides us with an intriguing sketch of the present state of European integration.

Leonard F. M. Besselink
University of Amsterdam
Amsterdam, The Netherlands

References

Janse, R. (2018). The evolution of the political criteria for accession to the European Community, 1957–1973, *European law journal: review of European law in context*, 24:1, 57–76.

Tamanaha, B. Z. (2004). *On the Rule of Law: History, Politics, Theory*, Cambridge University Press.

Leonard F. M. Besselink (Ph.D. at EUI) has been Professor of Constitutional Law at the Faculty of Law of the University of Amsterdam since 2012. He is affiliated to the Amsterdam Centre for European Law and Governance, ACELG, and is emeritus since September 2021. Prior to his position in Amsterdam he held the chair of European Constitutional Law at the University of Utrecht. Since 2021 he teaches at Luiss University's Law Department and School of Law, Rome. He is a member of the Royal Dutch Society of Sciences and Humanities, and was a member of the Royal Committee on the Constitution (Staatscommissie Grondwet 2008–2010) tendering advise to the Netherlands government on amending the Dutch Constitution to bring it up to date in various respects. He has participated in many research consortia and has published mainly in the fields of national constitutional law, European constitutional law and comparative constitutional law, with a particular thematic focus on the nexus between public international, European Union and national law, as well as issues of the rule of law and fundamental rights protection in Europe. He is one of the editors of the European Constitutional Law Review and among his many publications, he has authored a monograph on A Composite European Constitution (Europa Law Publishing, 2007).

Acknowledgments

This Volume has been drafted and funded in the framework of the European Union under Grant Agreement no. 101061621, RED-SPINEL—HORIZON-CL2-2021-DEMOCRACY-01, Work package no. 2. Views and opinions expressed are however those of the author(s) only and do not necessarily reflect those of the European Union. The European Union cannot be held responsible for them.

Contents

Notes on Contributors

Andrea Capati is a Postdoctoral researcher and teaching assistant in the Department of Political Science at LUISS Guido Carli University, Rome. His research interests lie in the institutions and policies of the Economic and Monetary Union, with a focus on financial assistance and fiscal integration. He obtained his Ph.D. in 2023 with a thesis titled "European Integration in the Pandemic Era: A 'Critical Junctures' Analysis of EU Financial Crisis Management following the Outbreak of COVID-19". Some of his recent publications have been featured in *Journal of European Integration*, *Politics and Governance* and *European Politics and Society*.

Lorenzo Cecchetti is Postdoctoral Research Fellow in EU Law at Luiss University. He holds a Law Degree (magna cum laude) from Luiss (2015), a Ph.D. in European Law from the University of Bologna, and a *Doctorat en Droi*t from the *Université Paris II* (2021). He has been Trainee Judicial Clerk in the Chambers of Judge Prof. Lucia Serena Rossi at the European Court of Justice (2019) and of Justice Silvana Sciarra at the Italian Constitutional Court (2022–2023). His main research interests are focused on EU Constitutional Law, EU Social Law, EU Internal Market Law and EU Procedural Law and he is working on a monograph on the fundamental labor rights and the Charter of Fundamental Rights of the EU. He has been Visiting Scholar at Durham University, Research Visitor at the University of Cambridge and Academic Visitor at the University of Oxford.

Thomas Christiansen is Professor of Political Science and European Integration at Luiss University, Rome. He previously held positions at Maastricht University, at the European Institute of Public Administration, at Aberystwyth University of Wales and at Essex University. He is Executive Editor of the *Journal of European Integration* and co-editor (with Sophie Vanhoonacker) of the "European Administration Governance" book series at Palgrave Macmillan. He has published widely on different aspects of European Union politics. He co-authored, with Emil Kirchner and Uwe Wissenbach, *The European Union and China* (London: Palgrave, 2019) and co-edited, with Emil Kirchner and Han Dorussen *Security Relations between the European Union and China* (Cambridge: Cambridge, 2016). *The Contestation of Expertise in the European Union* (London: Palgrave), co-edited with Johan Adriaensen and Vigjilenca Abazi, *The Making of European Security Policy*, co-edited with Roberta Haar, Sabina Lange and Sophie Vanhoonacker (London: Routledge) and *Security Relations between the European Union and Asian Partners*, co-edited with Emil Kirchner and Tan See Seng (London: Palgrave) were all published in 2021, followed by the publication of *The Routledge Handbook of Parliamentary Admnistrations* (London, Routledge), co-edited with Elena Griglio and Nicola Lupo, in 2023. In the period 2019–2023 he was academic coordinator of the EU-funded research network EAST (EU-Asia Security and Trade Relations) involving seven universities and think tanks across three continents.

Ylenia Maria Citino is a Postdoctoral Research Fellow of Public Law at Scuola Superiore Sant'Anna (Pisa) and a Member of the Center for Studies on Parliament (CESP). Prior to her current role, she served as a Post-Doc at Luiss University. She currently holds positions as a Contract Professor of Public Comparative Law at the University of Tuscia in Viterbo, of EU Law at the LUISS School of Government and of Comparative Parliamentary Law at the University of Luxembourg.

Dr. Citino contributed as a Visiting Researcher at the European Commission, DG CONNECT, and the Center for European Law at Maastricht University. Her doctoral thesis earned her the prize for the Best Doctoral Dissertation on Public Law by the Book Series "Sovranità, Federalismo, Diritti", a collaboration between the University of Insubria and the Gruppo di Pisa in 2019. She is an alumnus of the École Nationale d'Administration in France.

Ramona Coman is Professor in Political Science at the Université libre de Bruxelles, where she served as Director of the Institut d'études européennes (2014–2019) and as its President (2019–2023). She is the author of The Politics of the Rule of Law in the EU Polity Actors, Tools and Challenges (2022, Palgrave Studies in European Union Politics) and co-editor of the textbook Governance and Politics in the Post-Crisis European Union (2019). Her research focuses on dynamics of policy/ institutional change, democratization and Europeanization. Particular attention is devoted to the EU's rule of law policy tools and judicial reforms in Central and Eastern Europe. As of October 2022, she is the Principal Investigator of the Horizon Europe project "Respond to Emerging Dissensus: Supranational Instruments and Norms of European Democracy" (RED-SPINEL, 2022–2025) and the academic coordinator of the GEM-DIAMOND Marie Sklodowska Curie Action Joint Doctorate Network. She has published in several peer-reviewed journals, including Democratization, the New Political Economy, Journal of European Public Policy, The British Journal of Politics and International Relations, Journal of European Integration, Europe-Asia Studies, Perspective on European Politics and Societies, Revue française de Science politique, Politique européenne.

Katalin J. Cseres is Associate Professor of Law at the Amsterdam Centre for European Law and Governance (ACELG) and Program Director of the EU Law Masters at the University of Amsterdam. She is the Co-Director of The Good Lobby Profs initiative, which monitors the respect of the rule of law by holding the EU and national institutions and leaders accountable. Kati is Editor of the Journal Legal Issues of Economic Integration.

Kati's research investigates uneven power structures and relations in *(EU) competition law, consumer law, constitutional law and sector regulation (energy law)*. She interrogates how various sub-disciplines of law, formal and informal institutions structure power relations in the oversight of markets and which tools they provide for controlling power. She investigates how prevailing models of economic law and its enforcement can respond to challenges of growing political and corporate concentration as well as social inequalities.

Adriano Dirri is a Postdoctoral Research Fellow in Comparative Public Law at Luiss University, within the EU Horizon project RED-Spinel ("Responding to Emerging Dissensus: SuPranational Instruments and

Norms of European Liberal democracy"). Previously, he was Postdoctoral Researcher in Public Law at the University of Rome-"La Sapienza", lecturer at SciencesPo-Menton Campus in Law and Political Institutions and he benefited from a Scholarship of the University of Fribourg (Institute for Federalism) at the postdoctoral level. He was awarded of the Giancarlo Doria Prize for the best PhD thesis in 2021. He holds a Ph.D. in State Theory and Comparative Political Institutions at the University of Rome-"La Sapienza". He was Visiting Ph.D. Student at the University of the Western Cape-South Africa and Visiting Ph.D. Student at the Institute for Comparative Federalism at the Eurac Research. His main research interests are Comparative Constitutional Law, focusing on comparative federalism both in European and non-European Countries, especially in Africa. Currently is working on the European Union federalizing process as well as over the Rule of Law in the European Union in its interplay with the Conditionality Regulation.

Cristina Fasone is Associate Professor of Comparative Public Law at Luiss University, where she is also the Director of the BA in "Politics, Philosophy, and Economics", and Visiting Professor at Nicolaus Copernicus University of Toruń since 2020. She holds a Ph.D. in Comparative Public Law from the University of Siena and has been Max Weber postdoctoral fellow in Law (2013–2015), at the EUI. Holder of a Jean Monnet Module 2016–2019 "Parliamentary accountability and technical expertise: Budgetary Powers, Information and Communication Technologies and Elections" (PATEU), until January 2023 she has been the coordinator at Luiss research unit of the Horizon Europe Project RED-SPINEL. She was member of the Steering Committee of the ECPR Research Network on Differentiated Integration in the EU (2021–2023) and she is currently the co-coordinator of the Research Group on "Judicial Review and Electoral Law" of the International Association of Constitutional Law for which she has recently co-edited *Judicial Review and Electoral Law in a Global Perspective* (Hart Publishing, 2024). She has been Visiting Scholar at the Victoria University of Wellington, Georgetown Law Center, Uppsala University, Complutense University, the University of Copenhagen, Durham Law School.

Ylenia Guerra is Postdoctoral Research Fellow in Constitutional Law at Luiss University, within the EU Horizon project RED-Spinel ("Responding to Emerging Dissensus: SuPranational Instruments and

Norms of European Liberal democracy"). Previously, she was Postdoctoral Researcher in Constitutional Law at the University of Macerata. She holds a Ph.D. in Constitutional Law at the *Alma Mater Studiorum*-University of Bologna (with excellent marks) and an LL.M. in European Legal Studies from the College of Europe, in Bruges. She was Visiting Researcher at the University of Toulon, in the "Centre de Droit et Politique Comparés" (CDPC) and Visiting Researcher at the Max Planck Institut für ausländisches öffentliches Recht und Völkerrecht in Heidelberg, where she attended the Italian dialogues, presenting the first results of her research on the way of conditionality in Europe. Her research interests are concentrated on Constitutional Law, with a focus on the constitutional protection of the Environment, the theoretical dimension of future generations and their representation, as well as the intersection between the "Rule of Law" and the use of conditionality, in connection with the Horizon Project RED-Spinel.

Dora Hegedus is Ph.D. Candidate in the Department of Political Science at LUISS University in Rome, conducting research for a doctoral thesis with the provisional title "Towards a Europe of Subregions? Investigating the Illiberal Challenge of the Visegrad Group". Prior to coming to LUISS, she studied International Relations at Queen Mary University, and then worked at the Hungarian Embassy in London for two years before obtaining an M.Sc. degree in "Global Europe: Culture and Conflict" from the London School of Economics and Political Science. Her research interests include EU integration, subregionalism, democratic backsliding, the rule of law and Central Eastern European politics.

Nicola Lupo is Professor of Public Law and Director of the Center for Parliamentary Studies (Centro di studi sul Parlamento) at LUISS University in Rome. He has been the holder of a Jean Monnet Chair on "Understanding European Representative Democracy" (2018–2021) and visiting professor at several universities. His publications concern sources of law, parliamentary rules of procedures, legislative drafting, budgetary procedures, regional councils, EU parliamentary democracy. Among them, *The Constitution of Italy. A Contextual Analysis* (Hart, 2022, con Marta Cartabia), *Corso di diritto parlamentare* (Il Mulino, IV ed., 2023, with Luigi Gianniti) and *Il Parlamento europeo. Una introduzione* (Luiss University Press, II ed., 2024, with Andrea Manzella).

Alessandro Nato is Assistant Professor (Tenure Track) and former Postdoctoral Research Fellow at the Luiss University, Department of Law, Postdoctoral Research fellow and Assistant Professor at Faculty of Law, University of Gent. He holds a Ph.D. in Civil, Corporate, and International Law at the University of Genoa. His research interests concern EU Law. He is the author of the monograph "La Cittadinanza sociale europea ai tempi della crisi economica" [European social citizenship at the time of the economic crisis] (Cacucci editore: Bari, 2020). He was part of the research project Horizon 2020 RECONNECT (2019–2022), Hercule III BETKOSOL on the protection of EU financial interest (1 January 2021–30 June 2022), and EUARENAS. Furthermore, He was part of the teaching academic team of EUPRACT JM Chair led by Prof. Daniele Gallo, LUISS University. He is also Adjunct Professor in EU Law at University of Macerata, Department of Political Science (from 1 September 2022).

Giovanni Piccirilli is Associate Professor in Constitutional Law at the Law Department of LUISS University in Rome, where he is also Deputy director of the Center for Parliamentary Studies and Coordinator of the Executive Programme in Legislative drafting.

He holds a Ph.D. from the University of Genoa.

In 2016 he has been awarded of a Jean Monnet Module on "Legislative drafting in implementing EU law in Italy" by the EACEA. In 2019 he received funds from the Ministry of Education, University and Research as part of the consortium led by Scuola superiore Sant'Anna in Pisa on the topic "The challenge of Interlegality: A new perspective on Law".

He was Emile Noel Fellow at the Jean Monnet Center, New York University (USA, 2013), and visiting professor at the Institute of Advanced Legal Studies (UK, 2017), at the Center of European Studies, University of Florida (USA, 2012), and EUOSSIC Visitor at the Monash University (Australia, 2013).

Maciej Serowaniec is prof. NCU—Full Professor at Nicolaus Copernicus University in Toruń (Poland); Head of the Department of Constitutional Law of the Faculty of Law and Administration of NCU; Vice-Dean for International Cooperation of the Faculty of Law and Administration; A principal investigator of the project "Supreme Audit Institutions in the constitutional systems of the Member States of the European Union", funded by the National Science Center (grant No. 2018/02/X/HS5 /00047). Participated as a coordinator and investigator in the project "Responding to Emerging Dissensus: Supranational Instruments & Norms of European Liberal Democracy (Horizon Europe) and in the research project "BETKOSOL—Better Knowledge for Better Solutions", founded by the European Union's Hercule III Programme). Laureate of the European Court of Auditors Postgraduate Research Grant Programme. Laureate of the Scholarship of the Minister of Science and Higher Education for outstanding young scientists. A member of the ICON-S and Scientific Society in Toruń.

Marta Simoncini is Associate professor in administrative law at Luiss University. Marta holds a Ph.D. in administrative law (University of Pisa), a Laurea in Political Sciences, majoring law (University of Pisa) and a University Diploma in the same area (Scuola Superiore Sant'Anna in Pisa). Prior to joining Luiss University, Marta was an FWO postdoctoral fellow at King's College London and the University of Antwerp, a fellow in EU law at University College London and a Max Weber fellow at the European University Institute. Marta is also a fellow of the UK Higher Education Academy.

Her research interests cover European administrative law and governance, in particular the check-and-balances applicable to discretion. She published in peer-reviewed journals, including the Yearbook of European Law and Common Market Law Review. She authored two monographs for Hart Publishing (2018) and for Editoriale Scientifica (2010). She also co-edited a volume for Routledge (2017).

Pauline Thinus is a Ph.D. researcher at the Institute for European Studies (IEE-ULB) since 2022. Her research is focused on rule of law spending conditionality in the European Union throughout the 2021–2027 budgetary cycle. She holds a M.A. in European interdisciplinary studies from the College of Europe (Natolin, Poland) and a M.A. in European studies and political science from Sciences Po (Rennes, France). She has previously worked as an Academic Assistant at the College of Europe from 2020 to 2022 in the European Political and Governance Studies Department (Bruges, Belgium). She has also worked for the French Institute in Budapest in 2019–2020 as a lecturer in European and international relations at the Faculty of Law and Political Science in Szeged (Hungary).

List of Figures

List of Tables

CHAPTER 1

Introduction: Dissensus as a Trigger and Consequence of the Rule of Law Crisis in the EU

Cristina Fasone, Adriano Dirri, and Ylenia Guerra

1 The Context and the State-of-the-art in the Literature

Unfortunately, it is anything but new to claim that constitutional democracies and the entrenchment of the rule of law values are in crisis (Ginsburg & Huq, 2018; Graber et al., 2018). Over the last few years, the rule of law crisis in the EU has increased in scope and intensity, triggering the proliferation of academic work in the area. Some have particularly

C. Fasone · A. Dirri (✉) · Y. Guerra
Luiss University, Rome, Italy
e-mail: adirri@luiss.it

C. Fasone
e-mail: cfasone@luiss.it

Y. Guerra
e-mail: yguerra@luiss.it

C. Fasone et al. (eds.), *EU Rule of Law Procedures at the Test Bench*, Palgrave Studies in European Union Politics,
https://doi.org/10.1007/978-3-031-60008-1_1

engaged with the unfolding of the rule of law at the domestic level and the rise of illiberalism (Drinóczi & Bień-Kacała, 2021; Sadurski, 2019; Sajò, 2021; Sajò & Uitz, 2021). Others have considered the influence of the "polycrisis" in Europe on the rule of law (Wacks, 2021) and have engaged with the tension between democracy, underpinned by extreme majoritarianism and populism, and the rule of law principle in the broader EU context (Amato et al., 2021).

Scholars have further explored the EU rule of law crisis by looking at the problematic reception of supranational "counter-measures" at the Member State level, highlighting the deterioration of separation of powers at the domestic level and the lack of cooperation by national institutions (von Bogdandy et al., 2021). They have traced the evolution of the rule of law concept in the EU from its origins, unpacked the notion into its various components, and dealt with selected instruments like infringement proceedings, the rule of law conditionality regulation, and the EU external action (Pohjankoski et al., 2023).

Moreover, academic contributions have devised further rule of law mechanisms to be introduced in the EU and have advocated for refining the existing ones (Closa & Kochenov, 2016; Jakab & Kochenov, 2017; Södersten & Herkock, 2023). The scholarly solutions put forward have often served to orient institutional debates or form the basis for policymaking; this was the case for studies linking spending conditionality to rule of law purposes (Halmai, 2019; Kelemen & Scheppele, 2018). At times, the literature has even anticipated institutional needs. This is exemplified, for example, by research published just prior to the Polish national elections of October 2023 disclosing the paths to and difficulties of undergoing a second transition to democracy in countries that have experienced recent rule of law backsliding (Bobek et al., 2023),

This edited collection seeks to assess the variety of EU rule of law instruments as they function in their actual deployment by looking at their diverse nature and the mutual interplay between them. It aims to do so by taking as its starting point the study of the political dynamics of rule of law oversight in the EU, which will be framed according to the tension between consensus and dissensus (Coman, 2022).

2 Dissensus on the EU Rule of Law Instruments as a New Paradigm of Constitutional Analysis

The rule of law is a founding value of the EU and, together with other values enshrined in Article 2 TEU, forms its constitutional skeleton. The crisis of the rule of law, to which scholars have devoted considerable attention (for the most recent studies, see Pohjankoski et al., 2023; Södersten & Herkock, 2023; Spieker, 2023; von Bogdandy, 2024), has been an important test bench for the enforcement of several hard and soft law instruments in the EU.

On the one hand, these instruments were adopted in reaction to the rising dissensus against the rule of law principles seen at the national level with reforms undermining judicial independence and media freedom, for instance. On the other hand, the instruments themselves have become the targets of dissensus, for different reasons, by both the autocrats dismantling the constitutional democracy and those advocating for a prompt, coherent and decisive reaction by EU institutions surrounded instead by the rhetoric and practice of inaction (Emmons & Pavone, 2021: 1611 ff.).

Over the years, particularly since 2014, EU institutions have deployed an increasing number of instruments of varied nature as rule of law-related issues have gradually worsened within the EU (Closa & Kochenov, 2016; Jakab & Kochenov, 2017). These tools include mechanisms regulated under EU primary law (Part I) and legislation (Part II), soft law measures (Part III) and instruments linked to the EU budget and economic interests (Part IV). This volume aims to provide a comprehensive understanding of the interaction among the EU tools adopted or re-adapted to face the rule of law crisis, using dissensus as a new paradigm for constitutional analysis and as a form of contestation against liberal democracy that has become somewhat mainstream (Coman & Brack, 2023). The effort spent countering illiberal practices and rule of law deterioration in some EU member states through a growing arsenal of legal instruments devised by the EU has been the target of mounting academic and institutional dissensus. It is precisely this dissensus that is the object of the volume when analyzing existing EU rule of law instruments in action. The volume is not meant to endorse a specific or strict definition of dissensus nor to provide an analytic examination of each tool across time and space (for such an analysis, see, e.g., Coman, 2022: 37 ff.). Rather, it explores the emergence of contrasting academic views on the functioning of the various instruments, contestation of their enforcement and effectiveness, criticisms raised from within EU institutions, and potential conflicts, including inter-institutional conflicts, that have been triggered by the implementation of the various tools.

Framed this way, dissensus can materialize in different forms. It can be led by criticism of the doubtful enforcement of a particular tool, such as Article 7 TEU and the lack of follow-up on the activation of its paragraph 1 against Poland and Hungary; the volume looks at how the literature has dealt with this questionable stalemate (see R. Coman and P. Thinus in this volume). Dissensus can also be triggered by the interpretation of legal instruments, as has been the case for the reach and scope of the application of the Charter of Fundamental Rights (in particular Article 47) in combination with other Treaty provisions (see L. Cecchetti, Chapter 5 in this volume). This has also arisen for some procedures shaping the process of EU integration since its formation, like the infringement proceeding and the preliminary ruling procedure (PRP; see G. Piccirilli and L. Cecchetti in this volume). These tools have been adapted to serve the protection of the rule of law principles and have become channels of dissensus, either in the struggle between the EU and the Member State under review or between private parties and the national authorities contested, with the Court of Justice (CJEU) and national courts acting as arbiters in the disputes. The CJEU itself has been criticized, however, for its inconsistent and ambiguous attitude toward the rule of law and, especially, for its compliance with the standards of judicial independence (Kochenov & Bárd, 2022). The rise in the number of court cases dealing with rule of law issues in the EU (Pech & Kochenov, 2021) is proof of the level of dissensus currently experienced and the inability of politics to solve the issue, being that it is quite difficult to compromise on fundamental values such as the rule of law. Even when a (questionable) political compromise has been sealed, for example on the rule of law conditionality regulation (Baraggia & Bonelli, 2022; D. Hegedűs & T. Christiansen, in this volume; Sheppele et al., 2020), this has not prevented the use of strategic litigation in front of the CJEU (see cases C-156/21 and C-157/21).

The dissensus surrounding the use of the EU rule of law instruments is somewhat inherent in their design, especially for the binding instruments and those with the most far-reaching consequences in principle. They touch upon the sensitive area of domestic constitutional law, principles and values, which is closely related to the remains of national sovereignty and is typically used to resist EU law and policies. It was not by chance that the alleged variety of (national) definitions of the rule of law has been instrumentally mobilized to this end (Pech et al., 2020: 45 ff.), even though there is a clear and univocal understanding of the rule of law in the EU that was derived from the CJEU's case law and is now enshrined in Article 2 of Regulation No. 2020/2092 (Pech, 2022):

> It includes the principles of legality implying a transparent, accountable, democratic and pluralistic law-making process; legal certainty; prohibition of arbitrariness of the executive powers; effective judicial protection, including access to justice, by independent and impartial courts, also as regards fundamental rights; separation of powers; and non-discrimination and equality before the law.

Dissensus, also on legal measures, is certainly not new in the EU. As an example, the "jurisprudence of constitutional conflict" (Bobić, 2022; see also Martinico, 2022) at times featured the relationship between the CJEU and national constitutional judges, which tends to be quite destructive to the rule of law on the national level and moves away from the basic principle of sincere cooperation (Article 4, para 3 TEU: see, e.g. the Polish Constitutional Tribunal's ruling K 3/21, of 7 October 2021). The level of inter-institutional dissensus surrounding the rule of law has also increased, with the European Parliament being usually more vocal on rule of law concerns than the Council and the Commission. This was exemplified by the European Parliament's action for failure to act, under Article 265 TFEU, against the Commission for delaying the implementation of the rule of law conditionality Regulation, however problematic that was from the point of view of effectiveness (Platon, 2021).

Dissensus often has a negative connotation, made worse by the destructive nature of rule of law conflicts fueled by populism and legalism (Groussot & Zemkova, 2022). However, dissensus can also show a positive side being typically the outcome of pluralism and of different points of view, to be reconciled through democratic and political procedures. Dissensus can also enable EU institutions to engage in self-reflection and self-criticism when needed. The perspective of dissensus is also promising in that it enables the study of rule of law instruments from the perspective of how powers and competencies are effectively channeled in procedural terms. One of the major sources of tension between the domestic and the supranational levels of government is precisely the scope of EU action in this domain.

The volume looks at dissensus on the rule of law's toolbox as a problem targeting European integration, especially in its legal and constitutional dimensions. The growth and the broadening of the scope of such instruments, whether directly or indirectly dedicated to the protection of the rule of law, have proven not to be as effective as it was foreseen. Even the resort to the economic and financial leverage, which has marked an upgrade in the EU rule of law strategy is not exempted from some pitfalls and shortcomings. For example, in a recent Special Report, the EU Court of Auditors assessed the difficulties in the application of the new conditionality Regulation, mainly related to the requirement to establish a sufficient link between breaches to the rule of law principles and the protection of EU financial interests (European Court of Auditors, 2024: 5).

3 The Main Trends in EU Rule Toolbox's Dissensus

From the review of the various instruments three elements and trends seem to deserve special attention from the perspective of dissensus. First, the circumstance that the growing set of rule of law instruments is not necessarily promoting better results, as the detachment between the theory and the practice of the rule of law seems to prove. The relationship between the various instruments is to a large extent unsettled, thereby creating some confusion as to when it is appropriate to use each of them. Some tools, like the PRP or the rule of law conditionality regulation, are certainly complementary to the already existing ones, some being more generic (e.g., the infringement proceeding) and some being narrower in focus (e.g., the technical support instrument, on which see A. Dirri and Y. Guerra in this volume). In general, the dissensus can also be seen, at least from an academic perspective, as criticism and disappointment against the uncoordinated proliferation of soft law instruments (rule of law reports, rule of law dialogue, etc.: Part III) none of them alone is decisive to tackle rule of law problems. There is also the issue of overlapping between instruments as it was, just to mention one case, between the Cooperation and Verification Mechanism (see A. Dirri in this volume) and the Rule of Law Reports (see Y. M. Citino in this volume), with the former that has been embodied in the latter. At times, the overlapping, instrumental in creating synergies between the tools, as it is for the many conditionality regimes all targeting the lack of independence of the judiciary (RRF conditionality, Charter enabling condition under the CPR and the rule of law conditionality Regulation) if not well explained to the stakeholders and the public may create uncertainty, confusion and the allegation of an inconsistent approach by the Commission (see C. Fasone and M. Simoncini in this volume).

Second, there is a certain degree of disagreement and, hence, of dissensus, especially in the literature, on the qualitative and quantitative indicators setting the scoreboard for the assessment of the national performance on the rule of law and, in general, on how to check compliance with the rule of law principles in a systematic manner. For example, the EU Justice Scoreboard, which forms the basis for drafting the rule of law reports and part of the data grounding the elaboration of Country Specific Recommendations, has been contested both in terms of methodology and for the mechanism of data evaluation (see Y. Guerra in ths volume). If there is no convergence on the scoreboard to be used, then any position taken by the Commission can be subject to contestation and accused of arbitrariness and too broad discretion, which could run exactly in contrast to what the values of legal certainty and predictability the rule of law aims to represent.

The third element to consider is the extent to which the economic and financial leverage to deal with rule of law issues has become a central element of dissensus. This is clear, for instance, from the reach of the Country Specific Recommendations within the European Semester that have come to cover judicial reforms and the adoption of anti-corruption measures (see A. Capati and T. Christiansen in this volume) and from the way EU competition rules have been used to deal with problems of media freedoms (see K. Cseres in this volume). The increasing use of the economic leverage and of EU funds to tackle rule of law issues is also prompting a more active involvement of OLAF and, in the prospect of EPPO, as the fight against EU frauds and the protection of the rule of law principles can now more easily be paired (Rubio et al., 2023). Indeed, over the last five years and especially since the Next Generation EU package was adopted (see N. Lupo; C. Fasone and M. Simoncini in this volume), the rise of spending conditionality and the greater attention to the protection of the EU financial interests have indirectly led to further politicization and polarization of the debate on the rule of law. While this change is not necessarily problematic, as it triggers public debate and is conducive to alleviating rule of law problems, it may foster more divisions inside the EU between the East and West and between the North and South and could create disparities between European citizens across Member States. Relatedly, another contested dimension of spending conditionality refers to the alleged "democratic blackmail" it triggers (Baraggia, 2023), as it involves procedures directly affecting the rights and benefits of the citizens of a targeted Member State, punishing them for the faults of their government; the government is induced to adopt corrective measures in exchange for money. As has been effectively pointed out, the growing use of spending conditionality implies "trading" the rule of law and democracy for EU funds and recovery (Fromont & Van Waeyemberge, 2021). Moreover, the risks of ineffective enforcement of EU law have been pointed out: blocking EU funds could hamper the achievement of EU policy objectives and lead to a "simultaneous deterioration in other aspects of the rule of law" (European Court of Auditors, 2024: 50–52).

However, as some have argued, criticisms against the use of conditionality should be put in context considering the final aim of restoring the rule of law at the domestic level. Indeed, in the short- or medium-term, citizens certainly take advantage of EU spending conditionality to free themselves from the oppression of illiberal regimes, which otherwise could consolidate their power thanks to the clientelism and patronage fed through EU funds (Sheppele et al., 2021).

4 Structure and Contents

The volume is structured as follows. The first part reviews the EU primary law instruments intended to tackle rule of law problems and the dissensus surrounding their implementation. The most criticized tool by far, not only at the academic level, is Article 7 TEU; Ramona Coman and Pauline Thinus clearly highlight the striking difference between its design as a "nuclear option", especially its paras 2 and 3, and its use in practice (Chapter 2). To manage the deficiencies of Article 7 TEU's procedures, the infringement proceeding has been widely employed despite its general scope, not having been conceived specifically for rule of law problems (Article 258 TFEU). To this end, Giovanni Piccirilli emphasizes that the debate and dissensus have mainly focused on whether infringement proceedings are fit for the purpose, considering their low political profile compared to the "nuclear option" and their tailored focus on selected violations of EU law rather than on systemic deficiencies. Despite that, it is argued that the infringement proceedings might play a prominent role due to a consolidated practice given by decades of application, which would ensure an extremely concrete sanctioning system (Chapter 3). In the following chapter, Lorenzo Cecchetti guides us through the versatile use of the PRP (Article 267 TFEU) for rule of law purposes as a complementary rule to infringement proceedings. More precisely, Chapter 4 focuses on the value of the preliminary rulings to protect the independence of the judiciary in two sensitive fields: the controversial enforcement of the European Arrest Warrant and the exercise of the European mandate by national courts (Article 19 TEU). Linked to these judicial tools has been the Charter of Fundamental Rights: intended to uphold rule of law values, the guarantee of effective judicial protection and legal remedies (Article 47 of the Charter) was constructed as the basic right from which all others stem. Lorenzo Cecchetti underlines the tension between the use of the Charter to this end and the limited scope of its applications under Article 51, which has triggered some criticism of the effectiveness of the tool (Chapter 5). Consequently, he concludes that the criticism surrounding the Charter on this matter results from longstanding uncertainties that characterize both the nature of the Charter as a constitutional tool and the scope of application of Union law and, thus, of the Charter itself. As a result, the Charter continues to be the "shadow" of EU law. Last, Adriano Dirri (Chapter 6) highlights that the Cooperation and Verification Mechanism (CVM), though formally enshrined in EU primary law, in the Treaty of Accession of Bulgaria and Romania, has never been used as a standard for review by the ECJ (see the missed opportunity in the AFJR judgment, joined cases C-83/19, C-127/19, C-195/19, C-291/19, C-355/19, C-397/19, and in the *EuroBox-Promotion*, joined cases C-357/19, C-547/19, C-811/19, C-840/19, C-379/19). This de facto downgrading of the legal significance of the CMV legal basis has been coupled with the criticism of the effectiveness of the tool from the rule of law perspective, given the shortcomings in its application in Romania and Bulgaria. For example, as argued by Adriano Dirri, the CMV assessment has departed from the evidence produced by other monitoring tools such as the EU Justice Scoreboard, thereby amplifying the level of dissensus. Such shortcomings have led to the repealing of the CVM—first informally by the Rule of Law Reports and later formalized by two Decisions of the Commission in September 2023. The result was that "unresolved reforms covered by the Cooperation and Verification Mechanism had to be resumed" (European Court of Auditors, 2024: 29) under newly established instruments such as the Rule of Law reports and under the National Recovery and Resilience Plans (NRRPs), as argued by the European Court of Auditors.

The next part of the book is devoted to those legislative instruments indirectly dedicated to the protection of the rule of law, as they were conceived for the general purpose of supporting the correct enforcement of EU law and the EU budget. Adriano Dirri and Ylenia Guerra reflect on the multifaceted nature of the Technical Support Instrument (TSI), which aimed to provide Member States with technical assistance for the implementation of institutional and administrative reforms, particularly of those linked to the European Semester (Chapter 7). Proposed under the Multiannual Financial Framework 2021–2027 and covered by Regulation 2021/241 (the RRF Regulation), the TSI is now perceived as an additional instrument for fostering and strengthening the adoption of reform by Member States. It is also connected to the enhancement of the rule of law, predominantly through the consolidation of the national administrative capacity and the independence of the judiciary. Recently, the TSI has been extended to the promotion of the rule of law through the "Reinforce Democracy and the Rule of Law" Flagship Program aimed at supporting Member States to implement the policy and guidance provided by the EU Commission by strengthening the capacity of national authorities and enhancing their judicial systems.[1] Yet, the TSI has also been the target of criticism as it appears more directed to endorse fiscal consolidation and austerity than growth. As such, according to the European Court of Auditors, the instrument has not reached the targets for which it was created. Alessandro Nato, instead, focuses on the various legislative instruments protecting EU financial interests (e.g., Directive No. 2017/1371) and the emergence of a questionable "financial rule of law" in the EU (Chapter 8). In other words, the EU's recent approach to the rule of law has become increasingly steered by financial considerations. In this vein, the role of the European Anti-Fraud Office (OLAF) and the European Public Prosecutor Office (EPPO) has acquired prominence, as have the systems of administrative and criminal control.

[1] See Technical Support Instrument 2024 flagship project Reinforce Democracy and the Rule of Law, https://reform-support.ec.europa.eu/tsi-2024-flagship-reinforce-democracy-and-rule-law_en.

This shift, however, has also brought to the forefront new problems: if the OLAF and the EPPO are expected to contribute indirectly to the protection of the rule of law, the scope of action of these bodies may create new rule of law challenges. For example, the issue of identifying their specific mandates and arranging their mutual collaboration properly remains largely unsettled. Furthermore, the very limited avenues through which the EPPO can be subject to judicial review by the CJEU present additional concerns.

The third part of the volume shifts the focus to soft law instruments that have been devised over the last few years, mainly by the Commission. The tools discussed in this part define preventive mechanisms, meant to avoid the escalation of rule of law problems, that are not strictly tailored to the reach of the EU competencies. The rule of law framework and dialogue, launched in 2014 (Chapter 9), the EU Justice Scoreboard (Chapter 10) and the rule of law reports (Chapter 11) are intimately related to one another, and they are complementary to the binding tools. Dealing with the rule of law framework, Maciej Serowaniec discusses its subsidiary nature and the aim to target the systemic nature of the threat to the rule of law. The dialogue that can be activated by the Commission within this framework could even lead to an infringement proceeding or trigger Article 7 TEU. In practice, however, the flaws of this mechanism have been revealed. The mechanism was triggered only once, against the first judicial reforms in Poland in 2016. Overall, the procedure is intended to exert a shaming effect and place soft pressure on the Member State as well as to force the Member State under investigation to use an instrument in line with the principle of loyal cooperation. Dealing with reforms of the judicial system, the EU Justice Scoreboard is a soft law instrument established in 2013 and is now part of the EU rule of law toolbox. As clearly described by Ylenia Guerra, the Scoreboard provides a grid to assess the performance of national judicial systems. It monitors the effectiveness of member states' justice systems based on three elements: efficiency, quality and independence (perceived judicial independence but also structural independence). It provides member states with data each year to help them improve the effectiveness of their national justice systems. As such, it is based on a series of indicators measured through a complex mix of qualitative and quantitative methodologies, which have become a major source of disagreement among experts, between the Member States, and between Member States and the EU. This is of special concern as the critique against the reliability of the EU Justice Scoreboard's methodology can undermine its legitimacy and authoritativeness and impair the effectiveness of the rule of law reports, which indeed are drawn also based on the evidence produced through the Scoreboard assessment. Finally, Ylenia Maria Citino guides us through the design and use of the latest EU soft law instrument put forward, the rule of law reports launched for the first time in 2020, as part of the annual cycle of the rule of law mechanism. In this case, the criticism has revolved around both its too broad scope and lack of precision in targeting specific violations of the rule of law principles and its inability to stop or slow down the processes of autocratization taking place in certain Eastern countries. The rule of law reports draw on data collected through the EU Justice Scoreboard and the European Semester to foster a dialogue between EU institutions, the Member State concerned and the stakeholders. Aiming to respond to the allegations highlighting the too-abstract nature of the Commission's review, in the 2022 review cycle country-specific recommendations have been referred to in the reports (Chapter 12). Yet, especially with a view to the "incorporation" of the CVM into the rule of law reports—as the two instruments largely overlap today—a serious reflection on the added value of this tool, even more so after the RRF and the rule of law conditionality Regulation, is deemed desirable.

The fourth part of the volume engages with a variety of legal instruments, mostly embedded in binding provisions and, for competition law, also in Treaty provisions, next to soft law tools, all of them relying on economic leverage to foster compliance with the rule of law principles in the EU. Andrea Capati and Thomas Christiansen elaborate on the role of the European Semester as a framework for the indirect enforcement of the rule of law. In particular, Country Specific Recommendations and their widened scope have become the linchpins for steering a continuous assessment of the commitment and enforcement of rule of law principles through economic governance mechanisms, thereby fostering a lively debate on the desirability of such a mix that is not going to be fundamentally altered by the reform of the Stability and Growth Pact (Chapter 12). Drawing on this apparent contradiction, Cristina Fasone and Marta Simoncini deal with the spreading of conditionality as a tool of internal governance in the EU (Chapter 13). After reviewing the main types of conditionality regimes established under EU law, they discuss the problematic aspect of resorting to strict conditionality during the Eurozone crisis as an example of rule of law degradation. Focusing on the combination of multiple conditionality mechanisms under the Next Generation EU, they reflect on the hybrid nature and ambiguities of conditionality as a source of dissensus in the Union. To this end, they use the implementation of the Charter enabling condition under the CPR as a case study. Dora Hegedűs and Thomas Christiansen then focus on the process of adoption and the early implementation of the Rule of Law Conditionality Regulation (Chapter 14). In doing so, they accompany the reader through the complexity of the legislative procedure leading to the approval of the Regulation, highlighting the main points of dissensus, and then focus on the delayed enforcement of the measure, which also prompted controversies between the EU and the Member States, including actions for annulment in front of the CJUE. The authors point out that although Hungary eventually saw part of its funds suspended in December 2022, this has not produced the expected results. This shows, in turn, that the use of spending conditionality to defend the rule of law in the EU could remain vulnerable to political interference and possible blackmail. Nicola Lupo focuses on the Recovery and Resilience Facility as one of the major tools to tackle rule of law problems in today's EU (Chapter 15). Conceived to foster resilience and a speedy recovery from the pandemic through NRRPs, a set of specific reforms and investments, the Facility is becoming more effective than ad hoc instruments to address rule of law problems. Indeed, by making the EU payment conditional upon the satisfactory achievement of (super)milestones and targets, the design of the Facility aims to put even the most reluctant Member States, such as Hungary and Poland, on track to promote judicial reforms and anti-corruption policies and obliges the maintenance of the reforms achieved. Finally, Kati Cseres highlights the significance of EU competition rules for upholding the rule of law principles in the Union. Indeed, in Chapter 16 she emphasizes how by keeping the concentration of economic power under control, substantive norms of competition policy enhance the value of democratic competition and the protection of individual rights. Moreover, the decentralized system of enforcement of competition rules requires specific attention to ensure the autonomy and independence of national competition authorities from politics, as recently emphasized by the General Court in the *Spred-Pro* judgment. Last, EU competition law is also instrumental in protecting sound financial management under the rule of law conditionality regulation due to its influence on public procurement rules and can protect media pluralism by intervening in public broadcasting and state advertising through state aid provisions.

The concluding chapter will underline the many procedural linkages between the various tools reviewed, sum up the main points of dissensus in the state-of-the-art of EU rule of law instruments and recall proposals to expand the European toolbox further.

5 Contribution to the Research on the Rule of Law in the EU

This book has been written within the framework of the Horizon Europe Project "Respond to Emerging Dissensus: SuPranational Instruments and Norms of European Liberal Democracy" (RED-SPINEL), Work Package 2, with contributions from the research units of all partner institutions. It brings together a composite group of scholars in EU studies, including specialists in comparative law, constitutional law and political science, to offer a systematic inquiry into the strengths and weaknesses of the EU rule of law toolbox, reviewing each tool from the perspective of the dissensus it has triggered at the supranational level.

Coming ten years after the launch of the rule of law dialogue by the European Commission, this volume engages with the discussion surrounding the implementation of various EU instruments and contrasts the effectiveness of those of a general nature, which preceded the emergence of the EU rule of law crisis, with those that have been created ad hoc. It further compares and connects soft law and hard law measures.

The book seeks to highlight, through the topic of dissensus, the criticisms and dysfunctionalities that have characterized the armamentarium put in place by the EU to protect the rule of law. Indeed, it builds on the conceptual framework of dissensus provided within the RED-SPINEL Consortium (Coman, 2022; Coman & Brack, 2023), shifting the perspective of analysis from actors to procedures and instruments of EU internal governance and their mutual interaction. It intends to shed light on the effectiveness of each tool in relation to the others, emphasizing the interconnections, overlappings and synergies produced by their common goal of enforcing the European rule of law.

References

Amato, G., Barbisan, B., & Pinelli, C. (Eds.). (2021). *Rule of Law vs Majoritarian Democracy*. Hart Publishing.

Baraggia, A. (2023). Ricatto democratico. L'utilizzo della condizionalità a protezione dello stato di diritto. *Quaderni Costituzionali, 2*, 335–380.

Baraggia, A., & Bonelli, M. (2022). Linking Money to Values: The New Rule of Law Conditionality Regulation and Its Constitutional Challenges. *German Law Journal, 23*(2), 131–156.

Bobek, M., Bodnar, A., von Bogdandy, A., & Sonnevend, P. (Eds.). (2023). *Transition 2.0. Re-establishing Constitutional Democracy in EU Member States*. Nomos.

Bobić, A. (2022). *The Jurisprudence of Constitutional Conflict in the European Union*. Oxford University Press.

Closa, C., & Kochenov, D. (Eds.). (2016). *Reinforcing Rule of Law Oversight in the European Union*. Cambridge University Press.

Coman, R. (2022). *The Politics of the Rule of Law in the EU Polity: Actors*. Palgrave Macmillan.

Coman, R., & Brack, N. (2023). *Understanding Dissensus over Liberal Democracy in the Age of Crises: Theoretical Reflections*. Think Piece for the RED-SPINEL Working Paper Series.

Drinóczi, T., & Bień-Kacała, A. (Eds.). (2021). *Rule of Law, Common Values, and Illiberal Constitutionalism: Poland and Hungary Within the European Union*. Routledge.

Emmons, C., & Pavone, T. (2021). The Rhetoric of Inaction: Failing to Fail Forward in the EU's Rule of Law Crisis. *Journal of European Public Policy, 28*(10), 1611–1629.

European Court of Auditors, Special Report 03/2024. *The Rule of Law in the EU, an Improved Framework to Protect the EU's Financial Interests, but Risks Remain*, 21/02/2024.

Fromont, L., & Van Waeyemberge, A. (2021). Trading Rule of Law for Recovery? The New EU Strategy in the Post-Covid Era. *European Law Journal, 1–3*, 132–147.

Ginsburg, T., & Huq, A.Z. (2018). *How to Save a Constitutional Democracy*. The University of Chicago Press.

Graber, M. A., Levinson, S., & Tushnet, M. (Eds.). (2018). *Constitutional Democracy in Crisis?* Oxford University Press.

Groussot, X., & Zemskova, A. (2022). The Manifestations of the EU Rule of Law and Its Contestability: Historical and Constitutional Foundations. *Journal of Constitutional History, 44*(2), 93–110.

Halmai, G. (2019). The Possibility and Desirability of Rule of Law Conditionality. *The Hague Journal on the Rule of Law, 11*(1), 171.

Jakab, A., & Kochenov, D. (Eds.). (2017). *The Enforcement of EU Law and Values: Ensuring Member States' Compliance*. Oxford University Press.
Kelemen, R. D., & Scheppele, K. L. (2018, September 10). *How to Stop Funding Autocracy in the EU*. *Verfassungsblog*.
Kochenov, D., & Bárd, P. (2022). Kirchberg Salami Lost in Bosphorus: The Multiplication of Judicial Independence Standards and the Future of the Rule of Law in Europe. *Journal of Common Market Studies, 60*(1), 150–165.
Martinico, G. (2022). *The Tangled Complexity of the EU Constitutional Process. The Frustrating Knot of Europe* (2nd ed.). Routledge.
Pech, L. (2022). The Rule of Law as a Well-Established and Well-Defined Principle of EU Law. *The Hague Journal on the Rule of Law, 14*(2–3), 107.
Pech, L., Grogan, J., et al. (2020). *Meaning and Scope of the EU Rule of Law*. RECONNECT Working Paper, Work Package 7—Deliverable 2.
Pech, L., & Kochenov, D. (2021). *Respect for the Rule of Law in the Case Law of the European Court of Justice: A Casebook Overview of Key Judgments Since the Portuguese Judges Case*. SIEPS, 3.
Platon, S. (2021, June 11). Bringing a Knife to a Gunfight. The European Parliament, the Rule of Law Conditionality, and the Action for Failure to Act. *Verfassungsblog*.
Pohjankoski, P., Raitio, J., & Rosas, A. (2023). *The Rule of Law's Anatomy in the EU: Foundations and Protections*. Hart Publishing.
Rubio, E., et al. (2023). *The Tools for Protecting the EU Budget from Breaches of the Rule of Law: The Conditionality Regulation in Context*. Policy Department for Budgetary Affairs, Directorate-General for Internal Policies, PE 747.469.
Sajó, A. (2021). *Ruling by Cheating*. Cambridge University Press.
Sajó, A., & Uitz, R. (Eds.). (2021). *The Routledge Handbook of Illiberalism*. Routledge.
Sadurski, W. (2019). *Poland's Constitutional Breakdown*. Oxford University Press.
Sheppele, K. L., Kelemen, D., & Morijn, J. (2021). *The EU Commission Should Cut Funding to Hungary: The Legal Case*. Study Solicited by the Greens/EFA Group in the European Parliament.
Sheppele, K. L., Pech, L., & Platon, S. (2020, December 13). *Compromising the Rule of Law While Compromising on the Rule of Law*. *Verfassungsblog*.
Södersten, A., & Herkock, E. (Eds.). (2023). *The Rule of Law in the EU: Crisis and Solutions*, SIEPS, 1.
Spieker, L. D. (2023). *EU Values Before the Court of Justice*. Oxford University Press.
von Bogdandy, A. (2024, January 15). The European Renaissance of Republicanism: On the Future of EU Law in Light of Article 2 TEU. *Max Planck Institute for Comparative Public Law & International Law (MPIL) Research Paper* No. 2024-02.

von Bogdandy, A., Bogdanowicz, P., Canor, I., Grabenwarter, C., Taborowski, M., & Schmidt, M. (Eds.). (2021). *Defending Checks and Balances in EU Member States*. Springer.

Wacks, R. (2021). *The Rule of Law Under Fire?* Hart Publishing.

PART I

The Instruments Provided by EU Primary Law

CHAPTER 2

Key Political and Legal Debates on Article 7 TEU in Times of Dissensus Over the Rule of Law

Ramona Coman and Pauline Thinus

1 Introduction

Thirty years have passed since the adoption of the Copenhagen criteria by the European Council. This pivotal political moment has reshaped the future of the continent, marking a significant step forward in the gradual constitutionalisation of values and reinforcing the essence of the EU polity (Kochenov & Bárd, 2018). While Article 2 of the Treaty on the European Union (TEU) encapsulated the core identity of the Union and its member states (Besselink, 2016: 4), Article 7 TEU introduced by the Amsterdam Treaty equipped European institutions with a means to ensure that all member states respect these common values. Similar sanctioning provisions exist in other regional and international organisations for when members depart from common principles, even extending

R. Coman (✉) · P. Thinus
Université Libre de Bruxelles, Bruxelles, Belgium
e-mail: Ramona.Coman@ulb.be

C. Fasone et al. (eds.), *EU Rule of Law Procedures at the Test Bench*, Palgrave Studies in European Union Politics,
https://doi.org/10.1007/978-3-031-60008-1_2

to their exclusion.[1] Yet, Article 7 TEU only allows the "suspension of certain rights", as a result of a complex process. This mechanism was incorporated into the treaties in a particular context, linked not only to the eastern enlargement but also to the rise of radical right parties in the oldest EU member states. However, according to diplomats who attended the intergovernmental conferences that resulted in the drafting of Article 7 TEU, its initial purpose was to serve as a dissuasion tool, not only due to its highly political nature (Besselink, 2016: 13), but also because reaching the situation it was designed to mitigate was considered extremely unlikely (Heringa, 2018; Perakis, 2019). As Sadurski puts it, "the mechanism of Article 7 TEU in its original form was no more than a bark in practice" (quoted in Besselink, 2016: 14).

EU integration stands at a crossroad. The common values rooted in the constitutional traditions of the member states are under strain, facing challenges from political parties across various ideological corners in several countries. Although the European integration process has long been disputed, the Union has entered a new era marked by dissensus over liberal democracy and its core pillars. In the midst of multiple crises, common values are increasingly contested (e.g. Gora & de Wilde, 2022) or invoked with a meaning opposed to their original significance. Dissensus over liberal democracy is growing, as notably seen in debates over the rule of law (Coman, 2022). This dissensus takes the form of social, political and legal conflicts at both the EU and national levels, driven by political, social and legal actors (including state and non-state actors in different institutional and non-institutional arenas) seeking to maintain, replace or restructure liberal democracy (Coman & Brack, 2023).

Article 7 TEU has been debated at the European level in two key moments: in 2000, following the ascent to power of the FPÖ (Freiheitliche Partei Österreichs/Freedom Party) in Austria, and since the early 2010s, when the governments of Poland and Hungary initiated a process of de-Europeanisation (Coman, 2022: 6), moving towards autocratisation (Bárd & Kochenov, 2021: 41; Gora & de Wilde, 2022: 345). Both moments have highlighted the limits of this procedure, which this chapter sets out to discuss. Despite these radical transformations in Hungary and Poland, in the first half of the 2010s, EU institutional

[1] For instance, see Article 8 of the *Statute of the Council of Europe* (1949).

actors were reluctant to trigger Article 7 TEU. Commission President José Manuel Barroso advocated avoiding what he called the "nuclear option" in his 2012 and 2013 State of the Union addresses. What was seen as nuclear was the political sensitivity of the topic (Perakis, 2019), the high voting thresholds and the sanctions the instrument can lead to (e.g. Besselink, 2017). The use of this metaphor was criticised by academics who claimed that referring to Article 7 TEU as being something nuclear reinforced the unwillingness of EU institutions to act (Kochenov, 2021; Pech, 2020; Tichý, 2018). Triggered by the Commission in December 2017, following two years of unsuccessful dialogue with the Polish Law and Justice (PiS) government as part of the Rule of Law Framework, and in September 2018 by the European Parliament (EP) against Hungary after eight years of debates (Coman, 2022), Article 7 TEU is an ongoing process. The Council's "inability" or "unwillingness to make meaningful progress" (Pech & Jaraczewski, 2023: 6) has sparked significant scholarly and political discussions on the implications for European law and politics.

The objective of this chapter is to revisit the development of Article 7 TEU, with an emphasis on the major legal and political disputes it has ignited in a context of growing dissensus over liberal democracy. The chapter is structured as follows. The origins of Article 7 TEU are reviewed in Sect. 2, Sect. 3 covers the key political and legal controversies pertaining to Article 7 TEU since 2010, and in Sect. 4 current discussions on the stalemate of the procedure and the various "ways out" are examined.

2 The Rise: Back to the Origins of Article 7 TEU

The literature devoted to the origins of Article 7 TEU is rather limited (see Fig. 1). In the late 1990s and early 2000s, scholars primarily delved into its raison d'être in the EU polity, situating this provision in the specific political context of the enlargement of the EU towards Central and Eastern Europe and the constitutionalisation of its values (Bugarič, 2016; Kochenov, 2021; Moberg, 2020; Sadurski, 2010). However, the anticipation of the 2004 enlargement was just one reason for protecting the common values at the core of the constitutional traditions of the member states. Before this major event, the gradual rise of far-right parties in Western Europe since the end of the 1980s raised concerns among the heads of state or government in the European Council (Sadurski,

2010: 399). The Union was entering a new stage of external development (enlargement) and at the same time facing internal questions about the nature and the *finalité* of the EU (deepening). The accession of these new and potentially unstable democracies reinforced the idea of the need for an instrument to safeguard European values. This led to the introduction of Article 7 by the Amsterdam Treaty in 1997, as a mechanism that could sanction a member state for a "serious and persistent breach" of the values referred to in Article 2 TEU. Although the 1994–1995 Reflection Group and the 1996 Intergovernmental Conference initially discussed the potential exclusion of a Union member or the involvement of the Court of Justice of the EU (CJEU) in the case of such a breach, these options did not materialise in the end (Sadurski, 2010: 390).

In October 1999, just four years after Austria's accession to the EU, the FPÖ received 26.9% of the votes cast in parliamentary elections. The participation of this right-wing populist party with racist, xenophobic and Nazi tendencies (Happold, 2000: 954) in the Austrian government coalition in 2000 alarmed heads of state or government from France, Spain, and Belgium, where extreme right parties were gaining traction (Coman,

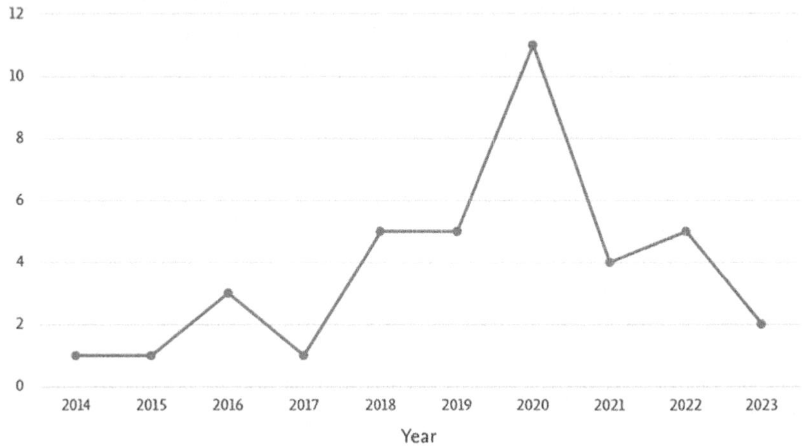

Fig. 1 Number of articles devoted exclusively to Article 7 TEU (data retrieved from Scopus)

2018; Cramér & Wrange, 2000; Merlingen et al., 2001). Following discussions about the perceived breach of common values in Austria, the fourteen EU member states of the time chose not to invoke Article 7 TEU. Instead, they decided to suspend their bilateral diplomatic relations with Austria. This circumvention of Article 7 TEU without dialogue with other institutions led to questions and criticism within the EP and the Commission. Although the EP supported the activation of Article 7 TEU against Austria despite internal divisions, the Prodi-led Commission opposed the idea of sanctions and regretted not being involved in the decision of the fourteen member states (Coman, 2018; Happold, 2000: 956). The Commission's president argued that "it is the duty of a strong supranational institution not to isolate one of its members" because "when one of its members is in difficulty, the whole Union is in difficulty" (Merlingen et al., 2001: 66). Discussions about the respect of common values in Austria also triggered debates in candidate countries from Central and Eastern Europe at that time. For instance, the Slovenian prime minister, Janez Drnovšek, argued that the EU action was "exaggerated" (Coman, 2018) and the former Czech Prime Minister Václav Klaus declared that "Brussels' arrogance was far more dangerous than Haider's rhetoric". The decision of the fourteen states to suspend diplomatic relations was aimed at creating a *cordon sanitaire* around the Austrian coalition government (Besselink, 2016: 7).

The debates in 1999–2000 foreshadowed the political and legal controversies surrounding the activation of Article 7 TEU, along with intra- and inter-institutional divisions. They also brought to light the limitations of the initial version of this provision, raised not only by the EP and the Commission in 2003 and 2004 but also in the report requested by the European Council to examine the situation in Austria. In this regard, the 2000 "Wise Men Report" recommended the development of a mechanism to monitor and evaluate the commitment of individual member states with respect to common European values. In response, the Treaty of Nice amended Article 7 TEU in 2001 to introduce a prevention mechanism. As a result, two mechanisms coexist within this provision. Article 7(1) addresses a "clear risk of a serious breach" of the values referred to in Article 2 TEU. Following a reasoned proposal adopted by one-third of the member states, by the European Parliament or by the European Commission, this risk can be confirmed by the Council through a majority of four-fifths of its members, after obtaining the EP's consent. Beyond the Council's requirement to "hear" the state concerned, the Lisbon Treaty added that it also "may address recommendations" through four-fifths majority voting. Under Article 7(2), "a serious and persistent breach" may be determined by the European Council acting by unanimity, based on a proposal of one-third of the member states or by the Commission, and after obtaining the EP's consent. If unanimity has been reached, Article 7(3) states that the Council, acting by a qualified majority, may decide to suspend certain rights deriving from the application of the treaties to the member state in question, including the voting rights of the representative of its government in the Council. Although this mechanism appears as a three-step procedure, it is possible to start directly with Article 7(2), as underscored by Kochenov (2017: 6).

The discussions regarding the respect of values in Austria opened a window of opportunity to address the limitations of Article 7 TEU and to tackle several remaining legal and political issues. Starting with legal considerations, in its 2003 Communication, the Commission focused on the conditions for applying Article 7 TEU, arguing that the scope of this article was "not confined to areas covered by Union law" (European Commission, 2003: 5). From a more political perspective, the Commission highlighted that the article gives "discretionary power to the Council both to determine that there is a clear threat of a serious breach and to determine that there is a serious and persistent breach" and, in the latter case, under Article 7(3), "it may decide to apply penalties, but it is not obliged to do so" (ibid.). The Commission also emphasised the political nature of Article 7 TEU, "which leaves room for a diplomatic solution", but insisted that "the Council's discretionary power cannot evade the democratic control by the EP" and deplored that the Treaty does not give the CJEU the power of judicial review (ibid.: 6). Although the CJEU is not explicitly mentioned in Article 7 TEU, scholars have underlined that its jurisdiction is not excluded, but rather limited to procedural aspects (Besselink, 2016: 13; Kochenov, 2017: 6). However, the window of opportunity of the 2000s closed without properly addressing these issues, which re-entered the EU's political agenda a decade later (Coman, 2022: 27), as discussed in the following sections.

3 Key Political and Legal Controversies in the 2010s

The academic debate on Article 7 TEU has flourished since the end of the last decade (see Fig. 1). A substantial body of research has emerged examining the transformation of the political regimes in Hungary and Poland, where the Fidesz and PiS governments rose to power with political programmes openly challenging liberal democracy and its core institutions and values. In 2014, Viktor Orbán announced his ambition to institute an "illiberal democracy", a concept many argued is a contradiction as democracy inherently relies on fundamental rights (Lacroix & Pranchère, 2019). In the name of the people and national sovereignty (Bakó, 2021), both PiS and Fidesz have challenged the foundations of national and supranational polities. They not only replaced provisions ensuring the independence of their judiciaries but also centralised power, limited pluralism and multiculturalism, reduced the space for civil society and implemented a series of policies in stark contrast to European values and principles (e.g. de Búrca, 2022), the respect of which was the precondition for accession to the Union.

This phenomenon received considerable attention in political science, with EU studies focusing on the implications for the Union, as well as its responses or lack of reaction (De Búrca, 2022; Moberg, 2020; Pech & Jaraczewski, 2023). Notably, scholars have devoted particular attention to the evolving rule of law policy and its instruments, including the Rule of Law Framework in the Commission (Kochenov & Pech, 2016) and the Rule of Law Dialogue in the Council (Sedelmeier, 2017; see also Serowaniec in this volume), the European Semester (see also Capati and Christiansen in this volume), the EU Justice Scoreboard (see also Guerra in this volume), and more recently, the Rule of Law Annual Report (Closa & Hernández, 2023; see also Citrino in this volume) and Regulation 2020/2092 (Baraggia & Bonelli, 2021; Bárd & Kochenov, 2021). The establishment of these instruments has encountered tensions and forms of dissensus, both at the legal and political levels, that is expressed in various institutional arenas (see Coman, 2022 for an overview). The Commission's Rule of Law Framework, established as a preliminary step before Article 7 TEU, was contested by the Legal Service of the Council, which argued that this provision "does not set a basis to further develop or amend the procedure" (Besselink, 2017). Regulation 2020/2092 was also challenged from the moment the Commission introduced this proposal in May 2018 to its adoption in December 2020, as illustrated by the action for annulment launched by Poland and Hungary in March 2021. In parallel, the Hungarian government challenged the EP's vote on the reasoned proposal triggering Article 7(1) TEU before the CJEU (Platon, 2022), along with many other decisions related to rule of law issues. All these instruments, either soft or hard, emerged from political and institutional compromises, with limited results in practice.

Against this backdrop, a large portion of the literature on Article 7 TEU focuses either on its politics (Closa, 2019, 2021; Coman & Thinus, 2024) or on its legal dimensions (Kochenov & Bárd, 2018; Perakis, 2019; Tichý, 2018), as this procedure "is a blend between law and politics" (Kochenov, 2017: 7). On the one hand, legal scholars have analysed domestic transformations that violate the rule of law (e.g. Bakó, 2021). Particular attention has been given to the legal interpretation of Article 7 TEU and its scope of application (Besselink, 2017; Tichý, 2018), procedural requirements (Kochenov, 2021; Perakis, 2019) or the types of sanctions that can be adopted (Besselink, 2017). Recommendations can be issued by the Council via the preventive branch through the same procedural steps but they remain optional (Pech & Jaraczewski, 2023). Pech's metaphor of a "Sisyphean procedure" (2020) illustrates the impression of an endless process with multiple steps and high hurdles, although the preventive and sanctioning mechanisms are independent of each other (Kochenov, 2021; Moberg, 2020).

On the other hand, from a political science perspective, Article 7 TEU serves as an ideal case to understand power relations between EU institutions, as well as their internal tensions and divisions. Within the EP, there have been vivid debates about this procedure. It took eight years for the institution to adopt a reasoned proposal to trigger the instrument against Hungary. While the Social Democrat, Green and Liberal groups, with the support of the Left, had been calling on the Commission and the Council to act since the beginning of the 2010s, the European People's Party, to which Fidesz belonged until 2021, was initially opposed or divided. Ideology, partisanship and rational calculations have been put forward to explain dynamics in the EP (Closa, 2021; Coman, 2022; Herman et al., 2021; Meijers & Van Der Veer, 2019), leading to a form of "authoritarian equilibrium" (Kelemen, 2020) or "mutual indulgence" (Bakó, 2021: 37). These internal debates eventually turned into a more consensual stance with the activation of Article 7 TEU and the regular adoption of resolutions on its continuation (De Búrca, 2022: 15). The role of the Commission as guardian of the treaties has also been scrutinised (Bárd & Kochenov, 2021; Closa, 2019; de Búrca, 2022: 13; Sedelmeier, 2017). Explanations of the Commission's initial reluctance to act focused on its preference for dialogue over sanctions and the anticipated degree of support in the Council (Closa, 2021). Dissensus has abounded not only in the EP and the Commission but also in the Council, where the norm of consensus has been increasingly challenged and where member states have been divided about how to deal with rule of law concerns, and especially Article 7 TEU (Coman & Thinus, 2024; Hernández, 2023; Puetter, 2022; Sedelmeier, 2017: 340). While alliances are not fixed in the Council, rule of law debates have enabled scholars to identify various dynamics, such as the opposition between old and new member states (Pech, 2020) and a coalition of "promoters of the rule of law" (Puetter, 2022). The positions of the member states on Article 7 TEU can be summarised in three categories: Poland and Hungary at one end of the continuum, the self-proclaimed "Rule of Law Friends" at the other, with several member states in between remaining silent or reluctant to take a stance. Political scientists have examined the opinions and actions of member states regarding the assertiveness of the Council in the Article 7 procedure (Closa, 2021), as well as the role of the rotating presidencies in moving it forward (Hernández, 2023; Tuominen, 2022). In addition, in examining the positions of populist governments in the Council, it has been argued that they challenge the norms or rules of the Council and reject compromises or solutions, while mainstream governments scarify policy reforms in order to uphold the fragile equilibrium or tackle disequilibrium in EU decision-making (Puetter, 2022; Zaun & Ripoll Servent, 2023).

The CJEU remains relatively understudied in the literature on Article 7 TEU, due to its limited role. Nevertheless, the Court's impact was crucial in various cases, including preliminary rulings concerning the independence of the judiciary and the rule of law in the EU. When the Court dismissed Hungary's action for annulment against the EP's reasoned proposal in 2021 (Platon, 2022), it affirmed its competence to rule on the legality of the decisions adopted by EU institutions through this mechanism. In the judgement of Hungary vs Parliament and Council C-156/21, the Court stated that numerous provisions in the treaties grant EU institutions the power to determine the existence of and, where appropriate, impose penalties for breaches of the values in Article 2 TEU

(Court of Justice of the EU, 2022). While validating the legality of Regulation 2020/2092, the Court also emphasised the nature of Article 7 TEU, stating, for instance, that this procedure covers all the values of the EU (paragraph 173) and allows "the Council to penalise serious and persistent breaches of values (...) with a view to compelling the member state concerned to put an end to those breaches" (paragraph 170). In this case, the EP and the Council received support from ten member states including Belgium, Denmark, Germany, Ireland, Spain, France, Luxembourg, the Netherlands, Finland and Sweden.

Overall, these studies shed light on the balance of power among European institutions in general, and particularly between the Council on the one hand and the EP or the Commission on the other. While Moberg (2020) sees the Article 7 TEU procedure as a hybridisation of intergovernmentalism and supranationalism, stressing the Commission's and the EP's roles, Priebus and Anders (2024) affirm the predominance of intergovernmentalism with only a few features of supranationalism, as actual control over the procedure remains in the hands of the (European) Council.

4 The Fall: A "Watered Down" or "Dead" Provision?

Article 7 TEU is currently at a standstill, despite the organisation of 13 hearings with Hungary and Poland (six with Poland, seven with Hungary) and several "state of play" updates. A limited yet flourishing literature delves into the institutionalisation of this procedure, that is, the conducting of hearings in the General Affairs Council and the informal development of the "state of play" format (Coman & Thinus, 2024; Pech, 2020). Given that Article 7 TEU is an instance of "incomplete contracting", member states were granted room of manoeuvre to decide on a course of action (Priebus, 2022). The initial hearings were organised without specific procedural rules until the adoption of final modalities in 2019. Scholars highlighted the Council's choice of "offender-friendly rules" protecting the rights of defence of the targeted countries, thus "watering down" the potential effectiveness of the procedure (Priebus, 2022). A hearing is a choreographed exchange of views rather than a debate: the Commission shares information on the domestic situation, the country concerned defends its position, and other Council members may ask questions. Some of them have preferred to remain silent, reluctant to confront another government, while the EP is completely excluded from the hearing (Coman & Thinus, 2024; Pech, 2020). A "state of play" is an informal format increasingly used since the Covid-19 pandemic that is not bound by any rules but serves as an update without a "questions and answers" session.

Beyond procedural aspects, understanding what happens during these meetings and the nature of these exchanges is fundamental. Hearings take place behind closed doors, and meeting minutes contain very little information. Drawing on interviews, scholars have sought to shed light on their content by analysing the role and positions of the Council's rotating presidency and of the Permanent Representations in Brussels. Article 7 TEU challenges an old diplomatic rule that prevents diplomats from criticising what happens in other member states or directly confronting one country in particular (de Búrca, 2022: 17). Some member states are more active than others in asking questions during hearings, such as the informal group of the "Rule of Law Friends", while Central and Eastern European governments tend to remain silent. Explanations include diplomatic or strategic alliances, different administrative and legal understanding of the issues at stake, and domestic politics (Coman & Thinus, 2024; Pech, 2020). The role of the Council presidency in dealing with the rule of law and Article 7 TEU is important. The presidency not only has a duty to act as an agenda-setter, but also to find compromises and solutions as an honest broker. Some presidencies have been proactive in adding rule of law concerns to their programmes and the Council's agenda; others have remained rather reluctant, but only a few included Article 7 TEU from the outset (Coman & Thinus, 2024; Hernández, 2023; Puetter, 2022; Tuominen, 2022). For instance, despite its written support of the Article 7 TEU procedure, the French Presidency considered that launching a vote in the Council would not be an effective decision (Agence Europe, 2022).

However, after five years Article 7 TEU is still ongoing, and hearings have yielded limited results. If the first hearings with the two countries were confrontational, over time they have become routine on the agenda of the Council presidency, which can opt for a state of play or a more formal hearing. Beyond political will, the dilemma is to achieve consensus when the positions of actors are fundamentally opposed. Council members are divided regarding the way to move forward with the procedure. The "Rule of Law Friends" group is inclined to maintain pressure on the member states concerned through a succession of hearings or the adoption of recommendations. Kochenov (2019: 93) argued that a four-fifths majority is not difficult to reach in this case, but Pech and Jaraczewski (2023: 6) observed that in practice, "the Council has proved unable or unwilling to address concrete recommendations to Poland and Hungary". Moreover, some diplomats hope for a move from the Commission, although from a procedural and political point of view the Council is responsible for the way forward. A formal means to terminate the procedure prematurely is the withdrawal of the Commission's or the EP's reasoned proposal. On 6 May 2024, the Commission actually announced its intention to withdraw its reasoned proposal against Poland, considering there is no longer a clear risk of a serious breach of the rule of law based on the measures adopted by the new Polish government. However, in case a vote is organised, the legal question is whether a lack of majority would lead to a return to the status quo (a succession of hearings and state of play updates) or to the end of the procedure for the country concerned. "Incomplete contracting" (Priebus, 2022) thus concerns how to end the Article 7 TEU procedure as well.

Therefore, some member states support a combination of Article 7 TEU with other instruments from the "rule of law toolkit", showing a particular preference for the Rule of Law Dialogue. Scholars also emphasise the potential of alternative mechanisms to effectively address rule of law breaches, such as an adaptation of infringement proceedings (Moberg, 2020) or the use of spending conditionality through Regulation 2020/2092 (Barragia & Bonelli, 2021, see Hegedűs and Christiansen in this volume) and the Recovery and Resilience Facility (see Fasone and Simonicini in this volume; see Lupo in this volume).

In the end, diplomats argue that a different outcome cannot be expected. Article 7 TEU was designed neither to be used nor to generate political change but to adopt recommendations or sanctions against (a risk of) systemic violations of the rule of law within a member state (Kochenov, 2021). More than a "watered down" mechanism (Priebus, 2022), Article 7 TEU seems to be a "dead" provision (Kochenov, 2021).

5 Conclusion: Towards a Revision of Article 7 TEU?

Institutional and academic actors have debated on the future of Article 7 TEU and how to make it more effective. They put forward options that either necessitate a treaty revision or additional modifications to the existing procedure. On the one hand, certain propositions focus only on the procedural aspects. Some scholars suggest important amendments, such as a complete rewriting of the article (Pech, 2020) or the proper inclusion of the CJEU, which would make the procedure more legal and less political (Perakis, 2019). In addition, a group of Franco-German experts has proposed the revision of the article to replace unanimity in Article 7(2) TEU with four-fifths majority voting by the European Council. The 12 experts recommend automatic sanctions five years after a reasoned proposal has been submitted, in case of inaction by the Council when the violation of common values persist. While they support the involvement of the Court of Justice in cases of dispute regarding the assessment of systemic value breaches, other proposals include implementing a clear set of complex indicators for a more appropriate and transparent assessment of the situation in the countries concerned (Bakó, 2021; Bugarič, 2016).

On the other hand, suggested improvements also address the way Article 7 TEU is implemented. The EP has on many occasions deplored that the situation in Poland and Hungary has continued to deteriorate despite the organisation of hearings in the Council. In its resolution adopted on 5 May 2022, the EP deplored that hearings are not organised in a regular, structured and open (transparent) manner, urging the Council to organise at least one per presidency, to include new developments in the discussions and to adopt "concrete recommendations" for the member state concerned.

In the end, as demonstrated through the example of Article 7 TEU, "material sanctions are difficult to use, owing to a combination of voting rules, member state preferences and party politics" (Sedelmeier, 2017). The situation in the member states concerned risk deteriorating in the absence of a decisive response from the Council and/or the European Council, despite the active role played by the EP and the use of various rule of law tools by the Commission. Even if the dynamic in Poland seems to change, a similar situation may unfold in other member states as long as the procedure remains "seriously defunct" (Puetter, 2022: 11) and the EU "in disequilibrium".

References

Agence Europe. (2022, January 27). Bulletin quotidien Europe N°12877.

Bakó, B. (2021). Hungary's Latest Experiences with Article 2 TEU: The Need for 'Informed' EU Sanctions. In A. von Bogdandy (Ed.), *Defending Checks and Balances in EU Member States* (pp. 35–69). Springer.

Baraggia, A., & Bonelli, M. (2021). Linking Money to Values: The New Rule of Law Conditionality Regulation and Its Constitutional Challenges. *German Law Journal, 23*(2), 131–156.

Bárd, P., & Kochenov, D. (2021). War as a Pretext to Wave the Rule of Law Goodbye? The Case for an EU Constitutional Awakening. *European Law Journal, 27*(1–3), 39–49.

Besselink, L. (2016). The Bite, the Bark, and the Howl: Article 7 TEU and the Rule of Law Initiative. *Amsterdam Law School Legal Studies Research Paper No., 2016-02*, 1–40.

Besselink, L. (2017). The Bite, the Bark, and the Howl: Article 7 TEU and the Rule of Law Initiative. In A. Jakab & D. Kochenov (Eds.), *The Enforcement of EU Law and Values: Ensuring Member States' Compliance* (pp. 128–144). Oxford University Press.

Bugarič, B. (2016). Protecting Democracy Inside the EU: On Article 7 TEU and the Hungarian Turn to Authoritarianism. In C. Closa & D. Kochenov (Eds.), *Reinforcing Rule of Law Oversight in the European Union* (pp. 82–102). Cambridge University Press.

Closa, C. (2019). The Politics of Guarding the Treaties: Commission Scrutiny of Rule of Law Compliance. *Journal of European Public Policy, 26*(5), 696–716.

Closa, C. (2021). Institutional Logics and the EU's Limited Sanctioning Capacity under Article 7 TEU. *International Political Science Review, 42*(4), 501–515.

Closa, C., & Hernández, G. (2023). *From Scrutiny to Implementation: Reinforcing the Impact of the Rule of Law Report*. European University Institute, School of Transnational Governance, Policy Brief 2023/05.

Coman, R. (2018). Protecting the Rule of Law and the State of Democracy at the Supranational Level: Political Dilemmas and Institutional Struggles in Strengthening EU's Input, Output and Throughput Legitimacy. In L. Tomini & G. Sandri (Eds.), *Challenges of Democracy in the 21st Century*. Routledge.

Coman, R. (2022). *The Politics of the Rule of Law in the EU Polity: Actors*. Palgrave MacMillan.

Coman, R., & Brack, N. (2023). Understanding Dissensus over Liberal Democracy in the Age of Crises: Theoretical Reflections. In R. Coman & N. Brack (Eds.), *Dissensus Over Liberal Democracy*, Working Paper Series N°1, RED SPINEL Project.

Coman, R., & Thinus, P. (2024). Article 7 TEU on the Agenda of the Council Rotating Presidencies. Still a "Nuclear Option" or Rather "A Talking Shop"? In R. Coman, O. Costa & V. Sierens (Eds.), *The EU Council Presidencies in Times of Crises*. Palgrave Macmillan.

Court of Justice of the EU. (2022, February 16). Hungary v Parliament and Council, C-156/21.

Cramér, P., & Wrange, P. (2000). *The Haider Affairs*. Faculty of Law, Stockholm University.

De Búrca, G. (2022). Poland and Hungary's EU Membership: On Not Confronting Authoritarian Governments. *International Journal of Constitutional Law, 20*(1), 13–34.

European Commission. (2003, October 15). Communication from the Commission to the Council and the European Parliament on Article 7 of the Treaty on European Union—Respect for and Promotion of the Values on Which the Union Is Based. COM (2003) 606 Final.

Gora, A., & de Wilde, P. (2022). The Essence of Democratic Backsliding in the European Union: Deliberation and Rule of Law. *Journal of European Public Policy, 29*(3), 342–362.

Happold, M. (2000). II. Fourteen Against One: The EU Member States' Response to Freedom Party Participation in The Austrian Government. *International & Comparative Law Quarterly, 49*(4), 953–963.

Heringa, A. W. (2018). Fundamental Rights, EU Membership, and Article 7 TEU. In A. Hatje, A., & L. Tichy (Eds.), *Liability of Member States for the Violation of Fundamental Values of the European Union* (pp. 59–72). Nomos.

Herman, L. E., Hoerner, J., & Lacey, J. (2021). Why does the European Right Accommodate Backsliding States? An Analysis of 24 European People's Party Votes (2011–2019). *European Political Science Review, 13*(2), 169–187.

Hernández, G. (2023, October 22). The Powers of the Presidency of the Council of the EU to Shape the Rule of Law Enforcement Agenda: The Article 7 Case. *Journal of Common Market Studies.*

Kelemen, D. (2020). The European Union's Authoritarian Equilibrium. *Journal of European Public Policy, 27*(3), 481–499.

Kochenov, D. (2017). *Busting the Myths Nuclear: A Commentary on Article 7 TEU*. EUI Working Papers, LAW 2017/10.

Kochenov, D. (2019). Article 7 TEU. In M. Kellerbauer, M. Klamert, and J. Tomkin (Eds.), *The EU Treaties and the Charter of Fundamental Rights - A Commentary* (pp. 88–98). Oxford.

Kochenov, D. (2021). Article 7: A Commentary on a Much Talked-About 'Dead' Provision. In A. von Bogdandy (Ed.), *Defending Checks and Balances in EU Member States* (pp. 127–154). Springer.

Kochenov, D., & Bárd, P. (2018, July 2018). *Rule of Law Crisis in the New Member States of the EU: The Pitfalls of Overemphasising Enforcement*. Reconnect Working Papers, pp. 1–28.

Kochenov, D., & Pech, L. (2016). Better Late than Never? On the European Commission's Rule of Law Framework and its First Activation. *JCMS: Journal of Common Market Studies, 54*, 1062–1074. https://doi.org/10.1111/jcms.12401

Lacroix, J., & Pranchère, J.-Y. (2019). *Les Droits de l'homme rendent-ils idiot?* Seuil.

Meijers, M. J., & Van Der Veer, H. (2019). MEP Responses to Democratic Backsliding in Hungary and Poland. An Analysis of Agenda-Setting and Voting Behaviour. *Journal of Common Market Studies, 57*(4), 838–856.

Merlingen, M., Mudde, C., & Sedelmeier, U. (2001). The Right and the Righteous? European Norms, Domestic Politics and Sanctions Against Austria. *Journal of Common Market Studies, 39*(1), 59–77.

Moberg, A. (2020). When the Return of the Nation-State Undermines the Rule of Law: Poland, the EU, and Article 7 TEU. In A. Bakardjieva Engelbrekt et al. (Eds.), *The European Union and the Return of the Nation State* (pp. 59–82). Palgrave Macmillan.

Platon, S. (2022). Is Silence Golden? The Abstention of MEPs and the Activation of Article 7 TEU against Hungary: Hungary vs. European Parliament. *CMLR, 59*(2), 543–560.

Pech, L. (2020). Article 7 TEU: From 'Nuclear Option' to 'Sisyphean Procedure'? In U. Belavusau & A. Gliszczynska-Grabias (Eds.), *Constitutionalism under Stress* (pp. 157–174). Oxford University Press.

Pech, L., & Jaraczewski, J. (2023). *Systemic Threat to the Rule of Law in Poland: Updated and new Article 7(1) TEU Recommendations*. CEU Democratic Institute. DI Working Papers, 2, pp. 1–105.

Perakis, M. (2019). *Exiting the European Union: Legal Procedure*. Cambridge Scholars Publishing.

Priebus, S. (2022). Watering Down the 'Nuclear Option'? The Council and the Article 7 Dilemma. *Journal of European Integration, 44*(7), 995–1010.

Priebus, S., & Anders, L. H. (2024). Fundamental Change Beneath the Surface: The Supranationalisation of Rule of Law Protection in the European Union. *Journal of Common Market Studies, 62*(1), 224–241.

Puetter, U. (2022). Consensus Politics and EU Disequilibrium: The German Council Presidency 2021 and the Rule of Law Mechanism. In S. Münch & H. Heinelt (Eds.), *EU Policymaking at Crossroads—Negotiating the 2021–2027 Budget* (pp. 233–250). Edward Elgar.

Sadurski, W. (2010). Adding Bite to a Bark: The Story of Article 7, EU Enlargement, and Jörg Haider. *Columbia Journal of European Law, 16*(3), 385–426.

Sedelmeier, U. (2017). Political Safeguards Against Democratic Backsliding in the EU: The Limits of Material Sanctions and the Scope of Social Pressure. *Journal of European Public Policy, 24*(3), 337–351.

Tichý, L. (2018). The Nature and Requirements for Liability of a Member State Under Article 7 TEU. In A. Hatje & L. Tichý (Eds.), *Liability of Member States for the Violation of Fundamental Values of the European Union*, Europarecht, Beiheft, 2018/1, pp. 87–108.

Tuominen, H. (2022). In Defence of Common Values: The Finnish EU Council Presidency 2019. *Cooperation and Conflict, 58*(1), 1–19.

Zaun, N., & Ripoll Servent, A. (2023). Perpetuating Crisis as a Supply Strategy: The Role of (Nativist) Populist Governments in EU Policymaking on Refugee Distribution. *Journal of Common Market Studies, 61*(3), 653–672.

CHAPTER 3

Ordinary Weapons for Exceptional Threats? Infringement Procedure and Rule of Law Crisis

Giovanni Piccirilli

1 A Traditional Tool of EC/EU Law

The infringement procedure is a key instrument of European law since its foundation (Mendrinou, 1996; Prete, 2017). It was foreseen by the original texts of the ECSC Treaty (Article 88) and the EEC Treaty (Article 169, identical to Article 141 EAEC Treaty), aimed at guaranteeing the respect and effectiveness of European law in all Member States. Its functioning has always been fundamentally the same, although some important changes have been passed through the years. As is well known, it is the Commission that can trigger a procedure based on the alleged failure of a Member State to fulfil an obligation under the Treaties. If the State does not comply with the reasoned opinion of the Commission, the case can be brought to the attention of the CJEU.

G. Piccirilli (✉)
Luiss University, Rome, Italy
e-mail: gpiccirilli@luiss.it

C. Fasone et al. (eds.), *EU Rule of Law Procedures at the Test Bench*, Palgrave Studies in European Union Politics,
https://doi.org/10.1007/978-3-031-60008-1_3

Currently, it is disciplined by Articles 258–260 TFEU, incorporating various amendments passed over time in order to make it more streamlined and effective, also in the light of the massive practice accumulated in its application. These multiple changes have sought to overcome some duplications envisaged in the original model, which had proved only partially effective in pushing Member States towards greater uniformity of EC/EU law (Kilbey, 2007). In particular, with the Treaty of Lisbon (taking up ideas already present in the unapproved Constitutional Treaty), the infringement procedure was modified in two distinct ways: on the one hand, the pre-litigation phase has been shortened (Article 260(2) TFEU) (Peers, 2012); on the other, the possibility of applying financial penalties already under the first infringement procedure was foreseen (Article 260(3) TFEU) (Várnay, 2017).

Already from these preliminary remarks, the potential of the infringement procedure as a deterrent is evident. Such a feature can have some importance in the case of its application with regard to rule of law violations.

2 *Pros and Cons* in Its Use with Regard to the Rule of Law Crisis

Thus, the infringement procedure is a tool that was conceived with the most general purposes, as the first and the main channel to highlight and possibly limit inconsistencies in the application of EU law by Member States. Consequently, its specific functionality in dealing with issues related to the rule of law is not to be taken for granted. Even the initial reaction of the Commission to the emerging situation of rule of law crisis in specific Member States was to affirm the necessity of a "better developed set of instruments" to tackle this challenge (Barroso, 2012), so implying the limits of the existing ones. This original consideration of unfitness of infringement procedures led to the creation of more dedicated instruments (Coman, 2022).

Considering the seriousness and the systematic nature of the violations of the rule of law in some EU countries, the use of an ordinary instrument like the infringement procedure may be seen as inadequate to the values put at risk by the Member State targeted by such a procedure. In the end, it would imply reacting to a comprehensive rule of law backsliding by a Member State of the EU in a way that is similar to the delay in implementing whatever minor directive. Just to have some figures, in the majority of the cases (54.8%), infringement procedures are initiated because of a simple time delay in the transposition of directives.[1] In other words, the question is twofold: whether the limited scope of infringement procedures, conceived to focus on a single act or law, may miss the bigger picture of systematic violations of the rule of law (von Bogdandy & Ioannidis, 2014); and whether such an ordinary instrument is proportionate to an extreme threat to the values referred to in Article 2 TEU. Moreover, its use can be seen as an underestimation of the constitutional tone of the conflict.

In the scholarly debate, the limits of using infringement procedures in this context have been underlined. Some authors claimed that they may lead only to symbolic effects, when the Member State concerned enacts only a formal compliance with a Commission's requests (Batory, 2016). Others pointed out that in the context of a rule of law crisis, infringement procedures may even be counterproductive, considering their impact on a compromised domestic public opinion (Schlipphak & Treib, 2016).

In the light of the evolution of the situation in Hungary, Romania and Poland, the debate on the possible use of infringement procedure offered further opinions, more open to its use upon the condition of introducing specific adaptations to make it more adequate to promote the rule of law (Besselink, 2017; Moberg, 2020). For example, its use in a more systemic way has been suggested in order to deal with multiple and composite threats, as is typical of risks concerned by rule of law backsliding (Scheppele, 2016). Then, a new interpretation of the procedural rules of the CJEU has been proposed, aimed at creating a fast track for the infringement procedures with implications related to the rule of law, so as to increase promptness and certainty of the penalty resulting from its violation (Bárd & Śledzińska-Simon, 2019). On the basis of this latter proposal, following some examples of further accelerated procedures, the duration of an infringement procedure may drop from an average of 40 months to some 6 months or so, enhancing its capacity of contrasting rule of law violations.

As can be seen, scholarly reflection on infringement procedure and its capacity to promote the rule of law, have been much more analytical if compared with the emphasis dedicated to the "nuclear option" of the Article 7 TEU, namely the ideal instrument specifically devised on

[1] European Commission, Single Market Scoreboard, Type of cases, situation at 1 December 2022.

the same subject. Without supporting formal amendments to Treaties' provisions, those proposals were in the sense of re-interpreting the tool, stretching to the maximum the potential of an existing and, so to speak, "ordinary" instrument.

However, the real advantage of using infringement procedures to contrast the rule of law crisis can be found exactly in its ordinary nature within the framework of institutes of EU law. The possibility of referring to a consolidated framework and a now widespread and well-known institutional praxis is certainly useful (Bakó, 2021; Heringa, 2018). Hence, the infringement procedure may bring in the set of tools managing the rule of law crisis the extremely effective leverage represented by fines (Pohjankoski, 2021), stressing not only its role as deterrent, but also the concreteness of its consequences in term of sanctions (Costamagna et al., 2020).

Some characteristics of the infringement procedure may offer answers to the limitations shown by the procedures of Article 7 TEU (Kochenov, 2021; see also Coman and Thinus in this Volume). In particular, the infringement procedure is a purely legal instrument, which can be activated by the Commission. Albeit subject to the discretion of the latter (Stone Sweet, 2004) it is not conditioned to filters of a political nature by the other Member States. The requirements for the activation of an infringement procedure are more concrete, as they are related to an effective violation of an obligation imposed by European law, not asking for "a clear risk of" a (serious) breach.

3 A New Understanding: A Tool Complementary with Article 7 TEU

The Commission also seems to have experienced a clear evolution in the interpretation of the functionality of the infringement procedure in relation to its ability to contain violations of the rule of law. Still in the Communication of January 2017 on *EU law: Better results through better application* it seemed to prefer the informal tools of the *Rule of Law Framework*, recognising that some threats in this field cannot be addressed through infringement procedures.[2] Later, probably due to the

[2] 2017/C 18/02, see p. 1.

problematic evolution that happened in some Member States (in particular in Hungary and Poland), the Commission changed its mind on this matter. The Communication *Strengthening the rule of law within the Union. In a blueprint for action* of July 2019, presented an action plan which, among other things, aims to respond effectively to violations of the rule of law through a wide-ranging use of powers of the Commission itself as "guardian" of the Treaties, in order to ensure compliance with what is provided by Union law in relation to the rule of law. In this perspective, the Commission announced a "strategic approach" to infringement procedures in this area. Such a strategic approach is not limited to the role of the Commission in activating infringement procedures (and in the timing to do so), but it also includes a more widespread involvement of the CJEU, through "requesting expedited proceedings and interim measures whenever necessary".[3]

This change of attitude on the side of the Commission has led to an emphasis on the complementarity between the general instrument of the infringement procedure and the more specific ones, such as that of Article 7 TEU. Indeed, these procedures are not mutually exclusive. In contrast with this conclusion, the nature as *lex specialis* for Article 7 TEU had been hypothesised (Kochenov & Pech, 2015), so to preclude the possibility of activating, for similar reasons or in any case against the same Member State, an infringement procedure relating to compliance with the rule of law once the Article 7 procedure has been triggered. This statement was challenged in the literature first (Schmidt & Bogdanowicz, 2018) and then overcome by the practice: both the Conclusions of Advocate General Tanchev in C-619/18 *Commission v Poland* (§48–51), as well as the aforementioned Communication of the Commission of 2019[4] clarified that these are complementary tools in the pursuit of the same goal.

The difference between Article 7 TEU and Article 258 TFEU is most evident both in regard to the preconditions and mechanisms for triggering the procedure and in terms of sanctions that can be applied to the State concerned, which are consistent with the political or legal nature of the instrument through which they are determined. Article 7 TEU foresees a decision by the Council, by a majority of four-fifths of its members,

[3] COM/2019/343 final, p. 14.

[4] See p. 9.

and the consent of the European Parliament. It is a quintessential political decision in the light of the bodies involved and the procedure for its decision. Its scope is wide and does not depend on an actual violation, it being related to "a clear risk of a serious breach by a Member State of the values referred to in Article 2". On the contrary, infringement procedures involve the Commission and the CJEU and its scope, as said, is to react to the failure to fulfil an obligation under the Treaties. Therefore, the nature and the procedure of the two procedures could not be more different. Instead, the objection related to the diverse scope of application of the two tools seems to be less decisive: at first glance, the mechanism of Article 7 TEU would appear to also be directed towards acts not covered by the principle of conferral, also involving the inner functioning of the Member State (Kochenov & Pech, 2015); however, an infringement procedure can also target a wide spectrum of a Member State's activities: practice has shown that acts generally affecting the functioning of the judiciary (i.e. the first and essential safeguard of compliance with the rule of law) end up being "attracted" under the EU competence, as they are functional to the application of European law as well[5] (Bárd, 2021).

In the light of this complementarity, as well as of the poor results of Article 7 TEU procedures in recent years (Puetter, 2022), the potential of infringement procedures in promoting compliance with the rule of law has drawn more and more attention, not only in the scholarly debate but also in the institutional practice.

4 The Most Recent Practice (with a Specific Attention to Poland)

In the last few years, the practice of infringement procedures aiming to protect the rule of law has been developing significantly. As said, the two most complicated situations are related to Hungary and Poland, although it seems possible to underline significant differences in their attitude towards the activism of European institutions.

Hungary followed a more conciliatory approach, even declaring that the institutional mechanism of the infringement procedure would have been the appropriate way to compose the legal conflict between national

[5] C-619/18, *Commission v Poland*, §50.

and EU law (Anders & Priebus, 2021). Later in the development of the relationships with the EU, in particular with regard to the many contestations concerning the migrants' crisis, a contribution to de-escalate the conflict came from the Hungarian Constitutional Court, which was able to favour the national Government without bringing the clash with EU law to extreme consequences (Kos, 2023).

Quite different is the situation with Poland, with multiple open issues concerning the independence of the judiciary (Granat, 2018).

In the last few years, several infringement procedures have been initiated. The first (launched on 3 April 2019) was on the new disciplinary regime of judges, considered harmful to the independence of Polish judges with respect to political power. The second (29 April 2020, moreover during the most difficult phase of the pandemic) was in relation to multiple acts on the functioning of the judicial system in Poland. The third (22 December 2021) is particularly interesting because it relates to the jurisprudence of the Polish Constitutional Tribunal on the primacy of Union law. In the first two cases, the Court of Justice already supported the Commission's objections.[6] Also the third case has been referred to the CJEU (15 February 2023): after a reasoned opinion sent in July 2022, the Commission did not find it to be satisfactory how Poland addressed the concerns related to Article 19(1) TEU, deciding to activate the subsequent step of the procedure (C-448/23).

As for the financial consequences of this strategy, the pressure put on Poland is potentially extremely high. Only with regard to the second case, the CJEU, upon the request of the Commission, ordered Poland to pay a fine of one million Euros per day for not having suspended the provisions relating to the Disciplinary Chamber of the Supreme Court.[7] Actually, Poland doesn't seem willing to fulfil this obligation, in a certain way confirming that this strategy of the Commission may determine an escalation in the clash between the Commission and the targeted Member State (Anders & Priebus, 2021).

The last development is a fourth infringement procedure in June 2023 related to the law passed only a few weeks before by the Polish Parliament establishing a State Commission for Investigating Russian Influences

[6] Cases C-791/19 and C-204/21.

[7] C-204/21, order issued on 27 October 2021. A subsequent order, issued on 21 April 2023 reduced the amount by a half.

on the Internal Security of the Republic of Poland from 2007 to 2022. Interestingly, beyond some more "classical" contestations related to the principle of legality, non-retroactivity of the sanctions and the right to an effective remedy before a tribunal, this last infringement procedure also encompassed the violation of the democratic principles. The possibility that decisions taken by that Commission could disqualify individual candidates from participating in the elections of October 2023 was at the core of the Commission's concerns (Wróblewska & Serowaniec, 2023). It was clear that one of the main targets was the leader of the opposition, former Prime Minister (and former President of the European Council) Donald Tusk, after whom the bill was renamed as "lex Tusk".

The prompt activation of the infringement procedure had an immediate impact in Polish politics. The parliament passed a new law amending the most controversial parts indicated by the Commission. The bill received the support of the President of the Republic and it was approved rapidly (with the signature of the President by the end of July 2023).

These facts have also to be considered in the bigger picture of the subsequent evolution of the Polish political system. A few months later, general elections have been won by the former opposition, bringing the same Tusk again as Prime Minister. It is undisputable that the whole story had a significant impact on the Polish public opinion and, at least in terms of effects, it has to be considered as a successful strategy by the Commission.

5 Conclusions: A Tool for a New Democratic Conditionality?

In conclusion, infringement procedure has been increasing its role in promoting the rule of law on an evident and somehow unexpected scale. Its results, in particular with regard to Poland, has not to be underestimated, being able to reduce the severity of the violation or any way to put pressure on national actors to a partial reconsideration of controversial national legislation.

The last case mentioned deserves specific attention, as it seems to open a new and stimulating perspective for the promotion of the rule of law and the other values enshrined in Article 2 TEU. The direct connection with the democratic principles in the context of an act introducing an infringement procedure is striking and, at least in these terms, does not seem to have precedents. This connection could perhaps appear contingent, in light of the effect of the measures of the inspection commission on the electoral rights of the people concerned. From a formal point of view, however, it cannot be ignored that the intertwining of the democratic principle and infringement procedure, according to the letter of Article 258 TFEU, means not only the identification of the former as an "obligation incumbent by virtue of the treaties", but also the activation of an instrument of EU law in order to promote and guarantee the effectiveness of that principle. In any case, the mention of the democratic principle in this matter appears most appropriate and agreeable, finally offering elements of clarity with respect to the Polish situation, in which it is the democratic principle itself, even before and even more than the characteristics of the rule of law, that result in a deep crisis.

Should this conjunction between prompt activation of infringement procedures concerning the promotion of the rule of law and connection to the democratic principle be further and effectively developed by the EC, we would find ourselves faced with a new perspective. Rather than attempting to identify new remedies with uncertain contours, the promotion of the values enshrined in Article 2 TEU (of *all* the values enshrined in Article 2 TEU) could rely on an already existing instrument, based on an institutional practice now consolidated over decades of application, which would now see immediate activation times and would ensure an extremely concrete sanctioning system.

The infringement procedure would thus end up being consolidated not only as a privileged tool for combating deviations from the rule of law, but as a procedural framework for a new form of democratic conditionality within the Union.

References

Anders, L. H., & Priebus S. (2021). Does It Help to Call a Spade a Spade? Examining the Legal Bases and Effects of Rule of Law-Related Infringement Procedures Against Hungary. In A. Lorenz & L. H. Anders (Eds.), *Illiberal Trends and Anti-EU Politics in East Central Europe*. Palgrave Macmillan.

Bakó, B. (2021). Hungary's Latest Experiences with Article 2 TEU: The Need for 'Informed' EU Sanctions. In A. von Bogdandy, et al. (Eds.), *Defending Checks and Balances in EU Member States*. Springer.

Bárd, P. (2021). In Courts We Trust, or Should We? Judicial Independence as the Precondition for the Effectiveness of EU Law. *European Law Journal, 27*(1–3), 185–210.

Bárd, P., & Śledzińska-Simon, A. (2019, May 2019). Rule of Law Infringement Procedures: A Proposal to Extend the EU's Rule of Law Toolbox. *CEPS Papers in Liberty and Security in Europe*, No. 2019-09, pp. 1–22.

Barroso, J. M. (2012, September 12). State of the Union 2012, Plenary Session of the European Parliament. *Strasbourg*. https://ec.europa.eu/commission/presscorner/detail/en/SPEECH_12_596

Batory, A. (2016). Defying the Commission: Creative Compliance and Respect for the Rule of Law in the EU. *Public Administration, 94*(3), 685–699.

Besselink, L. (2017). The Bite, the Bark, and the Howl: Article 7 TEU and the Rule of Law Initiative. In A. Jakab & D. Kochenov (Eds.), *The Enforcement of EU Law and Values: Ensuring Member States' Compliance*. Oxford University Press.

Coman, R. (2022). *The Politics of the Rule of Law in the EU Polity*. Palgrave Macmillan.

Costamagna, F., Miglio, A., & Montaldo, S. (Eds.). (2020). *EU Law Enforcement. The Evolution of Sanctioning Powers*. Giappichelli.

Granat, K. (2018). Political and Legal Enforcement of the Rule of Law in Poland. *Quaderni Costituzionali, 38*(4), 924–926.

Heringa, A. W. (2018). Fundamental rights, EU Membership, and Article 7 TEU. In A. Hatje & L. Tichy (Eds.), *Liability of Member States for the Violation of Fundamental Values of the European Union* (2018/1, pp, 59–72). Nomos.

Kilbey, I. (2007). Financial Penalties Under Article 228(2) EC: Excessive Complexity? *Common Market Law Review, 44*(3), 743–759.

Kochenov, D. (2021). Article 7: A Commentary on a Much Talked-About 'Dead' Provision. In A. von Bogdandy, et al. (Eds.), *Defending Checks and Balances in EU Member States*. Springer.

Kochenov, D., & Pech, L. (2015). Monitoring and Enforcement of the Rule of Law in the EU: Rhetoric and Reality. *European Constitutional Law Review, 11*(3), 512–540.

Kos, U. A. (2023). Signalling in European Rule of Law Cases: Hungary and Poland as Case Studies. *Human Rights Law Review, 23*(4), 1–37.

Mendrinou, M. (1996). Non-compliance and the European Commission's role in Integration. *Journal of European Public Policy, 3*(1), 1–22.

Moberg, A. (2020). When the Return of the Nation-State Undermines the Rule of Law: Poland, the EU, and Article 7 TEU. In A. Bakardjieva Engelbrekt, et al. (Eds.), *The European Union and the Return of the Nation State*. Palgrave Macmillan.

Peers, S. (2012). Sanctions for Infringement of EU Law After the Treaty of Lisbon. *European Public Law, 18*(1), 33–64.

Pohjankoski, P. (2021). Rule of Law with Leverage: Policing Structural Obligations in EU Law with the Infringement Procedure, Fines, and Set-Off. *Common Market Law Review, 58*, 1341–1364.

Prete, L. (2017). *Infringement Proceedings in EU Law*. Kluwer Law International.

Puetter, U. (2022). Consensus Politics and EU Disequilibrium: The German Council Presidency 2021 and the Rule of Law Mechanism. In S. Münch & H. Heinelt (Eds.), *EU Policymaking at Crossroads—Negotiating the 2021–2027 Budget* (pp. 233–250). Edward Elgar Publishing Limited.

Scheppele, K. L. (2016). Enforcing the Basic Principles of EU Law Through Systemic Infringement Actions. In C. Closa & D. Kochenov (Eds.), *Reinforcing Rule of Law Oversight in the European Union*. Cambridge University Press.

Schlipphak, B., & Treib, O. (2016). Playing the Blame Game on Brussels: The Domestic Political Effects of EU Interventions Against Democratic Backsliding. *Journal of European Public Policy, 24*(3), 352–365.

Schmidt, M., & Bogdanowicz, P. (2018). The Infringement Procedure in the Rule of Law Crisis: How to Make Effective Use of Article 258 TFEU. *Common Market Law Review, 55*(4), 1061–1100.

Stone Sweet, A. (2004). *The Judicial Construction of Europe*. Oxford University Press.

Várnay, E. (2017). Sanctioning under Article 260(3) TFEU: Much Ado About Nothing? *European Public Law, 23*(2), 301–316.

von Bogdandy, A., & Ioannidis, M. (2014). Systemic Deficiency in the Rule of Law: What It Is, What Has Been Done, What Can Be Done. *Common Market Law Review, 51*, 59–96.

Wróblewska, I., & Serowaniec, M. (2023). «Lex Tusk»—The Phenomenon of Constitutional Interpretation Hostile To The Constitution Itself. https://redspinel.iee-ulb.eu/lex-tusk-the-phenomenon-of-constitutional-interpretation-hostile-to-the-constitution-itself/?fbclid=IwAR2d2IgEQwMuOTkOvXNhhTwTcDQMRVUy1QmGSda7KX5syPtoEmrf8AlLbu8

CHAPTER 4

The Rising Value of the Preliminary Reference Procedure in the Rule of Law Protection

Lorenzo Cecchetti

1 Introduction

The preliminary reference procedure has shaped and continues to shape profoundly the European Union's (EU) legal order and the relationships between the EU and the Member States. As Baquero Cruz put it, the European integration process "would not have developed the way it has without the law and the Court" and, "[i]n turn, Union law and the Court of Justice would not be what they are without the preliminary rulings procedure" (Baquero Cruz, 2018: 54). This procedure is the "keystone" of the Union judicial system (Opinion 2/13, para. 176) and, in the literature, it has been defined as the "most important aspect of the work of the Court" (Brown & Jacobs, 1977: 131), the "jewel in the Crown" of the Court of Justice of the EU (CJEU or Court)'s jurisdiction (Langer, 2019:

L. Cecchetti (✉)
Luiss University, Rome, Italy
e-mail: lcecchetti@luiss.it

C. Fasone et al. (eds.), *EU Rule of Law Procedures at the Test Bench*, Palgrave Studies in European Union Politics,
https://doi.org/10.1007/978-3-031-60008-1_4

455), and the "genius" without which core principles, such as direct effect and primacy, could have not been conceived (Weiler, 2013: 11). These considerations on the importance of Article 267 TFEU for the European integration process hold true with regard to the rule of law crisis.

In light of these considerations, the objective of this chapter is specifically to briefly illustrate the role that this procedure has played in the context of the systemic threats to the rule of law over the last decade by paying particular attention to the potentialities and limits of this procedure highlighted by the academic literature. Interestingly, the preliminary reference procedure relates to the emerging dissensus in the EU from a twofold perspective. On the one hand, it has served as a procedural tool through which the dissensus—between the Member States and the EU as well as between national authorities—has been "channelled". This phenomenon does not only relate to the rule of law crisis: Article 267 TFEU has already been used to "question the limits of EU policies seen as intruding upon core national constitutional principles" (Dawson, 2020: 199). On the other hand, due to the inner characteristics of such a procedural tool and the EU legal order as a whole, the preliminary reference procedure has equally been the "subject" of dissensus. Most notably, in the context of the rule of law crisis, both the use of this procedure and some procedural aspects of Article 267 TFEU have attracted contrasting academic views. For instance, it has been pointed out that Article 267 TFEU has proved not to "bite" in the context of the rule of law backsliding, differently from the infringement procedure (see Giovanni Piccirilli's chapter in this volume).

The chapter unfolds as follows. Firstly, we will outline the basics of the preliminary reference procedure in order to explain *why* and *how* this tool, enshrined in the Treaties since the 1950s without experiencing any substantive amendments, has happened to play a role in protecting the value of the rule of law (Sect. 2). Secondly, we will examine the preliminary rulings rendered by the CJEU in the context of the rule of law crisis from the perspective of academics. To this end, we will adopt Kochenov's and Bárd's classification of the Court's case law, which distinguishes two "categories": (a) cases giving voice to the "*horizontal* rule of law *concerns*, leading to a significant refinement of the principle of mutual recognition" (Kochenov & Bárd, 2020: 245) in the Area of Freedom, Security and Justice ("AFSJ") (Sect. 3); and (b) those raising "*vertical* concerns related to the independence of the judiciary", that being cases affecting the cooperative relationship between the CJEU and national courts (Kochenov & Bárd, 2020: 245) (Sect. 4). On the basis of this case law analysis, which shall *not* be understood as exhaustive, we will offer some concluding remarks on the value of the preliminary reference procedure in the rule of law protection.

2 Why Has the Preliminary Reference Procedure Played a Role in the Protection of EU Values?

2.1 The "Enforcement Dimension" of Article 267 TFEU Within the Context of the EU Composite Judicial Architecture

As is well known, the preliminary reference procedure is today laid down in Article 267 TFEU, according to which the CJEU has the jurisdiction to give preliminary rulings concerning the *interpretation* or *validity* of Union law. Pursuant to Article 19(1) TEU, which sets the design of the EU judicial system, the Court has indeed the function to "ensure that in the interpretation and application of the Treaties the law is observed". Due to the particular nature of EU law and the decentralised judicial enforcement that characterises this legal order, EU law litigation occurs to a significant extent before courts of the Member States, which can be considered the "ordinary Union court[s] to hear and to determine all cases that do not fall within the jurisdiction of the [CJEU or, as the case may be, specialised courts]" (Lenaerts, 2023: 49). This is why, firstly, Article 267 TFEU proves to be pivotal to ensuring consistency, full effectiveness, the autonomy of EU law, and the particular nature of this legal order (Klamert & Schima, 2019: 175). Being a reference-based system, it is indeed necessary that a national court considers referring a preliminary question necessary to enable it to give judgement, thereby requesting the CJEU to give a ruling thereon. Secondly, such a setting also explains why, pursuant to the second subparagraph of Article 19(1), Member States are under a duty to "provide remedies sufficient to ensure effective legal protection in the fields covered by Union law", which is a specific expression of the duty of sincere cooperation today laid down in Article 4(3) TEU (Schütze, 2021: 412).

In such an EU composite judicial architecture, the national courts perform a "European mandate".[1] Article 267 TFEU thus represents "the central pillar of the Union's cooperative federalism for it combines

[1] On this concept, see Sect. 4 below.

the central interpretation of Union law by the Court of Justice with the decentralized application of European law by the national courts" (Schütze, 2021: 357). In this regard, it is worth noting that the roles and functions under Article 267 are traditionally conceived as "*separate* but *equal*" (Douglas-Scott, 2002: 228), i.e., the CJEU is in charge of the "interpretation" of EU law while the national courts are responsible for its "application". The CJEU has thus progressively developed a narrative of a "Europe of judicial cooperation" (Cecchetti & Gallo, 2023), according to which the preliminary reference procedure shall be considered a "dialogue" between national courts and the Court rooted in a "spirit of cooperation" (Case 16/65, *Schwarze*, 1095; Opinion 2/13, para. 176), of which the "spirit of mutual respect for the responsibilities of each partner" is the essential ingredient (Pescatore, 1971: 60). Nevertheless, the actual existence of a line between these two concepts has been questioned (Cohen, 1996: 422; Douglas-Scott, 2002: 228–229), and a "shift to a vertical hierarchy" between the CJEU and national courts has been highlighted (Craig & de Búrca, 2020: 510).[2]

Two additional clarifications seem to be necessary at this point. First, although Article 267 TFEU only refers to questions on the "interpretation" or "validity" of EU law, since *van Gend & Loos* (Case 26/62) is evident that preliminary questions can also concern the effects of certain provisions of EU law in the Member States. As stressed in the literature, uniform interpretation does not merely mean the "*unité de signification positive*" but also encompasses the "uniformity" of the effects that an EU law norm is endowed with in the Member States' legal orders ("*uniformité de la validité et de l'efficacité*") (Barav, 1977: 11–13; Pescatore, 1971: 54–56). Indeed, it has been apparent from the earliest CJEU's case law that, among the types of questions that national courts can refer to Luxembourg, there were questions on the compatibility between the national legal order and EU law. Second, and consequently, although overtly conceived for securing the uniform application of Union law throughout the Member States, the procedure under investigation has been used, de facto, to monitor the compatibility of national measures with EU law. By this means, the CJEU has been carrying out a judicial

[2] On the recent developments on the constitutional backbone of the preliminary reference procedure, see the contributions in Daniele Gallo and Lorenzo Cecchetti (eds), Special Issue: 'The Preliminary Ruling Procedure, Today: Revisiting Article 267 TFEU's Constitutional Backbone', in European Journal of Legal Studies, Issue No. 3, 2023.

review of Member State action (Tridimas, 2011), which proves essential for any federal-type structure (Mancini, 1989: 604 ff.). Tizzano defined it as the "alternative use" of the preliminary ruling procedure (Tizzano, 1995: 17). Considering the extent to which such "alternative use' has typically occurred, which arguably is one of the most frequent uses of this procedure (Broberg, 2017), it has been highlighted that the tool enshrined in Article 267 TFEU has become a sort of 'infringement procedure for European Citizens" (Pescatore, 2010: 7; de Witte, 2013: 95–97).

2.2 *The Paradigm Shift Brought About by* Associação Sindical dos Juízes Portugueses *in the Court's Role in Protecting the Rule of Law*

In the light of the foregoing, the preliminary reference procedure has been able to serve as a central instrument to tackle the challenges posed by the rule of law backsliding occurred in several Member States. It is indeed in the context of this procedure that several milestones in the history of the protection of the EU values by the CJEU have been laid down. The point of departure can be nothing but the well-known Court's ruling in *Associação Sindical dos Juízes Portugueses* ("*ASJP*") (Case C-64/16), rendered in February 2018, where the inner link between Article 2 TEU, Article 19 (1), second subparagraph, TEU, and Article 47 of the Charter of Fundamental Rights of the EU (the "Charter") was first clarified, "allowing it to exercise a level of scrutiny on domestic measures threatening the independence of the judiciary" (Muir et al., 2023: 9). After having stated that in "the fields covered by Union law", irrespective of Article 51(1) of the Charter, Member States must ensure that national courts meet the requirements essential to effective judicial protection, the CJEU held that they must (a) establish a system of legal remedies sufficient to ensure effective judicial protection and (b) ensure judicial independence of national courts and tribunals. The independence of national courts and tribunals—it was also stressed—"is, in particular, essential to the proper working of the judicial cooperation system embodied by the preliminary reference mechanism under Article 267 TFEU" (Case C-64/16, para. 43). Relying on its previous case law, and to a considerable extent on the principles affirmed in *Wilson* (Case C-506/04), the Court then specified that "[t]he concept of independence presupposes, in particular, that the body concerned exercises its judicial functions wholly autonomously, without being subject to any hierarchical constraint or subordinated to any other body and without taking orders or instructions from any source whatsoever, and that it is thus protected against external interventions or pressure liable to impair the independent judgment of its members and to influence their decisions" (Case C-64/16, para. 44). Following *ASJP*, the "independence" of the national courts in the context of Article 267 TFEU came back under the spotlight (see, e.g., Case C-274/14, *Banco de Santander*; and Case C-272/19, *Land Hessen*).[3]

The significance of the interpretation of the second subparagraph of Article 19(1) TEU provided for in such judgement has been unanimously acknowledged by academic literature. The Court's ruling has been defined, *inter alia*, as "creative" (Bonelli & Claes, 2018: 640), a "breakthrough" (Lenaerts, 2023: 71), and considered a "spectacular innovation reshaping the constitutional system of the Union" (Kochenov & Bárd, 2020: 245). The *ASJP* judgement was undoubtedly a paradigm shift, which has allowed the *Kirchberg* Court "to move to the centre of the stage in the Polish crisis", thereby—to some extent—tackling "[t]he difficulties in operationalising Article 7 TEU" (Bonelli & Claes, 2018: 639–640). From a broader theoretical perspective, it has been argued that *ASJP* opened "a new chapter of European constitutionalism", where the presumption that the strict enforcement of the acquis is sufficient to guarantee adherence to the values has been rebutted and where the inter-court dialogue concerns not only issues of "interpretation" and "validity" of EU law but the fundamental principles of the Union legal order (Kochenov & Bárd, 2020: 245).

The paradigm shift brought about by *ASJP* was swiftly followed by other seminal decisions, to a significant extent rendered upon references from national courts, on which the following sections focus. The "speed" characterising the steps forward down this line of jurisprudence has been highlighted by Scholars (CMLR Editorial Comments, 2019: 17). As mentioned in the introduction, however, we do not claim to be exhaustive.[4] Conversely, we will attempt to show the preliminary reference procedure's role in the context of the systemic threats to the

[3] We will come back on this aspect in Sect. 4 below.

[4] For a comprehensive account of the CJEU's case law on the rule of law crisis, see, e.g., Pech and Kochenov (2021) and the contributions in Muir et al. (2023).

rule of law by focusing on two main strands of the CJEU's case law, according to the classification offered by Kochenov and Bárd. Firstly, we will consider the cases that give voice to "*horizontal* rule of law *concerns*", leading to a significant refinement of the principle of mutual recognition' (Kochenov & Bárd, 2020: 245) in the context of the AFSJ (Sect. 3). Secondly, we will have a look at those cases where the European mandate of national courts and the cooperative relationship between the latter and the CJEU were at stake, which raised "*vertical* concerns related to the independence of the judiciary" (Kochenov & Bárd, 2020: 245).

3 The Independence of National Courts "On Trial": The European Arrest Warrant as a Test Bench

Let us begin with the "horizontal concerns" in the Area of Freedom, Security, and Justice. Here, the dissensus—channelled via Article 267—has been first and foremost expressed by national courts *in relation to* the independence of other Member States' courts. Most notably, soon after the Court's ruling in *ASJP*, the importance of the preliminary reference procedure as a means to enforce Union values has come under the spotlight in the context of the European Arrest Warrant ("EAW"), based on the principle of mutual recognition of judgements and judicial decisions in criminal matters and on "a high level" of mutual trust between the Member States. It is well known that these principles form the basis of the cooperation between the issuing national authority and the executing national authority provided for in the EAW Framework Decision. In turn, the preliminary rulings that the Court rendered upon request by courts worried about the independence of other Member States' courts have been the subject to dissensus, as we are about to see.

In *LM* (C-216/18 PPU), handed down in July 2018, the CJEU advanced the protection of the right to a fair trial, with specific regard to the right to an independent tribunal, in situations of systemic or general deficiencies as regards the rule of law (Spieker, 2023: 203 ff.). Most notably, building on its previous decision in *Aranyosi and Căldăraru* (Joined Cases C-404/15 e C-659/15 PPU), the Court held that—although mutual trust is the general rule—the executing judicial authorities can, after having applied a two-step procedure, suspend the surrender of the requested person. To this end, that authority shall, first of all, make a finding of general or systemic deficiencies in the protections provided in the issuing Member State and, second, "specifically and precisely [assess] whether, in the particular circumstances of the case, there are substantial grounds for believing that, following his surrender to the issuing Member State, the requested person will run that risk" (C-216/18 PPU, para. 68). In so doing, the principles affirmed in *ASJP*—with specific regard to the fundamental right to a fair trial as an essential element of the Union values—have been "decanted" into the EAW system.

Such a two-step assessment designed by the Court has been criticised by part of the academic literature. Several Scholars, for instance, have claimed the second prong of the test to be unpracticable in the context of the rule of law backsliding (Bárd & van Ballegooij, 2018; Bárd & Morijn, 2020; see also Biernat & Filipek, 2021; and Frąckowiak-Adamska, 2021). Conversely, other authors have placed emphasis on the fact that, undoubtedly, *LM* "has considerably reinforced Article 7 TEU" (Sarmiento, 2018: 386). Indeed, as Konstandinides put it, *LM* is "a small victory, but a victory nonetheless" (Konstadinides, 2019: 769). Interestingly, some Authors have highlighted that these developments wouldn't have been possible without the cooperation between the decentralised level of the composite "European judiciary", namely the cooperation of domestic courts and tribunals, and that such judicial cooperation served to offset the "inaction of the supranational and national political institutions" (von Bogdandy et al., 2021: 385–386).

Bonelli, moreover, disentangled three different "messages" from this judgement. Two of them directly concern the complementarity character of the judicial protection of the rule of law via Article 267 TFEU, and thus need to be briefly outlined. The first message is linked to the space dedicated to the Commission's reasoned proposal under Article 7(1) TEU, which was considered "particularly relevant" for the assessment to be conducted by national courts (in the first prong of the scrutiny) (Bonelli, 2021: 471). The second "message" or aspect to be recalled is the further emphasis placed on the respect of the political mechanisms available to safeguard EU values: the *Aranyosi* test is the exception since the general competence to suspend the application of the EAW in a specific Member State belongs to the Council and to the European Council only. In so doing, it has been argued that the Court seems to "well understand that ensuring democracy and the rule of law is not a task of judicial actors only" (Bonelli, 2021: 472). This second message, however, has also been interpreted as a step back from the forefront (Frąckowiak-Adamska, 2022: 148).

A second preliminary ruling, rendered by the CJEU in this context, is *L and P* (Joined Cases C-354/20 PPU and C-412/20 PPU), which, in essence, confirmed that *Aranyosi-LM* was still good law, despite the worsening of the rule of law situation in Poland. Indeed, in *L and P*, the Court firmly refused to give the green-light to Polish national courts to skip the second prong of the *Aranyosi-LM* test (the assessment of the particular circumstances of the cases). Nor is it accepted to consider that Polish courts are unfit for being qualified as "judicial authorities" under the EAW Framework Decision (Frąckowiak-Adamska, 2022: 115). Considering this refusal by the Court, some Authors considered quite understandable a "bottom-up resistance from national courts" refusing to give execution to EAW (Pech et al., 2021: 32–38; Pech, 2021: 162). Due to the Court's approach, it has been claimed that "[f]rom the point of view of the fight for the rule of law in the EU, the *L and P* (and *LM*) ruling cannot be rated highly" (Frąckowiak-Adamska, 2022: 148). In the same vein, Saenz Perez has concluded that the preliminary reference procedure "has not been an effective tool for the CJEU to develop a thick interpretation of the rule of law linked to fundamental rights. Instead, the Court has used Article 19(1) TEU and Article 267 TFEU to prioritise interpretations that safeguard the coherence and effective enforcement of EU law" (Saenz Perez, 2022: 532).

4 The Independence of National Courts "On Trial": The European Mandate of National Courts as a Test Bench

The *ASJP* ruling has profoundly impacted even the "vertical" (Craig & de Búrca, 2020: 510) relationship between the CJEU and national courts, with specific regard to limitations imposed by Member States on the possibility for these courts to exercise their "European mandate" (Claes, 2006). By "European mandate", we are referring to the national courts' possibility to *freely* (a) refer preliminary questions to the CJEU, (b) interpret national law in conformity with EU law, and (c) set aside national provisions that are not compatible with Union law norms having direct effect. Although this kind of limitation is not a new phenomenon in the Union legal system (consider, for instance, Case 106/77, *Simmenthal* or Case C-210/06, *Cartesio*),[5] those experienced in the context of the rule of law backsliding are characterised by a different "tone", as they are often coupled with the questioning of (some of) the constitutional principles of the EU legal order. Hence, even though they are linked to longstanding and multifaceted issues characterising the European integration process, the interpretation given to the second subparagraph of Article 19(1) TEU played a major role in protecting the national courts in their institutional capacity (Lenaerts, 2023), while the interpretation given to Article 267 TFEU served to protect the dialogue inherent in the preliminary reference procedure (Lenaerts, 2023). From this recent strand of case law, as aired in the literature, Article 19 TEU appears to be "the cement of the EU shared judicial space that glues together the two jurisdictions of the CJEU and of national courts tasked with the protection of individuals' EU rights and values" (Menzione, 2023).

Let us now recall the major preliminary rulings handed down by the CJEU in this regard by arranging them according to the Member State from which the preliminary questions originated. In relation to Hungary, suffice it to recall the Court's ruling in *IS* (Case C-564/19). With regard to Poland, *Miasto Łowicz* (Joined Cases C-558/18 and C-563/18), *A.B., C.D., E.F., G.H., I.J.* (Case C-824/18), *A.K. and others* (Joined Cases C-585/18, C-624/18 and 625/18), *YP and Others* (Joined Cases C-615/20 and C-671/20), Getin Noble Bank (Case C-132/22), and *Krajowa Rada Sądownictwa* (Case C-718/21) can be mentioned. As to the Romanian legal system, reference can be made to *Asociația* (Joined Cases C-83/19, C-127/19, C-195/19, C-291/19, C-355/19, and C-397/19), *Euro Box Promotion and Others* (Joined Cases C-357/19, C-379/19, C-547/19, C-811/19, and C-840/19), *RS* (Case C-430/21), and *Asociația "Forumul Judecătorilor din România"* (Case C-216/21). Closely connected issues have emerged in relation to the appointment of Maltese judges in *Repubblika* (Case C-896/19).

All these rulings, rendered in the context of the preliminary reference procedure, dealt with national rules or practices which are able, de facto or *de jure*, to hinder ordinary national courts from raising a preliminary question under Article 267 TFEU and/or to set aside national measures

[5] For an account of this phenomenon, see, e.g., Broberg and Fenger (2021, 83 ff.).

incompatible with EU law. Differently from previous case law on similar limitations, many of these recent cases are characterised by the need to ensure the independence of national judges and by the questioning—or, sometimes, by an actual denial (Palladino & Festa, 2022)—of the principle of primacy of Union law and of some of the essential prerogatives forming part of the rule of law.

As regards Romania, the issues concerned the reform introduced in 2017–2019 to the disciplinary, civil, and criminal liability of judges (for an overview of the requests for preliminary rulings submitted by Romanian judges and courts, see Călin, 2019). The preliminary ruling rendered in *Asociația I* laid very important principles for the protection of the rule of law in the EU: (a) it introduced the principle of progression towards achieving EU rule of law standards; (b) it extended the "judicial independence parameters for all types of judicial liability regimes, beyond the disciplinary one which has repeatedly appeared in the Polish case law"; and (c) it can be considered as "a strong restatement of the legally binding principle of primacy of EU law for constitutional courts" (Moraru & Bercea, 2022: 83). Nonetheless, according to the same Authors the "effective application" of these principles has been swiftly undermined by the Romanian Constitutional Court's case law (Moraru & Bercea, 2022: 83). These considerations proved right, as shown by the following "episodes" in the "Romanian saga" (Bellenghi, 2022). Among these cases, *RS* has been welcomed for having reaffirmed the core principles of EU law, including primacy, loyal cooperation and Article 267, and "interpretative autonomy" of the CJEU, while dealing with the concept of Member States' national identity under Article 4 (2) TEU (Gallo, 2022). In *Asociația II*, the CJEU, by reaffirming the principles stated in *Euro Box Promotion and Others*, held that the national legislation relating to the scheme for the promotion of judges is required to ensure compliance with the principle of the independence of judges.

In relation to Poland, the preliminary rulings rendered in this context have been considered *not* effective and useful to tackle the exacerbation of the issues in that Member State (Zelazna, 2019). *A.K. and Others*, for instance, has been considered by some commentators to "rais[e] more questions than it answers" (Leloup, 2020: 168–169). Nonetheless, in *YP and Others*, the CJEU affirmed that national courts must disapply resolutions of the Polish Disciplinary Chamber suspending, in breach of EU law, a national judge from his/her function, since—as stated in a previous judgement rendered in the context of an infringement procedure against

Poland—the independence and impartiality of the Disciplinary Chamber were not guaranteed. Other rulings concerned more precisely the use of Article 267 TFEU by Polish courts. For example, *Miasto Łowicz*, where the reference under Article 267 TFEU was considered inadmissible as the questions referred did not "concern an interpretation of EU law which meets an objective need for the resolution of those disputes, but are of a general nature" (para. 53), have reinforced the comments on a "timid" use of preliminary reference procedure, *i.e.*, the CJEU has been considered "less likely to engage with systemic issues on the rule of law in the preliminary ruling procedure" (Platon, 2020: 1866). In other words, it has been clarified that "even in the context of the crucial fight for judicial independence Article 267 TFEU is not a *passepartout* solution, since the courts must still find the 'substantive' link to EU law" (Scheppele et al., 2020: 70). In *Getin Noble Bank*, upon reference from a "new judge" appointed by the National Council for the Judiciary, the Court did not apply its case law on Article 19 TEU to the issue of admissibility of preliminary questions, preferring entering into such dialogue with national courts. The CJEU was thus criticised for having established a "presumption of independence", which was considered "a legal and strategic mistake" (Grabowska-Moroz, 2023; Kochenov & Bárd, 2022), although the rebuttable character of such presumption led other Authors to consider the Court's approach "cautious" and "wise" (Menzione, 2023: 257) and to stress that the principles affirmed in this judgement could have been read in line with the Court's previous case law on Article 19 TEU (Sánchez Frías, 2023). This is precisely what happened in the preliminary ruling recently rendered in *Krajowa Rada Sądownictwa*, where the presumption was considered rebutted in the light of the previous case law regarding the Chamber of Extraordinary Control and Public Affairs of the Polish Supreme Court, and the request for a preliminary ruling was thus considered inadmissible.

In *A.B., C.D., E.F., G.H., I.J.* (Case C-824/18), moreover, the CJEU "focused on the analysis of the right to an effective remedy under Article 19 (1) TEU as instrumental to ensuring effective legal protection for individuals in the field of EU law" (Saenz Perez, 2022: 351). Overall, these preliminary rulings on judicial independence in Poland have been read as primarily aimed at ensuring "the smooth operation of the EU's decentralised judicial system, including the preliminary reference procedure" (Bornemann, 2022: 662). The CJEU has thus applied one of its most characteristic interpretative yardsticks of Union law (Bonelli & Claes, 2018: 631; Bornemann, 2022: 662).

In the Hungarian case (C-564/19, *IS*), although the Court was confronted with a preliminary question on Article 19 TFEU, the ruling heavily relied on its case law on Article 267 TFEU, not even quoted in the order submitted by the referring court. Focusing on this equally effective—but arguably less conflicting—line of case law has been considered a "strategic choice" (Amalfitano & Cecchetti, 2023; Lattanzi, 2022). Other Authors, however, suggested that the preliminary ruling would not be "sufficient" or effective (Correra, 2022).

Finally, *Repubblika* (Case C-896/19), on the appointment of Maltese judges, shall not underestimated. As stressed by Łazowski, its true importance lies in the principle of non-regression, according to which Member States are precluded "from adopting national rules which would amount to a regression in their compliance with the standards of the rule of law" (Łazowski, 2022: 1804). According to some Authors, the Court's findings in this preliminary ruling have contributed to solving the so-called "Copenhagen dilemma" (Leloup et al., 2021).

5 Concluding Remarks

Undoubtedly, thanks to the preliminary reference procedure, the CJEU has played a pivotal role in "rescuing" judicial independence in the Union (Bonelli & Claes, 2018; Pech & Platon, 2018). As illustrated above, it is precisely in the context of this procedure that several milestones for the judicial protection of the rule of law and the EU values have been set.

This notwithstanding, many Scholars have considered the preliminary reference procedure as a "weak and tepid" tool to face many of the ongoing severe challenges to the Union values. For instance, Pech, Wachowiec, and Mazur have argued that, differently from the infringement procedure, preliminary rulings "have failed" to contain the irreparable damage done to judicial independence. Such an approach, they added, increased "the risk of (understandable) bottom-up resistance from national courts keen to prevent Poland's autocratisation from spreading to their systems via EU mutual trust-based mechanisms such as the European Arrest Warrant" (Pech et al., 2021: 32–38). Judgements like *L and P* have been deemed to nudge national courts towards this direction (Pech, 2021: 162). The use of preliminary reference procedure has been labelled as "timid", and the CJEU is generally considered "less likely to engage with systemic issues on the rule of law in the preliminary ruling procedure" (Platon, 2020: 1866).

In the context of the AFSJ (Sect. 3), the procedure "has not been an effective tool for the CJEU to develop a thick interpretation of the rule of law linked to fundamental rights" (Saenz Perez, 2022: 532). As brilliantly observed by the same Author, "the Court has used Article 19 (1) TEU and Article 267 TFEU to prioritise interpretations that safeguard the coherence and effective enforcement of EU law" (Saenz Perez, 2022: 532). Similar considerations seem to hold true in relation to the limitations on the European mandate of national judges (Sect. 4), where the Court's focus has been placed on ensuring "the smooth operation of the EU's decentralised judicial system, including the preliminary reference procedure" (Bornemann, 2022: 662).

To sum up this analysis, one could say that, differently from the infringement procedure, Article 267 TFEU has proved not to "bite" in the context of the severe crisis of Union values that some Member States have been experiencing. This was the main dissensus attracted by this procedural tool from the academic literature. Nonetheless, it should not be overlooked that it is precisely the preliminary reference procedure that—by interpreting EU law norms and channelling dissensus from national courts—allowed the creation of the essential "bridges" for enforcing the respect of the rule of law in the EU. This should, however, come as no surprise. It seems instead a necessary corollary of the procedure's inner rationale and objectives (outlined in Sect. 2 above). Differently from what happens in the context of the infringement procedure and Article 7 TEU, the important role played by the preliminary reference procedure has been possible thanks to the *cooperation* of national courts (in relation to specific cases, it has also been argued that these courts have abused of this channel of cooperation, see Pech & Platon, 2021), which have been traditionally considered as one of the "mighty allies" of the CJEU, along with the Commission (Mancini, 1989: 597)—each of them, of course, within the remit of their respective functions. Therefore, the preliminary ruling procedure shall be understood as a *complementary tool* to the procedure under Article 7 TEU (see Ramona Coman's and Pauline Thinus' chapter in this volume) and the infringement procedure (see Giovanni Piccirilli's chapter in this volume), a "mighty ally" of the other procedures rather than being a substitute for them and the single panacea for the crisis of the EU's founding values.

References

Amalfitano, C., & Cecchetti, L. (2023). The ItCC's Judgment No. 269/2017 Turns 5 Years Old: The ECJ's Approach to Dual Preliminarity. *Italian Journal of Public Law, 15*, 84–119.

Barav, A. (1977). Some Aspects of the Preliminary Rulings Procedure in EEC Law. *European Law Review, 2*, 3–25.

Bárd, P., & Morijn, J. (2020, April 18). Luxembourg's Unworkable Test to Protect the Rule of Law in the EU: Decoding the Amsterdam and Karlsruhe Courts' Post-LM rulings (Part I). *Verfassungsblog*. https://verfassungsblog.de/luxembourgs-unworkable-test-to-protect-the-rule-of-law-in-the-eu/

Bárd, P., & van Ballegooij, W. (2018). Judicial Independence as a Precondition for Mutual Trust? The CJEU in *Minister for Justice and Equality v. LM*. *New Journal of European Criminal Law, 9*(3), 353–365. https://doi.org/10.1177/2032284418801569

Bellenghi, G. (2022). A New Episode in the Romanian Saga: The Primacy of EU Law Over National Constitutional Jurisprudence. *EU Law Live*.

Biernat, S., & Filipek, P. (2021). *The Assessment of Judicial Independence Following the CJEU Ruling in C-216/18 LM*. In A. von Bogdandy et al. (Eds.), *Defending Checks and Balances in EU Member States*. Springer.

Bonelli, M. (2021). *Intermezzo in the Rule of Law Play: The Court of Justice's LM Case*. In A. von Bogdandy et al. (Eds.), *Defending Checks and Balances in EU Member States*. Springer.

Bonelli, M., & Claes, M. (2018). Judicial Serendipity: How Portuguese Judges Came to the Rescue of the Polish Judiciary. ECJ 27 February 2018, Case C-64/16, Associação Sindical dos Juízes Portugueses. *European Constitutional Law Review, 14*(3), 622–643. https://doi.org/10.1017/S1574019618000330

Bornemann, J. (2022). Judicial Responses to Autocratic Legalism: The European Court of Justice in a Cleft Stick? *European Papers, 7*(2), 651–670. https://doi.org/10.15166/2499-8249/592

Broberg, M. (2017). Preliminary References as a Mean for Enforcing EU Law. In A. Jakab & D. Kochenov (Eds.), *The Enforcement of EU Law: Ensuring Member State's Compliance*. Oxford University Press.

Broberg, M., & Fenger, N. (2021). *Preliminary References to the European Court of Justice* (3rd ed.). Oxford University Press.

Brown, N., & Jacobs, F. G. (1977). *The Court of Justice of the European Communities*. Sweet & Maxwell.

Călin, D. (2019). Ten Requests for a Preliminary Ruling Filed by the Romanian Courts for Maintaining the Rule of Law, a Common Value of all the European Union Member States. *Revista Forumul Judecătorilor, 2*, 69–123.

Cecchetti, L., & Gallo, D. (2023). The Reception of the Narrative of a Europe of Judicial Cooperation in the Italian Jurisprudence and Legal Doctrine: Cooperative Federalism in the Making. In A. Bailleux et al. (Ed.), *Les récits judiciaires de l'Europe: Diffusion et reception*. Bruylant.

Claes, M. (2006). *The National Courts' Mandate in the European Constitution*. Hart.

Cohen, J. C. (1996). The European Preliminary Reference and US Court Review of State Court Judgments: A Study in Comparative Judicial Federalism. *American Journal of Comparative Law, 44*(3), 421–461.

Correra, A. (2022). *Il giudice nazionale deve disattendere qualsiasi prassi giurisdizionale interna che pregiudichi la sua facoltà di interrogare la Corte di giustizia*. BlogDUE.

Craig, P., & de Búrca, G. (2020). *EU Law. Text, Cases, and Materials* (7th ed.). Oxford University Press.

Cruz, J. B. (2018). *What's Left of the Law of Integration?: Decay and Resistance in European Union Law*. Oxford University Press.

Dawson, M. (2020). How Can EU Law Respond to Populism? *Oxford Journal of Legal Studies, 40*, 183–213.

de Witte, B. (2013). *The Impact of Van Gend en Loos on Judicial Protection at European and National Level: Three Types of Preliminary Questions*. In A. Tizzano, J. Kokott, & S. Prechal (Organising Committee), *Court of Justice of the European Union. 50th Anniversary of Van Gend and Loos 1963–2013*. Luxembourg.

Douglas-Scott, S. (2002). *Constitutional Law of the European Union*. Pearson.

Editorial Comments. (2019). 2019 Shaping up as a Challenging Year for the Union, Not Least as a Community of Values. *Common Market Law Review, 56*(1), 3–22.

Frąckowiak-Adamska, A. (2022). Trust Until It Is Too Late!: Mutual Recognition of Judgments and Limitations of Judicial Independence in a Member State: L and P: Joined Cases C-354/20 PPU and C-412/20 PPU, Openbaar Ministerie v. L and P (Indépendance de l'autorité judiciaire d'émission). *Common Market Law Review, 59*(1), 113–150.

Frąckowiak-Adamska, A. (2021). Drawing Red Lines with No (Significant) Bites: Why an Individual Test Is Not Appropriate in the LM Case. In A. von Bogdandy et al. (Eds.), *Defending Checks and Balances in EU Member States*. Springer.

Gallo, D. (2022). Primato, identità nazionale e stato di diritto in Romania. *Quaderni Costituzionali, 2*, 374–378.

Gallo D., & Cecchetti, L. (Eds.). (2023). Special Issue: 'The Preliminary Ruling Procedure, Today: Revisiting Article 267 TFEU's Constitutional Backbone'. *European Journal of Legal Studies*, Issue No. 3.

Grabowska-Moroz, B. (2023). Judicial Dialogue About Judicial Independence in Times of Rule of Law Backsliding: Getin Noble Bank. *Common Market Law Review, 60*(3), 797–818.

Klamert, M., & Schima, B. (2019). Article 19 TEU. In M. Kellerbauer, M. Klamert, & J. Tomkin (Eds.), *The EU Treaties and the Charter of Fundamental Rights*. Oxford University Press.

Kochenov, D., & Bárd, P. (2020). The Last Soldier Standing? Courts Versus Politicians and the Rule of Law Crisis in the New Member States of the EU. In E. H. Ballin, G. van der Schyff & M. Stremler (Eds.), *European Yearbook of Constitutional Law 2019: Judicial Power: Safeguards and Limits in a Democratic Society*. Asser Press.

Kochenov, D. V., & Bárd, P. (2022). Kirchberg Salami Lost in Bosphorus: The Multiplication of Judicial Independence Standards and the Future of the Rule of Law in Europe. *Journal of Common Market Studies, 60*(1), 150–165.

Konstadinides, T. (2019). Judicial Independence and the Rule of Law in the Context of Non-Execution of a European Arrest Warrant: LM. *Common Market Law Review, 56*(3), 743–769.

Langer, J. (2019). Article 267 TFEU: Celebrating the Jewel in the Crown of the Community Legal Architecture and Some Hot Potatoes. In F. Ambtenbrink et al. (Eds.), *The Internal Market and the Future of European Integration. Essays in Honour of Laurence W. Gormley*. Cambridge University Press.

Lattanzi, U. (2022). Rinvio pregiudiziale ex art. 267 TFUE e procedimenti disciplinari nazionali nell'ambito della crisi del rule of law*: CGUE, sentenza del 23 novembre 2021, C-564/19, IS*, Diritti Comparati Blog.

Łazowski, A. (2022). Strengthening the Rule of Law and the EU Pre-accession Policy: Repubblika v. Il-Prim Ministru: Case C-896/19. *Common Market Law Review, 59*, 1803–1822.

Leloup, M. (2020). An Uncertain First Step in the Field of Judicial Self-Government. ECJ 19 November 2019, Joined Cases C-585/15, C-624/18 and C-625/18, A.K., CP and DO. *European Constitutional Law Review, 16*(1), 145–169.

Leloup, M., Kochenov, D., & Dimitrovs, A. (2021). Opening the Door to Solving the "Copenhagen Dilemma"? All Eyes on Repubblika v II-Prim Ministru. *European Law Review, 46*(5), 692–703.

Lenaerts, K. (2023). On Checks and Balances: The Rule of Law within the EU. *The Columbia Journal of European Law, 29*, 25–63.

Mancini, G. F. (1989). The Making of a Constitution for Europe. *Common Market Law Review, 26*(4), 595–614.

Menzione, S. (2023). *Article 19 TEU as the Cement of the EU Shared Judicial Space: An Analysis of the CJEU's Case-Law*. KU Leuven Thesis.

Moraru, M., & Bercea, R. (2022). The First Episode in the Romanian Rule of Law Saga: Joined Cases C-83/19, C-127/19, C-195/19, C-291/19, C-355/19 and C-397/19, Asociaţia 'Forumul Judecătorilor din România, and their Follow-Up at the National Level. *European Constitutional Law Review, 18*(1), 82–113.

Muir, E., Van Nuffel, P., & De Baere, G. (2023). The EU as a Guardian of the Rule of Law within its Member States. *The Columbia Journal of European Law, 29*(2), 1–23.

Palladino, R., & Festa, A. (2022). Il primato del diritto dell'Unione europea nei dissoi logoi tra la Corte di giustizia e le Alte Corti ungherese, polacca e rumena. Questioni sullo Stato di diritto, Eurojus.

Pescatore, P. (1971). L'interpretation du droit communautaire et la doctrine de l'acte clair, Bulletin de l'association des juristes européens.

Pescatore, P. (2010). Van Gend en Loos, 3 February 1963—A View from Within. In M. Poiares Maduro & L. Azoulai (Eds.), *The Past and Future of Eu Law: The Classics of EU Law Revisited on the 50th Anniversary of the Rome Treaty*. Hart.

Pech, L. (2021). Protecting Polish Judges from Poland's Disciplinary 'Star Chamber': Commission v. Poland (Interim proceedings). *Common Market Law Review, 58*(1), 137–162.

Pech, L., & Kochenov, D. (2021). Respect for the Rule of Law in the Case Law of the European Court of Justice: A Casebook Overview of Key Judgments since the Portuguese Judges Case. *SIESP Report*.

Pech, L., & Platon, S. (2018). Judicial Independence under Threat: The Court of Justice to the Rescue in the ASJP Case. *Common Market Law Review, 55*(6), 1827–1854.

Pech, L., & Platon, S. (2021). How Not to Deal with Poland's Fake Judges' Requests for a Preliminary Ruling: A Critical Analysis of AG Bobek's Proposal in Case C-132/20. *VerfBlog*. https://verfassungsblog.de/how-not-to-deal-with-polands-fake-judges-requests-for-a-preliminary-ruling/. https://doi.org/10.17176/20210729-020032-0

Pech, L., Wachowiec, P., & Mazur, D. (2021). Poland's Rule of Law Breakdown: A Five-Year Assessment of EU's (In)Action. *Hague Journal on the Rule of Law, 13*, 1–43.

Platon, S. (2020). Preliminary References and Rule of Law: Another Case of Mixed Signals from the Court of Justice Regarding the Independence of National Courts: Miasto Łowicz. *Common Market Law Review, 57*(6), 1843–1866.

Saenz Perez, C. (2022). What About Fundamental Rights? Security and Fundamental Rights in the Midst of a Rule of Law Breakdown. *New Journal of European Criminal Law, 13*(4), 385–554.

Sánchez Frías, A. (2023). A New Presumption for the Autonomous Concept of "Court or Tribunal" in Article 267 TFEU. *European Constitutional Law Review, 19*(2), 320–345.

Sarmiento, D. (2018). A Comment on the CJEU's Judgment in LM. *Maastricht Journal of European and Comparative Law, 25*(4), 385–387.

Scheppele, K. L., Kochenov, D. V., & Grabowska-Moroz, B. (2020). EU Values Are Law, After All: Enforcing EU Values Through Systemic Infringement Actions by the European Commission and the Member States of the European Union. *Yearbook of European Law, 39*, 3–121.

Schütze, R. (2021). *European Union Law* (3rd ed.). Oxford University Press.

Spieker, L. D. (2023). *EU Values Before the Court of Justice*. Oxford University Press.

Tizzano, A. (1995). La tutela dei privati nei confronti degli Stati membri dell'Unione europea. *Il Foro italiano, 118*(1), 13/14–31/32.

Tridimas, T. (2011). Constitutional Review of Member State Action: The Virtues and Vices of an Incomplete Jurisdiction. *International Journal of Constitutional Law, 9*(3–4), 737–756.

Weiler, J. H. H. (2013, May 13). *Revisiting Van Gend en Loos: Subjectifying and Objectifying the Individual*. In A. Tizzano, J. Kokott, & S. Prechal (Eds.), *50th Anniversary of the Judgement in Van Gend en Loos 1963–2013: Conference Proceedings, Luxembourg* (pp. 11–22). Office des publications de l'Union européenne.

von Bogdandy, A., Bogdanowicz, P., Canor, I., Rugge, G., Schmidt, M., & Taborowski, M. (2021). *A Potential Constitutional Moment for the European Rule of Law: The Importance of Red Lines*. In A. von Bogdandy, et al. (Eds.), Defending Checks and Balances in EU Member States. Springer.

Zelazna, E. (2019). The Rule of Law Crisis Deepens in Poland after A.K. v. Krajowa Rada Sadownictwa and CP, DO v. Sad Najwyzszy. *European Papers, 4*(3), 907–912.

Case Law

CJEU 5 February 1963, Case 26/62, *van Gend & Loos*, EU:C:1963:1.

CJEU 1 December 1965, Case 16/65, *Schwarze*, EU:C:1965:117.

CJEU 9 March 1978, Case 106/77, *Simmenthal* SpA, EU:C:1978:49.

CJEU 19 September 2006, Case C-506/04, *Wilson*, EU:C:2006:587.

CJEU 16 December 2008, Case C-210/06, *Cartesio*, EU:C:2008:723.

CJEU 18 December 2014, Opinion 2/13, *Accession of the European Union to the European Convention for the Protection of Human Rights and Fundamental Freedoms*, EU:C:2014:2454.

CJEU 5 April 2016, Joined Cases C-404/15 e C-659/15 PPU, *Aranyosi and Căldăraru*, EU:C:2016:198.

CJEU 27 February 2018, Case C-64/16, *Associação Sindical dos Juízes Portugueses*, EU:C:2018:117.
CJEU 25 July 2018, Case C-216/18 PPU, *LM*, EU:C:2018:586.
CJEU 19 November 2019, Joined Cases C-585/18, C-624/18 and 625/18, *A.K. and others*, EU:C:2019:982.
CJEU 21 January 2020, Case C-274/14, *Banco de Santander*, EU:C:2020:17.
CJEU 26 March 2020, Joined Cases C-558/18 and C-563/18, *Miasto Łowicz and Prokurator Generalny*, EU:C:2020:234.
CJEU 9 July 2020, Case C-272/19, *VQ v Land Hessen*, EU:C:2020:535.
CJEU 17 December 2020, Joined Cases C-354/20 PPU and C-412/20 PPU, *L and P*, EU:C:2020:1033.
CJEU 2 March 2021, Case C-824/18, *A.B., C.D., E.F., G.H., I.J. v Krajowa Rada Sądownictwa*, EU:C:2021:153.
CJEU 20 April 2021, Case C-896/19, *Repubblika*, EU:C:2021:311.
CJEU 18 May 2021, Joined Cases C-83/19, C-127/19, C-195/19, C-291/19, C-355/19 and C-397/19, *Asociația 'Forumul Judecătorilor din România' and Others v Inspecția Judiciară and Others*, EU:C:2021:393.
CJEU 23 November 2021, Case C-564/19, *Criminal proceedings against IS*, EU:C:2021:949.
CJEU 21 December 2021, Joined Cases C-357/19, C-379/19, C-547/19, C-811/19 and C-840/19, *Euro Box Promotion and Others*, EU:C:2021:1034.
CJEU 22 February 2022, Case C-430/21, *Proceedings brought by RS*, EU:C:2022:99.
CJEU 29 March 2022, Case C-132/22, *Getin Noble Bank*, EU:C:2022:235.
CJEU 13 July 2023, Joined Cases C-615/20 and C-671/20, YP and Others (Levée d'immunité et suspension d'un juge), ECLI:EU:C:2023:562.
CJEU 7 September 2023, Case C-216/21, *Asociația "Forumul Judecătorilor din România"*, EU:C:2023:628.
CJEU 21 December 2023, Case C-718/21, *Krajowa Rada Sądownictwa (Maintien en fonctions d'un juge)*, EU:C:2023:1015.

CHAPTER 5

Granting Rights, Preserving the Rule of Law? The Effectiveness of the Charter of Fundamental Rights

Lorenzo Cecchetti

1 Introduction

As is well known, the Charter of Fundamental Rights of the European Union (Charter) was solemnly proclaimed by the Parliament, the Council, and the Commission in 2000 and acquired the "same legal value as the Treaties" (Article 6(1) TEU) with the entry into force of the Lisbon Treaty in 2009. Today, the fundamental rights recognised by the Charter lie "at the heart of th[e] [Union's] legal structure" (Opinion 2/13, para. 169) and the "respect for human rights" is one of the values upon which the Union is founded (Article 2 TEU).

The idea to provide the European Union (EU) with its own "Bill of Rights", however, dates back in time and involved the drafting of several committee of experts' reports during the Nineties, such as the 1995

L. Cecchetti (✉)
Luiss University, Rome, Italy
e-mail: lcecchetti@luiss.it

C. Fasone et al. (eds.), *EU Rule of Law Procedures at the Test Bench*, Palgrave Studies in European Union Politics,
https://doi.org/10.1007/978-3-031-60008-1_5

so-called Pintasilgo Report, the 1998 *Comité de Sages* Report, and the 1999 so-called Simitis Report. Does this mean that fundamental rights were not protected *at all* in the Union before the Charter's proclamation? Of course, the answer to this question is in the negative. On the one hand, at the national level, both Member States' constitutions and international agreements protecting human rights to which they had entered into, first and foremost the European Convention on Human Rights (ECtHR), continued to apply to violation of human rights. On the other hand, with specific regard to the *sui generis* legal order established by the founding treaties and the legal acts adopted therein, after some years of hesitations, the Court of Justice of the European Union (CJEU or Court)—"nudged" by the Constitutional courts of some Member States—affirmed that "fundamental human rights [were] enshrined in the general principles of Community law and protected by the Court" (*Stauder*, Case 29/69, para. 7). It is against this backdrop that the European Council decided on drawing up a *written* catalogue of fundamental rights in order to make "their overriding importance and relevance more visible to the Union's citizens" (Cologne European Council of 3–4 June 1999, Conclusions of the Presidency, Annex IV).

Although the Charter has *not* transformed the Union into a "Human Rights Organisation" (von Bogdandy, 2000), it has unquestionably contributed to the development of the EU legal order (Muir, 2020). Hence, it *cannot* be seen as a mere (technical) "codification" of the existing situation. This is also confirmed by the *sui generis* Convention-based system used for its adoption (in this regard, see, e.g., Braibant, 2001; de Búrca, 2001). Poiares Maduro pointed out such a "double constitutional life" of the Charter by stressing that it reflected the "tension between its conception as a constitutional instrument for polity building and its conception as a simple consolidation of the previous fundamental rights *acquis* aimed at guaranteeing regime legitimacy" (Poiares Maduro, 2003: 269). In 2000, moreover, von Bogdandy already noticed that the Charter would have been part of "an ongoing process that has the potential to transform substantially the Union and its legal system" (von Bogdandy, 2000: 1308). Its "centralising force" was soon highlighted in the literature and linked to the importance placed—in drafting the Charter—on the delimitation of its "scope of application" (Eeckhout, 2002: 945), which remains a sensitive, open issue. This is also confirmed by the recent trends in the conditionality tools to combat the rule of law backsliding, such as the Charter enabling condition of the 2021 Common Provisions Regulation (see Cristina Fasone and Marta Simoncini in this volume).

Against this backdrop, this chapter aims to briefly illustrate the Charter's role in the context of the systemic threats to the rule of law that occurred over the last decade, by paying particular attention to its potentialities and limits as highlighted by the academic literature. Regarding the Charter, the interpretation of its Article 47 in combination with other EU law provisions played a pivotal role in the Court's response to the rule of law crisis. At the same time, such a joint interpretation of sources triggered some dissensus due to the sensitive character of its scope of application and the uncertainties surrounding this issue. Since the Charter is not a "procedural tool", it is worth noting that it could not be considered as completely detached from other tools analysed in this volume, such as the infringement procedure (Giovanni Piccirilli in this volume) and the preliminary reference procedure (Lorenzo Cecchetti in this volume).

This chapter is structured as follows. Firstly, we will look at Article 51 of the Charter, which regulates its "field of application" (Sect. 2). Secondly, we will outline the use of Charter by the CJEU in relation to the challenges posed by the rule of law backsliding occurred in several Member States, with specific regard to the protection of judicial independence (Sect. 3) and, briefly, beyond this issue (Sect. 4).

2 The (Material) Scope of Application of the Charter Under Its Article 51

Under Article 51(1), the Charter's provisions "are addressed to the institutions, bodies, offices and agencies of the Union with due regard for the principle of subsidiarity and to the Member States *only when they are implementing Union law*".[1] Therefore, "[t]hey shall [...] respect the rights, observe the principles and promote the application thereof in accordance with their respective powers and respecting the limits of the powers of the Union as conferred on it in the Treaties". Such provision, which rhymes with several other "safeguards" against centralising forces

[1] Emphasis added.

laid down or reinforced by the Lisbon Treaty,[2] is completed by Article 51 (2). According to this provision, "[t]he Charter does not extend the field of application of Union law beyond the powers of the Union or establish any new power or task for the Union, or modify powers and tasks as defined in the Treaties".[3] This key provision was not conceived by the Convention drafting the Charter overnight. The Explanation on Article 51—which serves as a "guidance in the interpretation of this Charter [and] shall be given due regard" (Article 52 (7) Charter)—states that "it follows *unambiguously* from the case-law of the Court of Justice that the requirement to respect fundamental rights defined in the context of the Union is only binding on the Member States when *they act in the scope of Union law*",[4] and refers to seminal preliminary rulings where the CJEU elaborated upon the scope of application of the EU fundamental rights.

Therefore, only *some* measures of the Member States fall within the EU fundamental rights' reach, and the major issues consist in assessing whether there is a sufficient link between a certain national measure and EU law (Lenaerts & Gutiérrez-Fons, 2021: 1713). The term "implementation" is normally considered as a synonym of "situation governed by EU law" (Lenaerts & Gutiérrez-Fons, 2021: 1713), which turns out to be the major determinant of the "material" scope of application of the EU fundamental rights.[5] This situation has led some authors to apply the so-called "doctrine of incorporation" of State action—developed in relation to the United States' federal system—to the EU legal order (Weiler, 1986, 1991) and to describe the EU constitutional architecture in terms of "selective incorporation" (Schütze, 2021: 476).

[2] Suffice it to recall the Early Warning System laid down in Protocol No. 2 attached to the Treaties, according to which Member States' National Parliaments are entrusted with the control over the respect of the principle of subsidiarity by draft legislative acts.

[3] The same concern is stated in Article 6(1)(2) TEU, pursuant to which "The provisions of the Charter shall not extend in any way the competences of the Union as defined in the Treaties".

[4] Emphasis added.

[5] As highlighted in the literature, the scope of application of the Charter, like any other legal rule, has four main facets: its "personal" scope, its "material" scope, its "temporal" scope, and its "territorial" scope, see Lazzerini (2018, 83 ff.).

In light of the foregoing, Article 51 of the Charter (and the CJEU's case law on which this provision is based) can be considered the "keystone" of the vertical allocation of powers between the Union and the Member States (Knook, 2005; Lenaerts & Gutiérrez-Fons, 2010). Since such vertical allocation had been profoundly impacted by the application of the general principles of Union law developed in the CJEU's case law, "competence creep" was considered an important issue in drafting the Charter (Prechal, 2010). Although a thorough analysis of the copious literature on Article 51 falls beyond the scope of this chapter (on this provision see, among others, Fontanelli, 2014; Gambardella, 2021; Hancox, 2013; Lazzerini, 2018; Spaventa, 2016; Tizzano, 2014; von Danwitz & Paraschas, 2017; Ward, 2021), three final remarks on this article seems necessary. First, it is reasonable to interpret Article 51 in line with the pre-Charter case law. As argued by Sarmiento, if the above-mentioned work of codification was to replace the Court's previous jurisprudence on the protection of fundamental rights as general principles of Union law, this intention should have been much more explicitly stated (Sarmiento, 2013: 1270). Second, the fact that the "scope of application" of EU law (i.e., the scope of the Member States' action that can be bound by EU law) is wider than the legislative competences conferred to the Union comes as no surprise today. This principle is also known as the "principle of *encadrement*" (Mengozzi & Morviducci, 2018: 92 ff.). Nevertheless, and this is the third remark, the scope of application of EU law—and thus that of the Charter that has been defined "the 'shadow' of EU law" (Lenaerts & Gutiérrez-Fons, 2021)—remains "nebulous" (Spaventa, 2018: 1002) and still is an open issue (Bartoloni, 2018), rather than "unambiguously" resulting from the CJEU's case law (cf. Explanation on Article 51). The Court's use of the Charter in the context of the rule of law backsliding that has recently occurred in several Member States proves to be a good litmus test of these uncertainties, as we are about to see.

3 Effective Judicial Protection and the "Independence" of National Judges and Courts

The point of departure of the Charter's role in facing the rule of law crisis is the interpretative preliminary ruling rendered by the CJEU in *Associação Sindical dos Juízes Portugueses* (Case C-64/16) ("*ASJP*") in 2018, outlined in the chapter on the preliminary reference procedure (see Lorenzo Cecchetti in this volume). For the purposes of this analysis, suffice it to recall that, in that judgement, the Court highlighted the inextricable knot between the value of the rule of law laid down in Article 2 TEU, Article 19(1)(2) TEU—which "gives specific expression" to that founding value—, and Article 47 of the Charter (*ASJP*, paras. 32 and 35).

In brief, Article 19(1)(2) TEU—following the Lisbon Treaty—reads "Member States shall provide remedies sufficient to ensure *effective legal protection* in *the fields covered by Union law*".[6] This provision—defined as the "cement" of the EU shared judicial space (Menzione, 2023)—thus imposes upon Member State a duty to ensure effective judicial protection (see Albors-Llorens, 2021: 1743), which is a specific expression of the duty of sincere cooperation today laid down in Article 4(3) TEU (Schütze, 2021: 412). The principle of the effective judicial protection of individuals' rights referred to in Article 19 TEU—carries on the CJEU—"is a general principle of EU law stemming from the constitutional traditions common to the Member States, which has been enshrined in [the European Convention on Human Rights], and which is now reaffirmed by Article 47 of the Charter" (*ASJP*, para. 35), titled "Right to an effective remedy and to a fair trial".[7]

[6] Emphasis added.

[7] Pursuant to Article 47 of the Charter, "Everyone whose rights and freedoms guaranteed by the law of the Union are violated has the right to an effective remedy before a tribunal in compliance with the conditions laid down in this Article. Everyone is entitled to a fair and public hearing within a reasonable time by an independent and impartial tribunal previously established by law. Everyone shall have the possibility of being advised, defended and represented. Legal aid shall be made available to those who lack sufficient resources in so far as such aid is necessary to ensure effective access to justice". According to the Explanation on Article 47, the fundamental rights protected in this provision correspond to those enshrined in Articles 6 and 13 of the European Convention on Human Rights.

Interestingly, in affirming these principles, the Court drew a distinction between the scope of application of Article 47 of the Charter—which must be limited to situations of "implementation" of Union law pursuant to its Article 51(1)—and "the material scope of the second subparagraph of Article 19(1) TEU, [which] relates to 'the fields covered by Union law'" (*ASJP*, para. 29). Such a distinction has been reiterated in following judgements, such as *Commission v Poland (Independence of the Supreme Court)* (Case C-619/18, para. 49). Here, however, the CJEU added a significant clarification by stating that "the second subparagraph of Article 19(1) TEU requires Member States to provide remedies that are sufficient to ensure effective legal protection, *within the meaning in particular of Article 47 of the Charter*, in the fields covered by EU law".[8] Yet, what does this clarification mean? In *A.B. and Others* (Case C-824/18, para. 143) and *Repubblika* (Case C-896/19, paras 45–46), the Court further explains that Article 47 of the Charter "must be *duly taken into consideration for the purposes of interpreting* the second subparagraph of Article 19 (1) TEU". In sum, after having *linked* the legal content of Article 19(1) TEU to that of Article 47 of the Charter in *ASJP*—so that the legal obligations stemming from the two provisions seemed already to overlap each other (Krajewski, 2018: 402)—, in *Commission v Poland*, the Court carried out an actual "*fusion*" of those two provisions (Torres Pérez, 2020b: 111) or, with Lenaerts, a "cross-fertilisation of its case law" (Lenaerts, 2023: 32).

Five major patterns can be identified in the academic reflection on these developments. First, it has been highlighted that this line of jurisprudence is based on a "wide material scope" of Article 19 TEU and of the principle of effective judicial protection (Editorial Comments, 2019: 17) that—to some extent—seems to go beyond the limits set in Article 51(1) of the Charter (Mori, 2021: 83; Vosa, 2023: 2022–2024; on these aspects see also Lazzerini, 2019; for proposals on how to limit the application of Article 19 TEU, see Prechal, 2022). Indeed, the organisation of justice falls within the competence of the Member States and is to some extent linked to the national identities of the Member States under Article 4(2) TEU. Such principle has been explicitly upheld by the CJEU itself in several recent judgements, even in the context of the rule of law crisis; see, for instance *RS* (C-430/21, paras. 38 and 43) and *Euro*

[8] Emphasis added.

Box Promotion and Others (Joined Cases C-357/19, C-379/19, C-547/19, C-811/19, and C-840/19, paras. 133, 216, 229). As regards such a distinction between the scope of application of Article 19(1)(2) TEU and the one of Article 47, even Scholars who considered it not to pose particular issues have noticed that, however, the Court decided not to "go into more details to explain such distinction" (Menzione, 2023: 11).

Second aspect: many Scholars, however, agree on considering the Charter in combination with Article 2 TEU and Article 19 TEU as "an efficient instrument (at least more efficient than Article 7 TEU) to counter the systematic, perpetual attacks committed by the illiberal States on the rule of law" (Groussot & Thor Pétursson, 2022: 241; see also Lenaerts, 2023). These authors have also highlighted that such an interpretation and application of Article 19 TEU has contributed to preserving the constitutional principles of the EU legal order (Gallo, 2022) and "to the development of the EU shared judicial space"(Menzione, 2023: 22).

A third aspect that has been highlighted in the literature is that such limited scope of the Charter has led the CJEU to prioritise the use of Article 19(1) TEU and Article 267 TFEU to tackle situations of violation of Union values in the Member States (Saenz Perez, 2022: 533). This preference for those "alternative" and "less contested" yardsticks can even be noted in relation to challenges to the rule of law in Hungary and Romania (Amalfitano & Cecchetti, 2022; Lattanzi, 2022; Moraru & Bercea, 2022: 102).

A fourth argument that Scholars have put forward is the need to reinforce the application of the Charter in the context of the rule of law crisis. It has been maintained that—"strikingly"—the Charter "has played only a slight and ambiguous role in this process" (Kochenov & Morijn, 2021: 760–761), mainly as "a 'sidekick' for Article 19 (1) TEU" (Pech & Kochenov, 2021: 222–223). These authors have also appreciated the use of the Charter in *A.K. and others* (Joined Cases C-585/18, C-624/18, and 625/18) (in relation to the notorious "Disciplinary Chamber" of the Polish Supreme Court) and called for "much more serious consideration [of the Charter] to ensure that the standards of the independence of the judiciary in the EU do not fall below the minimum standards laid down in the case law of the European Court of Human Rights" (Pech & Kochenov, 2021: 222–223).

In the same vein, fifthly, the expansion of the application of the Charter to purely domestic cases has been advocated by some Scholars, either by amending or interpreting extensively its Article 51(1) (Jakab & Kirchmair, 2022). Torres Pérez, for instance, contended that "[w]hile such an outcome might currently seem politically unsound, [...] a progressive case-by-case expansion of the applicability of the Charter to the Member States would be welcome from the standpoint of a robust notion of the rule of law in the EU" (Torres Pérez, 2020a).

Nevertheless, there is a second strand of case law in which the use of the Charter, including its Article 47, as a means to ensure the protection of the rule of law is instead welcomed, at least during a first phase. That being the cases of the use of Article 47 of the Charter in the context of the European Arrest Warrant ("EAW"), whose importance has been underlined by several Scholars (Anagnostaras, 2016; Łazowski, 2018: 12; Spieker, 2023: 203 ff.). These authors refer mainly to the CJEU's judgements in *LM* (Case C-216/18 PPU) and *L and P* (Joined Cases C-354/20 PPU and C-412/20 PPU), based on the principles affirmed in *Aranyosi and Căldăraru* (Joined Cases C-404/15 e C-659/15). The reason why these jurisprudential developments were, at least in a first phase, well received lies in the fact the "rigidity" of the grounds for non-execution laid down in the EAW Framework Decision had been under "academic siege" for some time already. As it has been said, in relation to the "*horizontal* rule of law *concerns*" arisen in the Area of Freedom, Security, and Justice—thanks to the preliminary reference procedure—the Charter allowed national judges to become "mouths of the rule of law" (Groussot & Martinico, 2020: 11–12). Nevertheless, the enthusiasm for these developments did not last long, as applying the second prong of the *Aranyosi-LM* test was soon considered impracticable (see further Lorenzo Cecchetti in this volume).

4 The Charter Beyond the "Independence" Criterion

Besides, it is worth recalling that the use of the Charter in infringement proceedings, which was an open issue until recently, proved successful (Bonelli, 2022: 40 ff.). This holds specifically true with regard to Hungary. Suffice it to recall *Commission v Hungary (Enseignement supérieur)* (Case C-66/18) and, most importantly, *Commission v Hungary (Transparency of associations)* (Case C-78/18), where the Court held that Hungary had failed to fulfil its obligations under Article 12(1) of the Charter, which is "one of the essential bases of a democratic and pluralist society, inasmuch as it allows citizens to act collectively in fields of mutual interest and in doing so to contribute to the proper functioning of public life" (Case C-78/18, paras. 110–112). In this context, the Court's approach of relying on the treaty provisions and on the Charter—rather than on Article 19 TEU—has been appreciated by some Scholars (Bonelli, 2021; Lenaerts, 2023; Marchioro, 2021; Morijn, 2022; Spieker, 2023: 198). It has been argued that such an approach "cleverly set a balance between two opposite needs, namely that of suppressing national rules and measures that grossly violate fundamental rights and threaten the rule of law, on the one hand, and of preserving a purely technical – and therefore apolitical – legal and judicial reasoning" (Marchioro, 2021: 38). The CJEU's concern for "upholding the rule of law and protecting the value of democracy" in *Commission v Hungary (Transparency of associations)* has been highlighted by other Scholars (Lenaerts, 2023: 27), although others noticed that, in this case, "fundamental rights remain[ed] a rather meek accessory to the internal market" (Spieker, 2023: 198).

5 Concluding Remarks

The Charter is a "complex beast", and its *material* scope of application lies among the most complex constitutional conundrums of the EU fundamental rights protection architecture. We have tried to show that the Charter has been of primary importance in the context of the rule of law backsliding occurred in several Member States, especially in combination with other EU provisions—such as Article 19 TEU—and thanks to other procedural tools provided for in EU law (i.e., the preliminary reference procedure and the infringement procedure). There is some consensus about the role that the principle of effective judicial protection today enshrined in Article 47 of the Charter, as well as on the Charter's importance in infringement procedures and in the context of the horizontal rule of law concerns arising within the EAW system. Conversely, to sum up, the dissensus has primarily regarded the following aspects: (i) the "nebulous" material scope of application of the EU fundamental rights protected in the Charter; (ii) the fact that the CJEU's legal reasoning on sensitive EU constitutional issues is "minimalist", "hermetic", methodologically questionable, and, at the same time, pro-integration; and, yet, seen from other viewpoints, (iii) the fact that the CJEU has not been sufficiently active (or proactive), and thus not incisive enough. Notwithstanding the seriousness of these constitutional issues, which should not be taken light-heartedly and whose importance ought not to be overlooked, these criticisms are certainly not alien to the academic reflection on the European integration process. In conclusion, the vast majority of those criticisms result from longstanding uncertainties surrounding the Charter as a peculiar constitutional tool in that process and the scope of application of Union law, and consequently of the Charter itself, which continues to be the "shadow" of EU law even at a time of rule of law-backsliding.

References

Albors-Llorens, A. (2021). The Asymmetrical Impact of Article 47 of the Charter on National and EU Remedies. In S. Peers, T. Hervey, J. Kenner, & A. Ward (Eds.), *The EU Charter of Fundamental Rights: A Commentary*. Oxford: Hart Publishing.

Amalfitano, C., & Cecchetti, L. (2022). *Sentenza n. 269/2017 della Corte costituzionale e doppia pregiudizialità: l'approccio della Corte di giustizia dell'Unione europea*. Eurojus.it.

Anagnostaras, G. (2016). Mutual Confidence Is Not Blind Trust! Fundamental Rights Protection and the Execution of the European Arrest Warrant: Aranyosi and Caldararu. *Common Market Law Review, 53*(6), 1675–1704.

Bartoloni, M. E. (2018). *Ambito d'applicazione del diritto dell'Unione europea e ordinamenti nazionali: Una questione ancora aperta*. Edizioni Scientifiche Italiane.

Bonelli, M. (2022). Infringement Actions 2.0: How to Protect EU Values before the Court of Justice, *European Constitutional Law Review*, *18*(1), 30–58.

Bonelli, M. (2021). 'European Commission v Hungary (Transparency of associations) (C-78/18): The "NGOs case": On How to Use the EU Charter of Fundamental Rights in Infringement Actions. *European Law Review, 2*, 258–271.

Braibant, G. (2001). *La Charte des droits fondamentaux de l'Union européenne. Témoignage et commentaires*. Seuil.

de Búrca, G. (2001). The Drafting of the European Charter of Fundamental Rights. *European Law Review, 26*(2), 126–138.

Editorial Comments. (2019). 2019 Shaping Up as a Challenging Year for the Union, Not Least as a Community of Values. *Common Market Law Review, 56*(1), 3–22.

Eeckhout, P. (2002). The EU Charter of Fundamental Rights and the Federal Question. *Common Market Law Review, 39*, 945–994.

Fontanelli, F. (2014). The Implementation of European Union Law by Member States Under Article 51(1) of the Charter of Fundamental Rights. *Columbia Journal of European Law, 20*(2), 194–247.

Gallo, D. (2022). Primato, identità nazionale e stato di diritto in Romania. *Quaderni costituzionali*, 374–378.

Gambardella, I. (2021). L'application de la Charte des droits fondamentaux de l'union européenne aux États membres: le critère de mise en oeuvre du droit de l'Union comme obstacle à son effectivité. Cahiers de droit européen, 241–286.

Groussot, X., & Thor Pétursson, G. (2022). Review Essay, Je t'aime...moi non plus: Ten Years of Application of the EU Charter of Fundamental Rights. *Common Market Law Review, 59*(1), 239–258.

Groussot, X., & Martinico, G. (2020, January 25). *Mutual Trust, the Rule of Law and the Charter: A New Age of Judicial Activism*. EU Law Live.

Hancox, E. (2013). The Meaning of "Implementing" EU Law Under Article 51(1) of the Charter: Åkerberg Fransson. *Common Market Law Review, 50*(5), 1411–1431.

Jakab, A., & Kirchmair, L. (2022). Two Ways of Completing the European Fundamental Rights Union: Amendment to vs. Reinterpretation of Article 51 of the EU Charter of Fundamental Rights. *Cambridge Yearbook of European Legal Studies, 24*, 239–261.

Kochenov, D., & Morijn, J. (2021). Strengthening the Charter's Role in the Fight for the Rule of Law in the EU: The Cases of Judicial Independence and Party Financing. *European Public Law, 27*(4), 759–780.

Knook, A. (2005). The Court, the Charter, and the Vertical Division of Powers in the European Union. *Common Market Law Review, 42*(2), 367–398.

Krajewski, M. (2018). Associação Sindical dos Juízes Portugueses: The Court of Justice and Athena's Dilemma. *European Papers, 3*(1), 395–407.

Lattanzi, U. (2022, January 27). *Rinvio pregiudiziale ex art. 267 TFUE e procedimenti disciplinari nazionali nell'ambito della crisi del rule of law: CGUE, sentenza del 23 novembre 2021, C-564/19, IS*. Diritti Comparati Blog.

Łazowski, A. (2018). The Sky Is Not the Limit: Mutual Trust and Mutual Recognition après Aranyosi and Caldararu. *Croatian Yearbook of European Law & Policy, 14*(1), 1–30.

Lazzerini, N. (2018). *La Carta dei diritti fondamentali dell'Unione europea – I limiti di applicazione*. Franco Angeli.

Lazzerini, N. (2019). Inapplicabile ma comunque rilevante? La Carta dei diritti fondamentali nella giurisprudenza recente della Corte di giustizia sull'indipendenza dei giudici. In AA. VV., *Temi e questioni di diritto dell'Unione europea*. Cacucci.

Lenaerts, K. (2023). On Checks and Balances: The Rule of Law Within the EU. *The Columbia Journal of European Law, 29*, 25–63.

Lenaerts, K., & Gutiérrez-Fons, J. A. (2010). The Constitutional Allocation of Powers and General Principles of EU Law. *Common Market Law Review, 47*(6), 1629–1669.

Lenaerts, K., & Gutiérrez-Fons, J. A. (2021). *The Place of the Charter in the European Legal Space*. In S. Peers, T. Hervey, J. Kenner & A. Ward (Eds.), *The EU Charter of Fundamental Rights: A Commentary*. Hart.

Marchioro, J. (2021). Role Models of Politics Disguised in Technique: Cases C-78/18 on Associative Transparency and C-66/18 on Academic Freedom in Hungary. *Bratislava Law Review, 5*(2), 23–42.

Mengozzi, P., & Morviducci, C. (2018). *Istituzioni di Diritto dell'Unione europea* (2nd ed.). CEDAM.

Menzione, S. (2023, December). *Article 19 TEU as the Cement of the EU Shared Judicial Space: An Analysis of the CJEU's Case-Law*. KU Leuven Thesis.

Moraru, M., & Bercea, R. (2022). The First Episode in the Romanian Rule of Law Saga: Joined Cases C-83/19, C-127/19, C-195/19, C-291/19, C-355/19 and C-397/19, Asociaţia 'Forumul Judecătorilor din România, and Their Follow-Up at the National Level. *European Constitutional Law Review, 18*(1), 82–113.

Mori, P. (2021). Il primato dei valori comuni dell'Unione europea. *Il Diritto Dell'unione Europea, 1*, 73–92.

Morijn, J. (2022). Separate Charter Invocation as a New Enforcement Method: The Lex NGO Case: Case C-78/18, Commission v Hungary. *Common Market Law Review, 59*, 1137–1168.

Muir, E. (2020). *The Added Value of the EU Charter of Fundamental Rights: At the Intersection of Legal Systems*. Jean Monnet Working Paper No. 15.

Pech, L., & Kochenov, D. (2021). *Respect for the Rule of Law in the Case Law of the European Court of Justice: A Casebook Overview of Key Judgments since the Portuguese Judges Case*. SIESP Report.

Poiares Maduro, M. (2003). The Double Constitutional Life of the Charter of Fundamental Rights of the European Union. In T. K. Hervey & J. Kenner (Eds.), *Economic and Social Rights Under the EU Charter of Fundamental Rights—A Legal Perspective*. Hart.

Prechal, S. (2010). Competence Creep and General Principles of Law. *Review of European Administrative Law, 3*(2), 5–22.

Prechal, S. (2022). Article 19 TEU and National Courts: A New Role for the Principle of Effective Judicial Protection? In M. Bonelli, M. Eliantonio, & G. Gentile (Eds.), *Article 47 of the EU Charter and Effective Judicial Protection, Volume 1: The Court of Justice's Perspective*. Hart.

Saenz Perez, C. (2022). What About Fundamental Rights? Security and Fundamental Rights in the Midst of a Rule of Law Breakdown. *New Journal of European Criminal Law, 13*(4), 526–545.

Sarmiento, D. (2013). Who's Afraid of the Charter? The Court of Justice, National Courts and the New Framework of Fundamental Rights Protection in Europe. *Common Market Law Review, 50*(5), 1267–1304.

Schütze, R. (2021). *European Union Law* (3rd ed.). Oxford University Press.

Spaventa, E. (2016). *The Interpretation of Article 51 of the EU Charter of Fundamental Rights*. Study on behalf of the PETI Committee, European Parliament. https://www.europarl.europa.eu/RegData/etudes/STUD/2016/556930/IPOL_STU%282016%29556930_EN.pdf

Spaventa, E. (2018). Should We "Harmonize" Fundamental Rights in the EU? Some Reflections About Minimum Standards and Fundamental Rights Protection in the EU Composite Constitutional System. *Common Market Law Review, 55*(4), 997–1023.

Spieker, L. D. (2023). *EU Values Before the Court of Justice*. Oxford University Press.

Tizzano, A. (2014). *L'application de la Charte des droits fondamentaux dans les Etats membres à la lumière de son article 51, paragraphe 1*, Il Diritto dell'Unione Europea, 429.

Torres Pérez, A. (2020a). Rights and Powers in the European Union: Towards a Charter That Is Fully Applicable to the Member States? *Cambridge Yearbook of European Legal Studies, 22*, 279–300.

Torres Pérez, A. (2020b). From Portugal to Poland: The Court of Justice of the European Union as Watchdog of Judicial Independence. *Maastricht Journal of European and Comparative Law, 27*(1), 105–119.

von Bogdandy, A. (2000). The European Union as a Human Rights Organization? Human Rights and the Core of the European Union. *Common Market Law Review, 37*(6), 1307–1338.

von Danwitz, T., & Paraschas, K. (2017). A Fresh Start for the Charter Fundamental Questions on the Application of the European Charter of Fundamental Rights. *Fordham International Law Journal, 35*, 1396–N/A.

Ward, A. (2021). *Article 51—Field of Application*. In S. Peers, T. K. Hervey, J. Kenner, & A. Ward (Eds.), *The EU Charter of Fundamental Rights. A Commentary* (2nd ed.). Hart.

Weiler, J. H. H. (1986). Eurocracy and Distrust. Some Questions Concerning the Role of the European Court of Justice in the Protection of Fundamental Human Rights Within the Legal Order of the European Communities. *Washington Law Review, 61*, 1103–1142.

Weiler, J. H. H. (1991). The Transformation of Europe. *Yale Law Journal, 100*(8), 2403–2483.

Vosa, G. (2023). Sulla problematica tutela dello Stato di diritto nell'Unione europea: spunti di diritto costituzionale e comparato a partire dal "caso Romania". *DPCE Online, 55*(4).

Case Law

CJEU 5 April 2016, Joined Cases C-404/15 e C-659/15 PPU, *Aranyosi and Căldăraru*, EU:C:2016:198.

CJEU 27 February 2018, Case C-64/16, *Associação Sindical dos Juízes Portugueses*, EU:C:2018:117.

CJEU 25 July 2018, Case C-216/18 PPU, *LM*, EU:C:2018:586.

CJEU 11 July 2019, Case C-619/18, *Commission v Poland (Independence of the Supreme Court)*, EU:C:2019:531.

CJEU 19 November 2019, Joined Cases C-585/18, C-624/18 and 625/18, *A.K. and others*, EU:C:2019:982.

CJEU 26 March 2020, Joined Cases C-558/18 and C-563/18, *Miasto Łowicz and Prokurator Generalny*, EU:C:2020:234.

CJEU 18 June 2020, Case C-78/18, *European Commission v Hungary (Transparency of associations)*, EU:C:2020:476.

CJEU 6 October 2020, Case C-66/18, *European Commission v Hungary (Enseignement supérieur)*, EU:C:2020:792.

CJEU 17 December 2020, Joined Cases C-354/20 PPU and C-412/20 PPU, *L and P*, EU:C:2020:1033.

CJEU 2 March 2021, Case C-824/18, *A.B. and Others (Nomination des juges à la Cour suprême - Recours)*, ECLI:EU:C:2021:153.

CJEU 20 April 2021, Case C-896/19, *Repubblika*, EU:C:2021:311.

CJEU 21 December 2021, Joined Cases C-357/19, C-379/19, C-547/19, C-811/19 and C-840/19, *Euro Box Promotion and Others*, EU:C:2021:1034.

CJEU 22 February 2022, Case C-430/21, *Proceedings brought by RS*, EU:C:2022:99.

Case Law

CHAPTER 6

The Cooperation and Verification Mechanism. The End of the "Exceptionalism"

Adriano Dirri

1 Introduction

The Cooperation and Verification Mechanism (CVM) was introduced in 2006 by the European Commission through the Decision 2006/928/EC for Romania and the Decision 2006/929/EC for Bulgaria. These Decisions, whose legal basis were Articles 37 and 38 of the Accession Treaty of Bulgaria and Romania, empowered the Commission to establish appropriate measures to address shortcomings and deficiencies of the two countries related to the rule of law at the time of their accession. Thus, it was "a strange and hoc beast in the EU legal order" (Dimotrovs & Kochenov, 2021: 6), created for Romania and Bulgaria, which did not satisfy many EU standards at the time of accession; therefore, it was an "exceptional" (Buzogány, 2021) legal regime for the two newcomers

A. Dirri (✉)
Luiss University, Rome, Italy
e-mail: adirri@luiss.it

C. Fasone et al. (eds.), *EU Rule of Law Procedures at the Test Bench*, Palgrave Studies in European Union Politics,
https://doi.org/10.1007/978-3-031-60008-1_6

which lasted formally until September 2023, when it has been repealed for Bulgaria with the Decision 2023/1785 and for Romania with the Decision 2023/1786.

Romania and Bulgaria were not part of the first phase of the fifth enlargement, which eventually took place in 2004, because they did not meet requirements set by the Copenhagen criteria. In fact, while negotiations with most Eastern European countries led to the acquisition of their membership status in 2004, for Bulgaria and Romania the path appeared to be slowed. Therefore, the EU Institutions were forced to set up an "exceptional" legal tool to tackle specific challenges of the two countries, which would have monitored and evaluated during the following years (Vachudova & Spendzharova, 2012: 2; Vassileva, 2020a).

The CVM has not proven to be effective and met several criticisms by EU Institutions and scholars. Despite the deficiencies of Romania and Bulgaria, the CVM "twilight" manifested only at the end of the last decade until it was eventually closed, because new tools for the rule of law oversight have been adopted by the EU. By recalling the context of the fifth accession (para. 2), this chapter explores the functioning of the CVM and highlights criticisms and dissensus that surrounded this tool since its inception (para. 3). The impact and poor results regarding Romania and Bulgaria will be scrutinised in turn (para. 4.1, 4.2). Finally, the concluding remarks will highlight the informal and formal "replacement" of the instrument within the broader effort of the EU in the protection of the rule of law, especially through the Rule of Law Reports (see Ylenia Citino in this volume) and the Recovery and Resilience Facility (RRF) (see Nicola Lupo in this volume).

2 The "Exceptionalism": The Post-accession Conditionality and the Sixth Enlargement

The enlargement that occurred in 2007 has to be considered the last step of the process begun by the European Council of Copenhagen in 1993. Nevertheless, the membership of Romania and Bulgaria was subjected to a different set up in comparison to the "big" 2004 enlargement (Hillion, 2004; Cremona, 2005); the accession of the last two post-Soviet countries has shown several political and legal features, which made their membership quite peculiar. First of all, the Commission and the European Council considered this enlargement the "second half" of the fifth, because politically it was considered the accomplishment of the inclusion of post-Soviet countries, a fact which was mirrored by the "symbolic act of ratification of the Accession Treaty" (Łazowski, 2007: 402). The EU Institutions were aware of the various shortcomings of the two countries at least 10 years before the accession eventually took place, as it is shown by the Opinion of the Commission in 1997, the Conclusion of the Helsinki European Council of 1999, where eventually Romania and Bulgaria were put among the candidate countries (Łazowski, 2007: 411).

In the conclusions of the 1999 Helsinki European Council, despite the initial enthusiasm in a big enlargement, it should be noted that while for many countries the European Council was satisfied of their progress, for Romania, Slovakia, Latvia, Lithuania, Bulgaria, and Malta the European Council decided to convene bilateral intergovernmental conferences with their governments on the conditions for the accession into the Union. Hence, it was pointed out that "in order to maintain momentum in the negotiations, cumbersome procedures should be avoided" (European Council, 1999). It might be argued that the European Council was aware of the countries' differences and difficulties, but nevertheless the priority was to go ahead.

The size of the challenges was significant and the Commission, in the last Report before the accession, raised several concerns despite some improvements. For example, it was noted that even though progress was assessed in areas such as judicial reform, corruption, money-laundering, and organised crime "further tangible results are needed" (European Commission, 2006). To this end the Commission asked for a "sustained support" from the EU and was (still) looking forward to welcoming Bulgaria and Romania as "fully-fledged members of the European Union". Consequently, in the same report the Commission clearly stated that it "will set up a mechanism for cooperation and verification of progress" in the abovementioned areas. This assessment triggered some dissensus between the European institutions since the Commission's concerns did not match with the enthusiasm showed by the European Parliament (EP), which insisted on the "speedy ratification of the Accession Treaty" (European Parliament, 2006). In the same Motion, the EP was animated more by "hopes" rather than tangible results, more focused on the progress made rather than over the reforms still needed. The enlargement was undoubtedly curbed by a deep faith in the integration of the Eastern European States in the common market, as well as their desire to be part of a common system of fundamental rights, despite relevant concerns raised by Member States such as Germany, France, and the Netherlands (Dimitrov & Plachkova, 2021: 174).

The Treaty of Accession of the two countries, in fact, embodied for the first time the possibility of a membership postponement of 12 months in case of clear evidence that the States were (still) "manifestly unprepared to meet the requirements of membership" (Article 39). Besides that, the Treaty contained two other safeguard clauses, Articles 37 and 38, which formed the legal basis for the CVM. Both gave mandate to the European Commission to adopt measures to tackle a serious risk respectively to the functioning of the internal market and in the area of Justice and Home Affairs (JHA). Hence, the Accession Treaty permitted the EU to adopt regulations or decisions establishing appropriate measures as well as specifying modalities which put them into effect; these were the legal bases of the CVM Decisions, which were adopted not more than three weeks before the 1 January 2007, the date of accession of the two countries.

In the CVM Decisions the rule of law is simply mentioned as a common principle to all Member States. It unveils that the purpose of the "exceptionalism" was to address critical shortcomings, without explicitly stating that both countries were unprepared for the full membership. In fact, the CVM Decisions empowered the Commission "to take appropriate measures in case of imminent risk that [...] would cause a breach in the functioning of the internal market by a failure to implement the commitments it has undertaken", alongside "the remaining issues in the accountability and efficiency of the judicial system and law enforcement bodies" (recital 4, 5, Decision, (2006/929/EC)). To this end, the Decisions established specific benchmarks to be monitored by the Commission and fulfilled by the two countries. Bulgaria had to meet European standards in a matter of independence and accountability of the judicial system; a more transparent and efficient judicial process by adopting a new civil procedure code; judicial system reforms; and corruption and organised crime had to be fought and put under control. Similarly, Romania was called to address the following issues: reform for enhancing judicial independence and accountability; integrity framework regarding incompatibilities and potential conflicts of interest; and anti-corruption policies.

The CVM fostered a dialogue between the two Member States under review and the Commission, whose assessment was published every six months in ad hoc reports where the benchmarks under scrutiny were being analysed. Hence, since 2007 the Commission started to evaluate the reforms enacted as well as progress related to the benchmarks; thus, the CVM was basically a tool for assessing, recommending, and addressing the authorities of the two countries over the obligations taken according to the Treaties of accession. The assessment was made by monitoring results and the adopted measures entered into force at time of accession; moreover, according to the same provision, such measures were supposed to be lifted when the commitments were fulfilled, but without specifying a timeframe or deadlines.

The methodology of the CVM reports was based upon the exchange of information between the governmental institutions of Romania and Bulgaria and the European Commission. The former were obliged to send detailed reports on the benchmarks to the Commission, which also received analyses from the EC Representation Office, Member States diplomatic missions in Bulgaria and Romania, and civil society organisations. The goal of the Commission was also to gather information independently on progress claimed by the governments. The assessments of the Commission were published every sixth months in detailed reports where the progress on the benchmarks was evaluated together with potential urgent measures to be taken before the subsequent report; in this manner the Commission specified the most demanding issues where the two countries had to intervene.

There were two types of report: the "progress report" published generally in July and the "technical report" in February. The "progress report" was a factual update, which resembled a "political report", since it did not provide precise assessments of results achieved but current normative trends in areas relevant to the benchmarks; moreover, it also laid down an overview of the assistance granted together with eventual gaps in the support to the two countries. The "technical report" instead outlined the information used by the Commission for setting up countries' assessment progress under the CVM; these sources were collected from relevant public authorities as well as from non-governmental organisations active in the areas of the benchmarks. The Commission reports were grounded on studies drafted by international institutions and independent observers such as the Venice Commission (see below). The technical report, to summarise, contained a deep analysis on the yearly recommendations as well as over those developments which might have affected the fulfilment of the CVM benchmarks.

3 Pitfalls and Shortcomings of the CVM "Exceptionalism"

It has been outlined that Romania and Bulgaria became members of the EU not without concerns or, better to say, warnings from their fulfilment regarding crucial aspects of the acquis; this means that they did not successfully meet legal, political, and economic criteria at the date of the accession. Hence, it must be pointed out that the Commission "was not in a position to call into question the political decision of 2002 to let these countries in" (Editorial Comments, 2006: 1498). It was clear that the option to deny the membership to Romania and Bulgaria was not on the table and the meaning was that it would have been mandatory for the EU Institution to find an acceptable juridical solution, given the huge amount of reform needed for the newcomers. In this context, while the Masters of the Treaties went ahead with the accession, the Commission tried a way out of this "very embarrassing situation" (Editorial Comments, 2006: 1500).

The legal solution was found in a specific post-accession conditionality tool addressing crucial rule of law issues like the accountability and efficiency of the judicial system and law enforcement bodies (Carp, 2014: 6). Perhaps, regarding these kinds of deficiencies, a more far-reaching wording in the Decisions would have been welcomed (Tanasoiu, 2012: 190), considering the relevance of the judiciary in granting the uniform application of the EU law. Despite that, the EU moved forward towards the "irreversible" enlargement at any cost, for not losing the (political) "momentum", in front of the failure of the Treaty establishing a Constitution for Europe in 2005.

Overall, the cost to pay was to admit that it would have been possible to design a different legal arrangement for the two "latecomers" (Dobrinsky, 2021); substantially the significance was that not all Member States would have been equal (Spernbauer, 2007). The problem was that while the adoption of the CVM Decisions should have occurred within a specific timeframe (three years from the accession), for the solution of the Rule of Law-related issues no deadline was set. Therefore, this special regime allowed for a specific derogation of the acquis Communautaire, whose standards were supposed to be met by the two countries once part of the EU.

Unsurprisingly, the CVM has been the target of several critiques by scholars focusing on their implementation in practice (Toneva-Metodieva,

2014). In fact, in the post-accession period Romania and Bulgaria found themselves in a sort of "limbo" with the acquis having been formally respected and the conditionality lost traction since the membership was ensured (Spendzharova & Vuchudova, 2014; Dimitrova, 2021), but the countries were not equipped with the same "rights" as other Member States, for example for what concerned the free circulation of people, which was denied until the CVM benchmarks were satisfied (Ganev, 2013; Levitz & Pop-Elches, 2010). In this regard, it is worth noting that, despite the repeal of the CVM in 2023, Romania and Bulgaria have just permitted to join the Schengen area only in air and sea borders as of March 2024.

From the methodological standpoint, it has been argued that the problem with the CVM lies in the absence of a system of sanctions and rewards (Gateva, 2015: 93). Thus, the main obstacle of the CVM seems to be the lack of an effective enforcement mechanism because the dialogue it entails has proven to be weak in terms of outcomes. Even more sharp criticism has been raised by those who underlined the incapacity of the CVM in bringing substantive reforms (Laurent, 2016: 12; Kochenov, 2014); for them, the CVM was based on an unrealistic definition of the Bulgarian and Romanian framework, coupled with a blind belief in the EU's "transformative power". Hence, the mistake was following a pure formal approach that disregards the "socio-structural changes that would guarantee respect for the rule of law", in order to infuse different political behaviour towards an accountable democracy. In addition, the enforcement was mainly considered an internal issue of the two countries (Dimitrov & Plachkova, 2021: 175–176). However, it is significant that, already in 2012, the Commission did not consider the CVM for the accession of Croatia in 2011 as well as for future candidates (Despost & Relji2011; Vachudova & Spendzharova, 2012: 13). To sum up, the Commission reversed its own decision and implicitly told the Member States to not speed up other accessions in the future.

Nevertheless, a minority of voices has spoken slightly in favour of the CVM on the ground of empirical evaluations, for example in the field of anti-corruption measures; indeed, despite the lack of sanctioning power, it has been argued that positive results have been registered given the institutional change witnessed and because the CVM operates as instruments of "social pressure" (Sedelmeier, 2014; Lacatus & Sedelmeier, 2020). Yet, as a matter of fact, the CVM has proven to be more effective where tangible consequences were foreseen as, for example, when

EU funds for Bulgaria were frozen in 2008 as well as the Decision to block the Schengen entry, which has triggered reform in both Bulgaria and Romania (Vachudova & Spendzharova, 2012: 13).

4 The CVM in Action in Bulgaria and Romania: A Comparison

4.1 Bulgaria

In Bulgaria, major concerns were related to the judicial system and specifically the prominent role of the General Prosecutor and the lack of internal checks and balances. In fact, at that time, the General Prosecutor had the power to issue binding orders concerning the work of every prosecutor and cases, to take over a case handled by another prosecutor and the power to promote and dismiss them. The autonomy and independence of the judges was tamed not only by the figure of the General Persecutor, but also by the appointing system of the whole Supreme Judicial Council, whose components were chosen by the Parliament with a simple majority vote. To this regard, two cases were evoked by the Council of Venice and by the European Commission: the so-called Kolevi case and the Yaneva Gate. The first one concerned the power of the General Prosecutor and was the object of the judgement of the European Court of Human Rights in 2009 (Kolevi v. Bulgaria). It is significant that the Court observed that, in the same period of the accession, "as a result of constitutional and legislative amendments of 2006, 2007 and 2009, the investigation service was integrated into the prosecution system and is now administratively subordinate to the Chief Public Prosecutor", as well as "that as a result of the hierarchical structure of the prosecution system and, apparently, its internal working methods, no prosecutor would issue a decision bringing charges against the Chief Public Prosecutor" (Kolevi v. Bulgaria, para. 135, 205).

The Yaneva Gate, instead, was a leak of a conversation between two judges who discussed how the Prime Minister and the General Prosecutor were able to instruct judges in the decisions of relevant cases (Vassileva, 2021). The issues involved were crucial for the Rule of Law, namely the status of the General Prosecutor's powers, judicial independence, and high level of corruption and it was directly quoted by the 2016 Report as one of the several corruption cases (European Commission, 2016: 11). Moreover, it should not be surprising that the Venice Commission was already aware of this issue, more than the European Institutions, as it may be read by the 2009 Opinion (Council of Venice, 2009), as well as by detailed reports over the new legislation amending the law on judicial power and the criminal procedure code (Council of Venice, 2010).

Instead, it has rightly been underlined that only the 2011 CVM report specifically asked for a reform of Bulgaria's prosecution system for the first time, a crucial aspect which was perhaps overlooked till then because of the priority to fight against corruption (Vassileva, 2020a). Besides that, only one year after the Commission published a worrisome report on crucial issues like the reform of the judicial system, independence, accountability and integrity of the judiciary, and efficiency of the judicial process, although some progress was made, the Commission, recalling the Kolevi case, raised concerns due to the lack of implementation of reforms in order for the process of improvement to become "irreversible". In the 2012 Report it was noted that, despite "important Constitutional reforms", "fundamental principles such as the independence of the judiciary have not always been respected to the full". Moreover, Bulgaria "has also been unable to properly introduce integrity into judicial promotions and appraisals", together with lack of transparency and relevant political influences. Overall, the reform of the judicial system as well as the improvement of the independence, accountability, and integrity of the judiciary and more efforts in persecuting organised crime and corruption, was recommended. Substantially, crucial aspects Rule of Law-related were still under threat five years since the accession (European Commission, 2012).

The application of the CVM to Bulgaria has become interesting due to the dissensus provoked by the decision of the Commission in 2018 to move away from the legal benchmarks of the judicial independence and of the General Prosecutor, which were considered solved. The closure of three benchmarks in 2018 and then the remaining three in 2019 (continued judicial reform, high-level corruption, general corruption) was not welcomed by scholars and experts such as Joeri Buhrer Tavanier, former European Commission's Resident Adviser to Bulgaria for the CVM. The Commission was considered "blind" and lenient on the unsolved problem of the Bulgarian judicial system as well as the governmental conduct over corruption (Vassileva, 2019) and, when the fulfilment of the CVM benchmarks was assessed by the Commission, the relevant NGO protested against the conclusions of the CVM monitoring process. It has appeared as a desire of the Commission to close the

CVM after Juncker declared in 2016 that Bulgaria would have fulfilled the benchmarks by 2019. In sharp contrast with that outcome was the EU Justice Scoreboard (see Ylenia Guerra in this volume) which painted a different picture of the Bulgarian judicial system (EU Justice Scoreboard 2019) and similar dissensus was manifested by the Commissioner for Justice Věra Jourová (Vassileva, 2019, 2020b).

Still more criticism came from the EP Assessment of the 10-year Cooperation and Verification (Chandler et al., 2018; Surubaru & Nitoiu, 2021), which was released in 2019, the same year of the CVM closure for Bulgaria. According to the EP Assessment the progress "toward some benchmarks has not been as rapid as was initially anticipated, and significant deficiencies remain"; in Bulgaria it was noted that, although reforms have been implemented in the area of the judicial system, some issues, such as the political influence on the judiciary, remain controversial. On Bulgaria, the Assessment did not forecast the ending of the CVM in a short period of time and proposed to continue with the Mechanism or with a similar framework (European Parliament, 2017: 8). The EP diverged from the desire of the Commission to close the CVM and recommended that "much remains to be done if the CVM benchmarks are to be achieved" (European Parliament, 2017: 9). Despite this detailed assessment and other criticisms outlined above, the Commission decided to close the Bulgarian CVM stating that "the progress made by Bulgaria under the CVM is sufficient to meet Bulgaria's commitments made at the time of its accession"; at the same time, the reforms implementation "will feed into the future dialogue with the Commission in the framework of the comprehensive rule of law mechanism" (European Commission, 2019: 13).

4.2 Romania

Similarly, a few years after the accession, Romania did not show any progress on the Rule of Law path and even more concerns were expressed about the events in the country, with reference to intimidation of judges, the undermining of the Constitutional Court, and the overturning of established judicial procedures, as well as checks and balances. Because of that, in 2012 the Commission called for "urgent action needed to demonstrate commitment to the rule of law and judicial independence" meaning a rigorous implementation of the recommendations under the CVM (European Commission, Press Release, 2012). The report of the same year stressed that since 2007 there have been progress and setbacks, which meant that the progress was still at the initial stage. In the 2012 CMV Report on Romania, the Commission was "extremely concerned by the indications of manipulations and pressure which affect institutions, members of the judiciary, and eventually have a serious impact on society as a whole" (European Commission, 2012: 3). Therefore, in this Report, the Commission's concerns were quite similar to those of the scholars about the effectiveness of the CVM; this represented a first implicit admission of the CVM shortcomings and ineffectiveness (Dimitrov & Plachkova, 2021: 178). Similarly, the Venice Commission highlighted the same issues and harshly criticised some measures taken by the Romanian Government and Parliament for being "problematic from the viewpoint of constitutionality and the rule of law"; such measures included the limitations of the competences of the Constitutional Court and the suspension of the President of the Republic. In addition, the Venice Commission criticised the extensive recourse to government emergency ordinances (Venice Commission, 2012: 18).

The Romanian case was increasingly worrisome given the results published by the 2017–2019 reports, which were characterised by a "waning reform momentum" as it was admitted years later by the European Commission (2022: 1). During these years the Venice Commission assessed a proper "setback", due to the adoption of the Justice Reform whose measures weakened the legal guarantees for judicial independence. Again, the Council of Europe emphasised more than the EU Institutions the danger to the principle of the rule of law that was derived from the reforms but also from the extensive use of emergency ordinances to adopt such a legislation (Venice Commission, 2019: 15). In this period, the Commission paved the way to re-open issues previously considered fulfilled such as judicial independence and judicial reform included in benchmark one (European Commission, 2017: 3, 8, 12).

By contrast, valuable progress was assessed in the 2021 and 2022 reports with many tasks considered completed. The 2022 report set the "end" of the CVM: on the one hand, the Commission has considered sufficient the progress made by Romania related to the benchmarks set in the CVM but, on the other hand, it has recalled that the EU has developed new tools for upholding the rule of law. Among them there are those considered relevant for supporting the Romanian reform process and "as a result, there are a number of monitoring tracks now in place looking at issues covered by the CVM benchmarks"; the Commission specifically mentions the Rule of Law Reports (see Ylenia Citino in this volume), where the areas covered previously by the CVM are assessed and evaluated for each Member State. Similarly, in the conclusion of the 2022 Report it is argued that "it is important that Romania continues to work consistently [...] within the annual Rule of Law Report cycle and with the support of other parts of the EU rule of law toolbox". Moreover, the last report of 2022 stated that "it is important that Romania continues to work consistently on translating the remaining commitments specified in this report into concrete legislation and on continued implementation, within the annual Rule of Law cycle [...]" (European Commission, 2022: 29).

However, other questions have been raised over the relationship between the ending of the CVM and the Rule of Law annual Reports. This "overlap", at least for Romania, raised concerns about the binding nature of the CVM (Dimotrovs & Kochenov, 2021). The occasion came in six preliminary references (see Lorenzo Cecchetti in this volume) promoted by the national association of judges and prosecutors (joined cases C-83/19, C-127/19, C-195/19, C-291/19, C-355/19, and C-397/19), who were questioned over the binding effects of the CVM reports and indirectly the primacy of the EU law. The preliminary references asked the Court of Justice to clarify the legal nature and effects of the CVM which, according to the referring judges, was considered binding for Romania. Therefore, the applicants questioned the compatibility of key aspects of the Justice Reform with the EU law, such as the organisation of the Judicial Inspectorate and the Section within the Public Prosecutor's Office for the investigation of offences committed within the judicial system (the SIIJ) and the rules governing the personal liability of judges.

It is interesting to note that different points of view on the CVM emerged between the Advocate General (A.G.) Bobek and the CJEU. Whereas the A.G. held that the CVM is part of the binding EU law and as such proposed to use the CVM as one of the parameters of the judgement, the Grand Chamber of the CJEU grounded its reasoning mainly on Article 19 TEU, which "covered" and "subsumed" the CVM (Kadlec & Kosar, 2022: 1833). Without going into deep analysis of the judgement (Moraru & Bercea, 2022), the Bobek reasoning was grounded in the CVM itself, which has basically "regulated" the Romanian membership according to the Accession Treaty; instead, the Court proved the binding nature of the CVM in connection with Articles 2 and 19(1) TEU given the jurisprudence occurred for the time being. In the judgement, the CVM Decision was "binding in its entirety on Romania, as long as it has not been repealed. The benchmarks in the Annex to Decision 2006/928 are intended to ensure that Romania complies with the value of the rule of law, set out in Article 2 TEU" (par. 178). In the judgement, the CJEU strongly called for a combined reading of Article 2 TUE, Article 19 (1) TEU and the Decision 2006/928, which "must be interpreted as precluding national legislation adopted by the government" with the aim of weakening the independence of the judiciary. It was the case of the functioning of the SIIJ as an instrument of political pressure and intimidation towards judges; in addition, the Court was concerned about the capacity of the SIIJ to alter the course of certain criminal investigations or judicial proceedings over acts of high-level corruption (para. 215–219). Thus, the CVM was recognised as a piece of hard law, relying not only in the Accession Treaty but more notably on the basis of Articles 2 and 19 TUE, even though these dispositions were not in force at the time of the Accession.

In the subsequent judgement *EuroBox-Promotion*, the Court answered to five preliminary rulings in the matter of corruption and tax fraud to value added tax (joined cases C-357/19, C-547/19, C-811/19, C-840/19, C-379/19) and stated clearly the binding nature of the CVM by saying that "it must be recalled from the outset that Decision 2006/928 is an act adopted by an EU institution, namely the Commission, on the basis of the Act of Accession, which falls within the scope of EU primary law, and specifically constitutes a decision within the meaning of the fourth paragraph of Article 288 TFEU" (*EuroBox Promotion*, para. 156). Thus, according to the Court the connection between the CVM and the compliance with the EU values constitutes "a precondition for the accession to the European Union of any European State applying to become an EU member. It is in that context that the CVM was established by Decision 2006/928 in order to ensure that the value of the rule of law is complied with in Romania" (*EuroBox Promotion*, para. 161) (Weber, 2022).

5 Concluding Remarks: The End of the CVM "Exceptionalism" or Substance over Form

The CVM recommendations, already closed for Bulgaria in 2019, was also lifted for Romania in 2022. What matters here is that the formal closure of the Mechanism occurred in September 2023. Despite the repealing Decisions set just at the end of the CVM, some remarks may be drawn from the recitals which may enlighten the context in which the CVM was repealed.

Regarding Bulgaria, for example, it is significant that the Commission was aware that the last outstanding specific commitment concerning the accountability and criminal liability of the General Prosecutor under the last report of October 2019 has been recently "finalised" under the Bulgarian National Recovery and Resilience Plan (NRRP) (recital 8, Decision 2023/1785). In fact, this reform which previously was one of the benchmarks to be fulfilled by Bulgaria under the CVM, actually is a relevant milestone of the Bulgarian NRRP. Thus, it might be argued that the task has "shifted" from the CVM to the Bulgarian NRRP; therefore, one may also think that the Commission has admitted the shortcomings of the CVM for the simple reason that a subsequent tool, the RRF, seems to be more efficient. To this regard, it should be noted that the Commission acknowledged adamantly that "the evolution of the Union's rule of law landscape has given a new context for the Commission's cooperation with Bulgaria" (recital 11, Decision 2023/1785). Despite that, at the time of writing—February 2024—it should be noted that Bulgaria is poorly implementing its Plan (European Parliament, 2024) and is still waiting for the second payment, which is subject to the assessment of the Commission. Among the tasks which are being evaluated there is the abovementioned milestone, whose completion was expected for the second quarter of 2023. Similar remarks were made for Romania, where the Commission emphasised the role of the Romanian NRRP in the achievement of reforms already set by the CVM, especially those aimed at strengthening the independence of the judicial systems (recital 8, Decision 2023/1786; European Commission, 2024: 111).

In conclusion, the CVM has been contested since its inception and it has not worked as expected, given the fact that Bulgaria and Romania are still struggling with the critical issues acknowledged at the accession. The CVM deficiencies have attracted criticism not only by academics, but also by some EU Institutions. Therefore, it is possible to argue that the Commission has chosen the best "moment" to replace the CVM Decisions, taking advantage of the establishment of the RRF (European Commission, 2024: 111). Perhaps the main legacy of this tool has been the benchmark set for specific countries in order to fully meet the obligations of the Treaties, especially related to the rule of law. Moreover, by assessing that the CVM has not worked well, it is argued that the EU should be more cautious in evaluating new candidates and to firmly assess the full compliance with the EU values and rule of law before the accession.

References

Official Institutional Documents

Commission Decision (EU) 2023/1786 of 15 September 2023 Repealing Decision 2006/928/EC Establishing a Mechanism for Cooperation and Verification of Progress in Romania to Address Specific Benchmarks in the Areas of Judicial Reform and the Fight Against Corruption.

Council of Europe. (2009). Venice Commission—515/2009—Opinion on the Draft Law Amending and Supplementing the Law on Judicial Power of Bulgaria.

Council of Europe. (2010). Venice Commission—591/2010—Opinion on the Draft Law Amending the Law on Judicial Power and the Draft Law Amending the Criminal Procedure Code of Bulgaria.

Council of Europe. (2012, December 17). Venice Commission—Opinion No. 685/2012.

Council of Europe (2019, June 24). Venice Commission—Opinion No. 950/2019.

European Commission. (2006, September 26). Communication from the Commission, COM(2006) 549 final, Monitoring Report on the State of Preparedness for EU Membership of Bulgaria and Romania Brussels.

European Commission. (2012, July 18), Press Release, Romania: Urgent Action Needed to Demonstrate Commitment to Rule of Law and Judicial Independence.

European Commission. (2016, January 27). Report from the Commission to the European Parliament and the Council, on Progress in Bulgaria under the Co-operation and Verification Mechanism, COM(2016) 40 final.

European Commission. (2024, March 21). Commission Staff Working Document—Mid-term evaluation of the Recovery and Resilience Facility. *Accompanying the document Communication from the Commission to The European Parliament, The Council, The European Economic and Social Committee*

And the Committee of the Regions Mid-Term Evaluation of the Recovery and Resilience Facility: Strengthening the EU through ambitious reforms and investments. (COM(2024) 82 final), SWD(2024) 70 final.

European Court of Human Rights. (2009, November 5). Kolevi v. Bulgaria—1108/02 Judgment.

European Parliament Resolution on the Accession of Romania to the European Union (2006/2115(INI)). (2006, December 22).

European Parliament. (2024, February 1), BUDG-ECON—Scrutinising Implementation of the Recovery and Resilience Facility.

Helsinki European Council. (1999 December 10 and 11). Presidency Conclusions.

Report from the Commission to the European Parliament and the Council, On Progress in Bulgaria under the Cooperation and Verification Mechanism SWD (2012) 232 final.

Report from the Commission to the European Parliament and the Council on Progress in Romania under the Co-operation and Verification Mechanism. (2017 November 15). COM(2017) 751 final.

Report from the Commission to the European Parliament and the Council on Progress in Romania under the Cooperation and Verification Mechanism. (2022 November 22). COM(2022) 664 final.

Bibliography

Buzogány, A. (2021). Beyond Balkan Exceptionalism. Assessing Compliance with EU Law in Bulgaria and Romania. *European Politics and Society, 22*(2), 185–202.

Carp, R. (2014). The Struggle for the Rule of Law in Romania as an EU Member State: The Role of the Cooperation and Verification Mechanism. *Utrecht Law Review, 10*(1), 1–16.

Chandler, C., Lale-Demoz, E., Malan, J., & Kreutzer, S. (2018, January). Assessment of the 10 Years' Cooperation and Verification Mechanism for Bulgaria and Romania, Study requested by the CONT Committee, European Parliament, Directorate General for Internal Policies of the Union, PE 603.813.

Cremona, M. (2005). EU Enlargement: Solidarity and Conditionality. *European Law Review, 30*(1), 3–22.

Despost, A., & Reljić, D. (2011, June). *Croatia Rush to Join the EU. Hasty Admission Would Damage the Country, Other Candidate Countries and the EU*. German Institute for International and Security Affairs (pp. 1–4).

Dimitrov, G., & Plachkova, A. (2021). Bulgaria and Romania, Twin Cinderellas in the European Union: How They Contributed in a Peculiar Way to the

Change in EU Policy for the Promotion of Democracy and Rule of Law. *European Politics and Society, 22*(2), 167–184.

Dimitrova, A. L. (2021). Understanding Europeanization in Bulgaria and Romania: Following Broader European Trends or Still the Balkan Exceptions? *European Politics and Society, 22*(2), 295–304.

Dimitrovs, A., & Kochenov, D. (2021, June 5). Of Jupiters and Bulls: The Cooperation and Verification Mechanism as a Redundant Special Regime of the Rule of Law. In *EU Law Live* (Week End Edition, p., 61).

Dobrinsky, R. (2021). Bulgaria and Romania: The Latecomers to the Eastern Enlargement. In M. Landesmann & I. P. Székely (Eds.), *Does EU Membership Facilitate Convergence? The Experience of the EU's Eastern Enlargement—Volume I* (pp. 239–281). Springer.

Editorial Comment. (2006). *Common Market Law Review, 43*, 1497–1501.

Ganev, V. I. (2013). Post-Accession Hooliganism: Democratic Governance in Bulgaria and Romania after 2007. *East European Politics and Societies and Cultures, 27*(1), 26–44.

Gateva, E. (2015). *European Union Enlargement Conditionality*. Palgrave Macmillan.

Hillion, C. (2004). *EU Enlargement: A Legal Approach*. Hart.

Kadlec, O., & Kosarˇ, D. (2022). Romanian Version of the Rule of Law Crisis Comes to the ECJ: The AFJR Case Is Not Just About the Cooperation and Verification Mechanism. *Common Market Law Review, 59*, 1823–1852.

Kochenov, D. (2014). Overestimating conditionality. In I. Govaere, E. Lanon, P. Van Elsuwege & S. Adam (Eds.), *The European Union in the World: Essays in Honour of Marc Maresceau* (pp. 541–556). Martinus Nijhoff Publishers.

Lacatus, C., & Sedelmeier, U. (2020). Does Monitoring Without Enforcement Make a Difference? The European Union and Anti-Corruption Policies in Bulgaria and Romania after Accession. *Journal of European Public Policy, 27*(8), 1236–1255.

Laurent, P. (2016). The EU as a global rule of law promoter: The consistency and effectiveness challenges. *Asia Europe Journal, 14*(1) 7–24. https://doi.org/10.1007/s10308-015-0432-z

Łazowski, A. (2007). And Then They Were Twenty-Seven...A Legal Appraisal of the Sixth Accession Treaty. *Common Market Law Review, 44*, 401–430.

Levitz, P., & Pop-Eleches, G. (2010). Monitoring, Money and Migrants: Countering Post-Accession Backsliding in Bulgaria and Romania. *Europe-Asia Studies, 62*(3), 461–479.

Moraru, M., & Bercea, R. (2022). The First Episode in the Romanian Rule of Law Saga: Joined Cases C-83/19, C-127/19, C-195/19, C-291/19, C-355/19 and C-397/19, Asociaţia Forumul Judecătorilor din România, and Their Follow-Up at the National Level, EU. *European Constitutional Law Review, 18*(1), 82–113.

Sedelmeier, U. (2014). Anchoring Democracy from Above? The European Union and Democratic Backsliding in Hungary and Romania After Accession. *Journal of Common Market Studies, 52*(1), 105–121.

Spendzharova, A. B., & Vuchudova, M. A. (2014). Catching Up? Consolidating Liberal Democracy in Bulgaria and Romania after EU Accession. In T. A. Borzel & T. Risse (Eds.), *From Europeanisation to Diffusion* (pp. 39–58). London: Routledge.

Spernbauer, M. (2007). Benchmarking, Safeguard Clauses and Verification Mechanisms—What's in a Name? Recent Developments in Pre- and Post-Accession Conditionality and Compliance with EU Law. *Croatian Yearbook of European Law and Policy, 3*, 273–306.

Surubaru, N. C., & Nitoiu, C. (2021). One Decade Onwards: Assessing the Impact of European Union Membership on Bulgaria and Romania. *European Politics and Society, 22*(2), 161–166.

Tanasoiu, C. (2012). Europeanization Post-Accession: Rule Adoption and National Political Elites in Romania and Bulgaria. *Southeast European and Black Sea Studies, 12*(1), 173–193.

Toneva-Metodieva, L. (2014). Beyond the Carrots and Sticks Paradigm: Rethinking the Cooperation and Verification Mechanism Experience of Bulgaria and Romania. *Perspectives on European Politics and Society, 15*(4), 534–551.

Vachudova, M. A., & Spendzharova, A. (2012). The EU's Cooperation and Verification Mechanism: Fighting Corruption in Bulgaria and Romania after EU Accession. In *SIEPS—European Policy Analysis* (pp. 1–20).

Vassileva, R. (2019, October 24). So Why Don't We Just Call the Whole Rule of Law Thing Off, Then? On Tomatoes, Tomahtoes, and Bulgaria's Cooperation and Verification Mechanism. *Verfassungsblog*.

Vassileva, R. (2020a, September 12). On Coins, Parallel Universes and the Cooperation and Verification Mechanism. *Verfassungsblog*.

Vassileva, R. (2020b). Threats to the Rule of Law: The Pitfalls of the Cooperation and Verification Mechanism. *European Public Law, 26*(3), 741–768.

Vassileva, R. (2021, June 9). Framing and Raiding. Bulgaria's Kafkaesque Prosecutor's Office. *Verfassungsblog*.

Weber, F. (2022). The Identity of Union Law in Primacy: Piercing Through Euro Box Promotion and Others. *European Papers, 7*(2), 749–771.

PART II

The Tools Offered by EU Legislation

CHAPTER 7

Strengthening the Rule of Law Through Administrative Support: The Technical Support Instrument and Its Precedents

Adriano Dirri and Ylenia Guerra

1 Introduction

Administrative support for structural reforms may be considered an instrument of soft law which may have direct and practical effects on Member States' administrations (Da Silva et al., 2018). At the same time, it may have an indirect effect in prompting the EU policies across the Member States and leading to more uniformity in capacity building as well as in the implementation of EU tasks (Láncos et al., 2023). The evolution of the various programmes of administrative support, which eventually led to the Technical Support Instrument (TSI), shows that the EU tended to expand the purposes of this kind of tool: from targeting specific

A. Dirri (✉) · Y. Guerra
Luiss University, Rome, Italy
e-mail: adirri@luiss.it

Y. Guerra
e-mail: yguerra@luiss.it

C. Fasone et al. (eds.), *EU Rule of Law Procedures at the Test Bench*, Palgrave Studies in European Union Politics,
https://doi.org/10.1007/978-3-031-60008-1_7

Member States to broad and cross-cutting tasks within the Recovery Resilience Facility (RRF) (see Nicola Lupo in this volume), the administrative support is actually intertwined with all the main policies of the EU. The state of play might be summed up as follows: the EU asks for reform and when the Member States are ready to comply with them, they can benefit from administrative support in the implementation of such reforms.

This section provides an overview of the evolution and significance of the TSI. This tool is currently grounded in its predecessors (infra) and the legal bases are found primarily in Article 197 (2) of the Treaty on the Functioning of the European Union (TFEU), where it is stated that the Union supports the efforts of the Member States to improve their administrative capacity to implement Union law. Additional legal bases are found in Articles 120 and 121 TFEU, as well as in Article 175 TFEU, which asks Member States to coordinate their economic policies to achieve economic, social and territorial cohesion. The second section analyses the evolution of the administrative support of the EU, from pursuing merely economic objectives to a broad array of reforms; the third section explores the main features of the TSI, while the fourth will consider critical remarks especially related to the previous stronger link between structural reforms support and the budget consolidation. In the conclusive remarks it will be emphasised that this tool is currently being part of the RRF in the implementation of the NRRPs, thus in connection with hard law more directly involved in the enforcement of the EU values and the rule of law (Magnus et al., 2023: 2).

2 Finding the Connection Between the TSI and the Rule of Law

Looking at the functioning of the TSI, the issue on the table is how it is related to the protection and promotion of the rule of law. As we will emphasise below, currently the TSI is not related to the protection of the rule of law except in one case on the implementation of the judicial academy in Croatia,[1] which represents a marginal case of a direct

[1] 2021 TSI, "Promotion of the rule of law and Fundamental rights through high-quality online trainings in the Croatian judiciary". Through this project the "Commission provided technical support to the Judicial Academy in Croatia to improve methodology, tools and expertise to design and deliver high-quality online trainings, with focus on

support to the national judiciary personnel. Actually, the TSI is the EU programme that provides a tailored technical expertise for the Member States in the design and implementation of their reforms. It is demand driven and it represents an important tool in helping the Member States against the consequences of the pandemic. Therefore, this tool should be considered mainly as a support programme for structural reforms rather than protection of the rule of law. Nevertheless, it is interesting to note that it has only recently become (*infra*) part of the European rule of law toolbox. In fact, it is worth recalling the previous "versions" of the TSI, whose purposes were gradually broadened.

Hence, the TSI is not at all a new mechanism, and it was originally nothing more than an ad hoc measure specifically created for providing technical assistance to Greece and Cyprus in implementing their economic adjustment programmes. At the beginning, there were two task forces within the Commission, the Task Force for Greece (TFGR) and the Support Group for Cyprus (SGCY) respectively in 2011 and in 2013, and both were deemed necessary to provide technical assistance.

The mandate ended in 2015 and 2016 and the Commission evaluated the results positively; nevertheless, the European Court of Auditors was of a different opinion, since it highlighted the shortcomings of the TFGR, mainly the low influence of the assistance despite the efforts made. Several recommendations were raised, and this gave way to an overall revision of this kind of assistance; the consequence, as also noted by the European Parliament (EP), was the introduction, in 2017, of a permanent structure with clear objectives, the Structural Reform Support Programme (SRSP), as it was also previously endorsed by the Court of Auditors. It is noteworthy that the dawn of the technical assistance was evaluated well by the Commission, under whose auspices the task forces were created, and badly by other EU Institutions; it is also interesting that the path undertaken by the Commission after this first stage was in line with those reports that criticised the measures adopted, thus promoting a "novel approach" (Ongaro, 2022: 9).

The shift in the European Commission (EC) approach changed with the abovementioned SRSP, upon which it might be argued the TSI is

human rights and the rule of law. The project was implemented by the Council of Europe in cooperation with the Commission and with the support of the Office of the Representative of the Republic of Croatia before the European Court for Human Rights" (https://reform-support.ec.europa.eu).

based (Dolls et al., 2019). The EU intervention moved from a single member target towards "supporting cross-cutting modernization of the administrative system as a whole"; for the purposes of this new role the EC established the Directorate General for Structural Reform Support (SRSS) (Ongaro & Kickert, 2020: 2). Hence, it indicated the desire of the EC to adopt a supporting and facilitating role together with the development of a conditionality role, which eventually led to the adoption in 2020 of, among others, the Regulation 2020/2092 (see Fasone and Simoncini in this volume; see Hegedus and Christiansen in this volume).

The SRSP, since 2017, has contributed to the implementation of more than 1400 technical support projects in all MS (see EU Regulation 2017/825 as amended by Regulation EU 2018/1671). The SRSP, with a budget of €142.8 million for the period 2017 to 2020, set up a European programme to provide support for institutional, administrative and growth-enhancing structural reforms in the EU Member States. The scope of the SRSP was to substantially assist the Member States in the journey of reforms. The Regulation expressively highlighted the Union's considerable experience in providing Member States with capacity building in certain sectors (e.g. taxation, customs and support to small and medium-sized enterprises) and in relation to the implementation of cohesion policy (recital 6). In this regard, the Commission sets the support Programme upon request by any Member State in a wide range of areas related to, for example, cohesion, competitiveness, justice systems, public procurement as well as rural development and fisheries (recital 9). As expressed in the mentioned regulation:

> Reforms are by their very nature complex processes that require a full chain of highly specialised knowledge and skills, as well as a long-term vision. As their effects often take time to materialise, structural reforms in a wide range of public policy areas are challenging. Designing and implementing them in a timely and efficient manner is therefore crucial, whether for crisis-hit or structurally weak economies. In this context, Union support in the form of technical assistance has been important in supporting the economic adjustment of Greece and Cyprus in recent years. (Regulation 2017/825, recital 4)

This evolution was consolidated by the TSI as a new EU "funding line to support public administrative reforms in the Member States" (Ongaro & Kickert, 2020: 4). The TSI has become part of the Multiannual Financial Framework (MFF) 2021–2027 and of the RRF which has been enacted by Regulation 2021/240. It is an additional measure to provide technical expertise and administrative support to EU Member States, with the purpose to implement their own reforms especially related to the National Recovery and Resilience Plans (NRRPs) (Dermine, 2022: 91). Hence, it might be argued that the European Institutions found the way to connect this administrative support to a more explicit design related to strengthening the rule of law throughout the RRF and NRRPs (Spinaci, 2021).

Indeed, the ultimate goal is supporting a "sustainable and fair economic recovery and convergence, achieve resilience, reduce poverty and inequality [...]" (Regulation 2021/240, recital 8). More precisely, the objective should be to assist national authorities in developing reforms "and to prepare, amend, implement and revise recovery and resilience plans under Regulation (EU) 2021/241" (Regulation 2021/240, recital n. 9). An additional feature of the present TSI refers to the budget which has increased significantly if compared to similar instruments (*infra*); in fact, EUR 864 million have been allocated for the period 2021–2027, and it suggests that this tool is likely to play a key role in the implementation of the MFF and the NRRPs (EuLawLive, 2021). At the time of writing, the TSI and its predecessors have helped the implementation of more than 1500 projects in Member States; in March 2023 only, the Commission has approved 151 projects to support the implementation of up to 326 cutting-edge reforms in 2023. Overall, under the call for the year 2023, the TSI has supported 321 projects, including multi-country projects. Thus it seems that the TSI aims at strengthening cooperation among Member States through cross-country projects, with 33 multi-country and 10 multi-regional projects (Magnus et al., 2023).

More recently, at the 3rd annual meeting of the Technical Support Instrument, the Commission launched a new call for proposals under the TSI 2024 cycle. This new call aims to provide technical assistance to Member States for the design or implementation of reform projects in 2024: "In particular, Member States can submit requests for technical support in a broad range of areas, such as green and digital transition, diversity, public and private finance, migration, business environment, health, skills and education" (see the TSI portal). Indeed, many of the areas of intervention are those of the National Recovery and Resilience Plans (NRRPs). Moreover, under the TSI, since 2022, the EC has manifested the desire to strengthen the administrative performance and coordination in the implementation of selected projects based on the needs of the Member States, often included in each NRRP, as well as on top priorities of the EU. Through a vertical consultative process, every year several "Flagship Technical Support Projects" have been selected by the Commission and each Member State can submit its request for administrative support. Among the 2024 Flagship Technical Support Projects, it is worth mentioning that it is possible to ask for support in the area "Reinforce Democracy and the Rule of Law" with the main objective of "strengthening the capacity of the national authorities with the ensuing enhancement of their judicial systems". Hence, from this brief overview, the broadening of the scope of the current TSI has been a signal of the EU to harmonise the administrative support as well as to find and reach a common ground for the EU intervention in and according to the needs of the Member States.

3 The Main Features of the TSI

The type of support is very broad (Hecser & Molitor, 2022), meaning that Member States could ask for assistance in implementing resilience-enhancing reforms in the context of EU economic governance (also in relation to the European Semester) (see Capati and Christiansen in this volume) and by virtue of implementing EU law; preparing, amending, implementing and revising National Recovery and Resilience Plans under the Recovery and Resilience Facility; implementing economic adjustment programmes; implementing reforms undertaken at their own initiative. Furthermore, the Regulation specifies that the TSI asks for strong cooperation from and with the Member States in the improvement of their administrative capacities, since the general objective of the instrument is the promotion of "the Union's economic, social and territorial cohesion by supporting Member States' efforts to implement reforms" (Regulation 2021/240, Articles 3, 4). All in all, the TSI provided technical expertise on the drafting and implementation of the NRRPs or upon request by Member States, beyond the NRRPs. This might mean that the TSI, being strictly connected to the NRRPs, is subjected to conditionality mechanisms since the TSI is designed to support the implementation of projects under the umbrella of various European funds (Schramm et al., 2022: 5).

The object of the tool is also very broad since it includes, among others, green and digital transition, health and long-term care, education, public administration and governance, competitiveness, financial sector and social and labour protection. Some of the projects mentioned will become "projects in the spotlight", i.e. selected projects from different policy areas and different countries which, on the basis of effective implementation, show promising results on the ground and have the potential to be replicated across the EU. In this way, the Commission aims to promote best practices.

The procedure is quite simple: a Member State can demand to receive technical support via the submission of a request to the Commission. Later the Commission evaluates the request and starts a dialogue with the national Coordinating Authorities to assess the country-specific needs. The concrete support can be guaranteed by the Commission itself (in-house expertise) or with other technical support such as experts from EU Member States' national administrations, international organisations, private firms and consultancies and individual experts from the private sector.

A case that deserves to be highlighted here looks at the 2024 flagship technical support projects, which has been previously taken into account. A flagship is "selected on the basis that they are largely needed across Member States and are linked to top EU priorities the Member States are in the process of implementing. As such, they aim at supporting Member States in achieving resilience and growth enhancing reforms". In particular, the Commission has explained that the new centrality of the rule of law is related to three main aspects: the fight against corruption, the protection of children and the strengthening of the judicial system in the Member States. In this line of support the non-exhaustive measures are listed in Table 1.

This example sheds light on the desire of the Commission to combine the overall purposes of the RRF, which requests several reforms from the Member States in order to get access to their reserved grants and loans, with the administrative support which is granted on the basis of the needs of each Member State.

Table 1 2024 flagship type of measure[2]

Type of measure	*Area of objectives*
Development of action plans and support to the implementation of targeted actions regarding the quality and efficiency of justice systems, such as digitalisation of justice	General measure, digitalisation
Needs assessment reports in terms of increasing capacity of evidence-informed policymaking in governance and public administration in Member States	General measure, organisation
Developing national strategies and action plans	General measure, organisation
Piloting the implementation of proposed strategies/ action plans	
Capacity building of administration to implement proposed strategies/action plans	General measure
Identification of existing EU good practices and gap analysis	General measure
Developing a data-driven framework to identify irregularities and to address fraud and corruption risks in public expenditure	Corruption and fraud
Guidance on using Artificial Intelligence (AI) as an anti-corruption and fraud-detection tool	Corruption and fraud
Realisation of proof of concepts of AI business solutions for anti-corruption and fraud-detection	Corruption and fraud
Assessment of existing initiatives, national policy frameworks, organisational structures and financial support mechanisms in terms of science-for-policy ecosystem as a way to prevent fraud and corruption in policymaking, identifying gaps and needs and producing actionable policy recommendations	Corruption and fraud
Support to the development and promotion of multidisciplinary intervention centres for child victims and witnesses of violence and more integrated child protection systems	Children protection

(continued)

[2] The table is based on the information provided by the official website of the European Commission on the TSI (https://reform-support.ec.europa.eu/tsi-2024-flagship-reinforce-democracy-and-rule-law_en).

Table 1 (continued)

Type of measure	*Area of objectives*
Developing methodologies for conducting assessment of corruption risks in relevant sectors	Corruption
Support for the development of institutional capacity, aimed at improving the effective implementation of ethics and integrity instruments (such as on financial disclosure, codes of conduct, lobbying, whistleblowing, anti-bribery compliance programmes)	Corruption
Support for the development of institutional capacity, aimed at improving the detection, investigation, prosecution and adjudication of high-level corruption cases	Corruption

4 A Critical Evaluation of the TSI and Its Predecessors

The TSI has attracted some criticism by scholars. For example, in light of the not always positive outcomes, an alternative framework to the TSI has been suggested, in which Member States agree on convergence targets and roadmaps, along with a specific timeframe for achieving such common targets (Dolls et al., 2019). In other words, some have supported a limitation of the target indicators to a small set of structural outcome variables, such as per capita income and the unemployment rate. This will not only allow for better policy targeting but also for greater flexibility in achieving these targets. At the same time, just before the pandemic, some suggested the development of a different narrative for the EU structural reform support, more in association with the Cohesion Policy. Indeed, the role of the TSI was questioned above all with regard to the interplay with the Cohesion Policy (CP), because the Commission was quite reluctant to connect structural reforms with the purpose of the CP. For example, back in 2018 it was argued that positive outcomes were observed by the ongoing negotiations on the 2021–2027 MFF due to the increasing effort to highlight "the added value of Cohesion Policy in promoting economic capability, territorial balance and social inclusiveness in the EU" (Huguenot-Noel et al., 2018: 26). In fact, others also noted in the past decade that structural reforms were often connected to budget consolidation, which was the priority of the European Institutions; in addition, the same scholars demanded the promotion of reforms through the budget conditionality, with the inclusion of cohesion funds mainly for safeguarding the rule of law. The auspice was a "correction of the EU's policy recommendations in which it tended to lean toward budget consolidation" (Bayer & Breitenfellner, 2018: 108).

Similarly, during the process of approval of the Regulation EU 2017/825, the European Parliament (EP) favoured the use of SRSP funding for strengthening economic, social and territorial cohesion (Widuto, 2017: 3). Nevertheless, regarding the level of the political debate, it seems that criticism has never triggered an actual dissensus within and among the national and EU Institutions. For instance, from the EP debate it has emerged that TSI should not be used as an excuse to prescribe austerity policies through country-specific recommendations and the use of the most far-reaching measures of the European Semester (see 9-0173/2020—Geese, Karas & Pîslaru).

The BUDG-ECON joint committee of the EP requested an additional financial amount of €1.45 billion for the TSI. It also stressed that Member States should be entitled to use part of their Recovery and Resilience Facility budget for the instrument to strengthen the technical assistance available to them to prepare and improve their recovery and resilience plans. In addition, the report pointed out that the Instrument should be applied in full accordance with the rules on the protection of the EU budget, considering the respect for the rule of law (Widuto, 2019; Spinaci, 2021).

National Parliaments have expressed similar views. In particular, the Portuguese Parliament welcomed the establishment of a programme offering technical and financial assistance for reforms that were considered crucial for convergence and competitiveness (Widuto, 2019). The Czech Senate supported the establishment of the TSI but warned that a situation where the programme could lead the Member States to condition their reform efforts on the availability of EU financial support should be avoided (Widuto, 2019). It highlighted that efforts should be motivated by national needs and EU support should only be supplementary. Moreover, in a more general resolution on the governance of the euro area on 23 June 2018, the French National Assembly supported the EU's efforts to strengthen structural reforms and the use of instruments for this purpose under the new MFF.

All in all, the main problem that emerged from the TSI for Member States has been its link with policies for fiscal consolidation and reduction of public expenditures rather than those fostering growth and cohesion policy.

5 Concluding Remarks

To conclude, the evolution of the TSI tool has shown that initially it was not properly linked to the rule of law; rather, it was purposely created to address specific (and contested) economic issues in Greece and Cyprus and only afterwards did it become more linked to structural reforms in all Member States. The role of the TSI was boosted by the NRRPs as a supporting tool for the implementation of the plans. Still, its connection with the rule of law may be considered weak since the main purpose is represented by the administrative support for the Member States; this also leads to questioning how much the TSI and its predecessors have been envisaged as ad hoc tools or as "structural" tools for administrative support; in fact, the TSI has evolved from targeting specific countries to an all-encompassing instrument in support of and at the disposal of all Member State administrations; what matters here is to highlight that the Commission, in helping structural reforms for Member States, is pursuing both the administrative harmonisation as well as the support to specific projects when a country asks for it. Hence, the TSI may be considered an effort to strengthen a sort of multilevel administration governance with the purpose of making the implementation of the reforms timely and more efficient. To this end, the Commission will be launching another ancillary initiative—the Public Administration Cooperation Exchange (PACE)—to strengthen the administrative capacity of Member States. In the end it may be argued that the NRRPs have been given a chance to rethink and rework the entire rationale of the TSI, grounded on the new MFF and on the NRRPs and its goals.

References

Bayer, K., & Breitenfellner, A. (2018). What Is the Appropriate Role of Structural Reforms in E(M)U Deepening? *Focus on European Economic Integration, Oesterreichische Nationalbank (Austrian Central Bank), Q3*, 102–112.

Da Silva, A. D., Givone, A., & Sondermann, D. (2018). When Do Countries Implement Structural Reforms? In N. F. Campos, P. De Grauwe, &

Y. Ji (Eds.), *The Political Economy of Structural Reforms in Europe*. Oxford University Press.

Dermine, P. (2022). *The New Economic Governance of the Eurozone*. Cambridge University Press.

Dolls, M., Fuest, C., Krolage, C., Neumeier, F., & Stöhlker, D. (2019). Incentivising Structural Reforms in Europe? A Blueprint for the European Commission's Reform Support Programme. *Intereconomics, 1*(2019), 42–46.

EULawLive. (2021). Technical Support Instrument now officially published, 18th February 2021.

Hecser, A., & Molitor, P. (2022, November). Economic governance support unit (EGOV), *In-Depth Analysis—Technical Support Instrument: Main features*, PE 659.652.

Huguenot-Noel, R., Hunter, A., & Zuleeg, F. (2018, October 18). Strengthening cohesion in the EU: How can structural reforms contribute? Discussion Paper—Sustainable Prosperity for Europe Programme.

Lancos, P. L., Xanthoulis, N., & Arroyo Jiménez, L. (2023). *The Legal Effects of EU Soft Law*. Edward Elgar Publishing.

Magnus, M. et al. (2023, October). European governance and EMU scrutiny unit. In-Depth Analysis—Technical Support Instrument: Latest developments. PE 747.871.

Ongaro, E. (2022). The Long and Winding Road Towards the EU Policy of Support to Member States Public Administration Reform: History (2000–2021) and Prospects. *Public Policy and Administration*, 1–24.

Ongaro, E., & Kickert, W. (2020). EU-driven Public Sector Reforms. *Public Policy and Administration, 2*(2020), 117–134.

Schramm, L., Krotz, U., & De Witte, B. (2022). Building 'Next Generation' after the Pandemic: The Implementation and Implications of the EU Covid Recovery Plan. *Journal of Common Market Studies, S1*(2022), 114–124.

Spinaci, S. (2021, March). European parliamentary research service. *Briefing—Technical Support Instrument 2021–2027*. PE 659.332.

Widuto, A. (2017, June). Structural reform support programme 2017–2020. *Briefing, European Parliamentary Research Service,* European Parliament.

Widuto, A. (2019, March). European parliamentary research service. *Briefing—Reform Support Programme 2021–2027*. PE 625.150.

CHAPTER 8

The Role of OLAF and EPPO in the Protection of the Rule of Law

Alessandro Nato

1 Introduction

Recital No. 1 of Directive No. 2017/1371 set up the definition of the protection of the Union's financial interests. According to this definition, the protection of EU financial interests "concerns not only the management of budget appropriations but extends to all measures which negatively affect, or which threaten to negatively impact its assets and those of the Member States, to the extent that those measures are of relevance to Union policies". Furthermore, the EU financial interest is defined by Article 2, Directive No. 2017/1371 as "all revenues, expenditure and assets covered by, acquired through, or due to: (i) the Union budget; (ii) the budgets of the Union institutions, bodies, offices and agencies established pursuant to the Treaties or budgets directly or indirectly managed and monitored by them".

A. Nato (✉)
University of Teramo, Teramo, Italy
e-mail: anato@unite.it

C. Fasone et al. (eds.), *EU Rule of Law Procedures at the Test Bench*, Palgrave Studies in European Union Politics,
https://doi.org/10.1007/978-3-031-60008-1_8

Before EU Regulation No. 883/2013 safeguarding the financial interests of the European Union was an important but not central issue, not least because the European budget was much smaller than those of the Member States themselves (Berlin et al., 2017; Crijns & Haentjens, 2022; White, 1998). There has also always been very little interest from the legal and economic sciences in the study of this topic, which has been investigated mainly from the angle of criminal law, to combat fraud (Izzi & Jimenez Galli, 2016; Pizzolante, 2019; Venegoni, 2018). Nevertheless, it has recently become crucial to defend the EU's financial interests, even becoming, as it were, a fundamental component of the European Union legal system. This shift in perspective is linked to the increase in the financial endowment of the Union through its new tools and in the rise of spending conditionality (see Fasone and Simoncini in this volume; see Hegedűs and Christiansen in this volume; see Lupo in this volume). The EU budget is the financial instrument that allows the European Institutions to translate their policies into concrete reality (Benedetto, 2013; Laffan, 1997). After the Next Generation EU, the EU budget was almost doubled, though temporarily, and the EU institutions and Member States understood that it was necessary to strengthen the protection of this vital interest.

The protection of the financial interests of the EU has had an effect in the multilevel collaboration between criminal control and administrative control. The protection of EU financial interests has increased the national and supranational collaboration between institutions that conduct administrative investigations and those that conduct criminal investigations. Notwithstanding, some questions arise: but which are the supranational bodies and agencies that protect the EU's financial interest? How do these help protect the EU's financial interests, and how is this connected to the rule of law?

To answer these questions a central stage is occupied by the role and the cooperation between the European Anti-Fraud Office (henceforth OLAF) and the European Public Prosecutor Office (henceforth EPPO). The next few paragraphs will try to answer these questions and examine both positive and negative aspects—the latter related to judicial protection—connecting them to rule of law and OLAF and EPPO actions.

2 OLAF and EPPO in the EU Legal System

Protecting the financial interest of the European Union has become central to the follow-up of the European integration process. Also, the protection of this European financial interest is a relevant tool for restoring proper respect for the rule of law in the multilevel EU legal system. In fact, European institutions aim to check that European funds are properly spent and intervene in cases of mismanagement. In the latter cases, the institutions provide recovery of the sums disbursed. However, this operation can allow them to put pressure on national governments to also enforce the rule of law in domestic legal systems. Indeed, such a system, by ensuring continuous control of the internal apparatuses and the actions of the national executives responsible for the management of European funds, makes it possible to restore the proper functioning not only of the management of funds, but also of respect for fundamental values.

In this regard, it is worth examining two key EU bodies for the protection of the EU financial interest, which in the light of the policy against rule of law backsliding promoted by the European institutions over the past decade can play a first-order role in achieving this goal. Reference is made to the OLAF and the EPPO.

The scope of OLAF's action covers any fraud, administrative irregularities, or other detrimental activity that can damage the financial interests of the EU. To respect the division of roles derived from the principle of guarantee—similar to that which inspires the work of the judiciary—with a distinction between investigative and adjudicative activities, OLAF has the power to conduct investigations, but it does not issue sanctions. It can formulate a report and recommendations at the end of the investigations. The Court of Justice—see T-289/16, Inox Mare srl, par. 28—clarified that such a recommendation has no binding legal effect on EU or Member States authorities. It is a decision of the EU institution or Member States' authorities to apply OLAF's recommendation and to proceed to take administrative or judicial action (Cahn, 2023: 329; Kratsas, 2012: 65).

On 1 June 2021, the EPPO, the missing pillar in the EU anti-fraud architecture, became operational. It was the Lisbon Treaty that provided the long-sought legal basis for the creation of the EPPO: Article 86 TFEU. This rule allows the Council, by unanimous decision and subject to approval by the European Parliament, to establish the European Public

Prosecutor's Office "from Eurojust". It also allows a group of at least nine Member States to request a Council decision and establish the EPPO through enhanced cooperation. The Lisbon Treaty itself places before Article 86 TFEU, two provisions of equally fundamental importance: Articles 82 and 83 TFEU. These norms in specifying the guidelines outlined in Article 325 TFEU, enshrine the Union's legislative competence to dictate common minimum rules aimed at the approximation of the criminal, substantive, and procedural side of national legislation (Lopez, 2021: 700). Affecting these normative bases with a distinctly derogatory character are Article 86 and the Regulation establishing the European Public Prosecutor's Office, which finds legitimacy in it.

EPPO is a rare case for enhanced EU cooperation. In fact, 22 EU Member States currently participate in it. Poland and Hungary remain outside this enhanced cooperation. This divergence shows how such a control instrument can serve not only to protect the financial interests of the EU, but also to protect the rule of law in the Union. In fact, the EPPO has the characteristics and the powers to engage in an in-depth dialogue with the judicial system of the Member States and to test its state of independence and autonomy from the fund management bodies and internal executives daily. The work of the EPPO in this regard can serve as an early warning light on the tightness of the values inscribed in Article 2 TEU within the national legal systems. The creation of the European Public Prosecutor is intended to overcome the previous level of integration, which was based on the need to implement judicial measures beyond the borders of the territory in which they were issued. Conversely, with the entry into the era of the European Public Prosecutor, the identification, prosecution, and indictment of the perpetrators and accomplices of the crimes within its jurisdiction will be carried out based on a single set of rules, by means of decisions with immediate effect, capable of direct enforcement, and therefore capable of disregarding recognition by national bodies (Lopez, 2021: 703).

Indeed, the EPPO represents an innovation in the EU legal framework (Ligeti, 2020: 33; Oberg, 2021: 164; Sicurella, 2023: 19). Before it was set up, the EU had no power to investigate and bring to judgement the perpetrators of crime against EU financial interests. Existing EU bodies—such as OLAF, Eurojust, and Europol—do not have, and cannot be given, the mandate to conduct criminal investigations and do not have coercive powers if the Member States refuse to carry out OLAF's investigations (see Bellacosa & De Bellis, 2023: 26). Therefore, only national authorities could investigate and prosecute EU fraud, but their jurisdiction ends at national borders. The EPPO fills this institutional gap considering the transnational nature of most fraud affecting the EU financial interests (see Bellacosa & De Bellis, 2023: 26). After enhanced cooperation, in 2017 20 Member States adopted the Council Regulation (EU) 2017/1939, establishing the EPPO. This regulation is now binding in its entirety and is directly applicable in 22 Member States.[1]

The primary aim of the EPPO is to investigate and prosecute crimes affecting the EU's financial interest in a more efficient and effective way than the Member States could do individually through a specialised and well-equipped office (Varvaele, 2018: 17). To this end, the European Public Prosecutor is "competent in respect of the offences against the financial interests of the Union provided for in Directive EU, 2017/ 1371" as implemented in national law, irrespective of whether the same criminal conduct could be classified as another type of offence under national law (see Article 22(1), EU Regulation 2017/1939). These offences have a direct impact on the EU budget, as they deprive the EU of huge amounts of resources and are detrimental to all EU citizens (De Amicis & Kostoris, 2018: 240). Moreover, the European Public Prosecutor has jurisdiction over any other offence that is inextricably linked to criminal conduct within the scope of Article 22, par. 1, EU Regulation 2017/1939. The EPPO is integrated into the national legal framework. From a structural point of view, the EPPO has two tiers: central and decentral, meaning national. The central level of the EPPO, based in Luxembourg, consists of: the Chief European Prosecutor; 22 European Prosecutors (one from each participating EU country), two of whom are deputies to the Chief European Prosecutor (currently the European Prosecutors of Germany and Italy); and the Administrative Director. The Chief European Public Prosecutor and the 22 European Public Prosecutors form the College of the EPPO. The decentralised level of the EPPO consists of the Deputy European Public Prosecutors in the 22 participating EU Member States. The central level supervises the investigations and prosecutions carried out at national level by the Deputy European Public Prosecutors, who are completely independent of their national

[1] The first 20 Member States were: Austria, Belgium, Bulgaria, Croatia, Cyprus, Czech Republic, Estonia, Germany, Greece, Spain, Finland, France, Italy, Latvia, Lithuania, Luxembourg, Portugal, Romania, Slovenia, and Slovakia. In 2018, Malta and the Netherlands joined the EPPO.

authorities. The EPPO and OLAF's field of operation are nonetheless closely linked. The common aim of both bodies is to increase fraud detection at EU level and to maximise the recovery of damages to the EU budget. Moreover, both EU bodies are combining their investigative and other capacities to improve the protection of the EU financial interests. To avoid duplication of effort, the working arrangement between OLAF and the EPPO is of utmost importance for their relationship. At present, the annual activity report of the two agencies for 2021 shows that the cooperation between OLAF and the EPPO is running smoothly and that any obstacles are being resolved without major problems (see OLAF, The OLAF Report 2021, 1, 37 (2022); EPPO, 2021 Annual Report, 1, 88 (2022)).

Cooperation between these two EU bodies could turn into a useful complementarity for the strengthening of their action. Complementary with the European Public Prosecutors means that OLAF can conduct administrative investigations into the same facts as the EPPO. This allows OLAF to address essential aspects of the protection of the financial interests of the EU, such as recommendations for rapid recovery, the adoption of administrative precautionary measures and the development of systemic recommendations for improvements where shortcomings are identified in administrative investigations (e.g. concerning procurement procedures). These investigations are carried out in close and mutually agreed cooperation with the EPPO. OLAF may assist the EPPO in its investigations by providing operational, forensic, and analytical expertise and tools to enhance the activities of OLAF and the EPPO in full respect of the applicable procedural guarantees. In 2021, for example, OLAF investigators supported the EPPO by acting as expert witnesses in complex cases and by providing forensic analysis and extensive documentation of relevant EU projects and programmes. This cooperation will ensure that OLAF becomes a reliable operational partner for the EPPO and that all available means are used to protect taxpayers' money against fraud and other irregular activities (see OLAF, The OLAF Report 2021, 1, 37 (2022)).

However, unambiguous criticism (see Bellacosa & De Bellis, 2023: 26; Klement, 2021: 51) regards the case of complementary investigations between the OLAF and the EPPO. On this point, recently the OLAF guidelines intervene to fix the problem. Article 12 of the OLAF Guidelines provides that the agency regulation establishes that it can conduct a complementary investigation into the same facts as the EPPO criminal investigation, where the EPPO does not object to such investigation.

Such investigations are opened either on OLAF's initiative or on the EPPO's request, to facilitate the adoption of precautionary administrative measures or of financial disciplinary or administrative action.

Though, in more general terms, it is the very role of the administrative arm of the system that will need to be reassessed in a context in which the EPPO acts.

From this viewpoint, it has been argued that two different visions of OLAF's role could theoretically be considered. On the one hand, OLAF could be transformed into a sort of "EPPO investigatory arm", responding to the EPPO's priorities and orders—supporting a unification between the two agencies insofar as this solution would provide a more efficient allocation of resources (Bellacosa & De Bellis, 2023: 26; Kratsas, 2012: 95). On the other hand, OLAF and the EPPO could work as two autonomous bodies, while the main operative support to the EPPO should come from the national authorities (Bellacosa & De Bellis, 2023: 26; Weyembergh & Brière, 2018: 75–76). The primary role of OLAF and the EPPO is to protect the financial interest of the European Union. Therefore, we can consider them as indirect tools for the protection of the rule of law.

Nevertheless, when we look at the functioning of OLAF, especially before the case law of the Court of Justice, and of the EPPO, the rule of law profiles that relate to judicial protection come to the fore.

It is concerning that judicial oversight of OLAF's actions is still very weak and that damages actions—recourse procedure under Article 340 TFEU—are often the only remedy available to those under investigation. This lack of protection has been a constant source of concern since the creation of OLAF. The jurisprudence of the European Courts has been particularly active and progressive in protecting the rule of law in the context of OLAF investigations. In particular, the General Court of the EU has given some very innovative judgements in this area.

Although OLAF has many areas of activity—such as coordination, assistance, monitoring, improving cooperation with and between Member States, and developing anti-fraud policy—its investigative function is paramount. When OLAF conducts internal and external investigations, it should of course do so with integrity, impartiality, and professionalism and, above all, with respect for the fundamental rights and freedoms of the individual (Groussot & Popov, 2010: 642). Unfortunately, this is not always the case in practice. Indeed, OLAF is in a delicate position and must balance the effectiveness of its investigations with the so-called "culture of accountability" (Groussot & Popov, 2010: 642).

As Groussot and Popov point out, the Court of Justice of the EU played a key role in improving OLAF's accountability and restoring the inconsistencies that it produced with respect to the rule of law (Groussot & Popov, 2010: 642). Indeed, the General Court affirmed in the *Nikolaou* case law (T-259/03:139–187) that the person under investigation cannot invoke the fundamental right of defiance to gain access to the OLAF investigation file and the final report, since these acts cannot be considered as adversely affecting him or her. However, the Court underlined two other obligations that OLAF has towards the person under investigation. On the one hand, the person concerned must be informed promptly of the existence of an investigation, provided that this does not harm the investigation. On the other hand, if OLAF intends to draw conclusions referring to a person under investigation by name, that person must be able to express his or her views on all facts concerning him or her. Interestingly, the plaintiff did not have to prove the exact circumstances of the leakage to establish that the leakage was attributable to OLAF, although the burden of proof for a claim for compensation pursuant to Article 340, par. 2 TFEU normally rests with the plaintiff (Groussot & Popov, 2010: 642).

In the *Giraudy* case law (T-23/05:165), the General Court changed previous jurisprudential direction and recognised that a culture of accountability has developed within the institutions of the Union, which responds to the concern of the public to be informed and to be certain that maladministration and fraud are detected and, where appropriate, duly remedied and punished. The consequence of this requirement is that officials and other servants holding positions of responsibility in an administration such as the Commission must consider the possible existence of a legitimate need to provide the public with a certain amount of information. It is clear that such a requirement may be in conflict with the fundamental rights of individuals. This jurisprudence has allowed for the healing of critical profiles between OLAF and the rule of law (Groussot & Popov, 2010: 643). In other words, it was the intervention of the Court of Justice that made it possible to remedy the problem of judicial review of OLAF's acts.

Concerning the rule of law profiles affecting the EPPO, which are related to judicial protection, it is appropriate to devote an in-depth discussion in the next section.

3 EPPO and Rule of Law: A Possible Infringement?

EPPO grounds some problems with the rule of law. The EPPO Regulation presents a significant rule of law deficit in terms of judicial protection by establishing very limited jurisdiction of the Court of Justice in reviewing EPPO acts, which is linked to the reliance of the EPPO on the legal orders of Member States in terms of the applicability of national law and criminal justice mechanisms (Mitsilegas, 2020: 260; Zivic et al., 2022: 408). In other words, these rule of law concerns arise from limiting the jurisdiction of the CJEU as regards the acts of the EPPO. The version of the EPPO Regulation in force has brought limited changes to the Commission proposal introducing a very limited review of EPPO acts by the Court of Justice (see Mitsilegas & Giuffrida, 2020: 115). Indeed, it is the national courts, not the CJEU, that are empowered to examine, according to the requirements and procedures laid down by national legislation, the acts intended to produce legal effects against a third party.

This limited review is justified because of the unique nature of the EPPO in relation to other EU agencies (see recital 86 of Council Regulation EU 2017/1939; Mitsilegas, 2020: 260). Undeniably, Article 86, par. 3, TFEU allows the Union legislature to determine the rules applicable to the judicial review of procedural measures taken by the EPPO in the performance of its functions. For this reason, recital 86 of Council Regulation EU 2017/1939 affirms that the competence granted to the Union legislature reflects the specific nature of the tasks and structure of the EPPO and requires special rules regarding judicial review. Moreover, the limited review of the EPPO is linked to the reliance of this tool on the legal orders of Member States in terms of the applicability of national law and criminal justice mechanism (see Mitsilegas, 2020: 260). Recital 87 of Council Regulation EU 2017/1939 states that, according to Article 86, par. 2, TFEU, the EPPO exercises its functions of prosecutor before the competent courts of the Member States. Consequently, acts undertaken by the EPPO during its investigations are closely related to the prosecution which may result therefrom, and thus have effects in the legal order of the Member States. In many cases the acts will be carried out by national law enforcement authorities acting under the instructions of the EPPO, in some cases after having obtained the authorisation of a national court.

As emerged from the exam of recital 87 of Council Regulation EU 2017/1939, it is therefore appropriate to consider that procedural acts of the EPPO that are intended to produce legal effects towards third parties should be subject to review by the competent national courts in accordance with the requirements and procedures laid down by national law (see Wade, 2021: 267). This should ensure that the procedural acts of the EPPO that are adopted before the indictment and intended to produce legal effects against third parties (a category which includes the suspect, the victim, and other interested persons whose rights may be adversely affected by such acts) are subject to judicial review by national courts. Procedural acts that relate to the choice of the Member State whose courts will be competent to hear the prosecution, which is to be determined based on the criteria laid down in this Regulation, are intended to produce legal effects regarding third parties and should therefore be subject to judicial review by national courts, at the latest at the trial stage (see Wade, 2021: 267).

Also, recital 87 of Council Regulation EU 2017/1939, which contains a kind of authentic interpretation of Article 42, par. 1 of EU Regulation 2017/1939, states that actions before competent national courts for failures of the EPPO to act are those regarding procedural acts which the EPPO is under a legal obligation to adopt, and which are intended to produce legal effects towards third parties. Where national law provides for judicial review concerning procedural acts which are not intended to produce legal effects vis-à-vis third parties or for legal actions concerning other failures to act, this Regulation should not be interpreted as affecting such legal provisions. In addition, Member States should not be required to provide for judicial review by the competent national courts of procedural acts which are not intended to produce legal effects against third parties, such as the appointment of experts or the reimbursement of witness costs. In other words, appealable acts of the EPPO must be procedural acts and must be intended to produce legal effects vis-à-vis third parties, i.e. vis-à-vis the suspect, the victim, and other interested persons whose rights might be affected by such procedural acts (Article 42, par. 1, EU Regulation 2017/1939). The meaning of the expression procedural acts can be deduced, both from recital 87, which expressly refers to acts taken prior to the indictment such as, for example, investigative measures under Article 30 EU Regulation 2017/1939, and recital 89 EU Regulation 2017/1939, which refers more explicitly to the EPPO's decision taken in the exercise of its functions, aimed at conducting investigations, prosecutions, or bringing cases to trial. The legal concept of an act intended to produce legal effects vis-à-vis third parties reproduces verbatim an expression used in the second sentence of Article 263, par. 1, TFEU, and thus constitutes an autonomous notion in EU law, which as such is independent of similar notions of a challengeable act in national law and must therefore be interpreted uniformly throughout the EU (see Pawel Dworzecki, C-108/16:28-30; Traversa, 2019: 37).

To sum up, as highlighted in the literature, the EPPO regulation "relies on national courts and not on the Court of Justice for the review of procedural acts of the EPPO that are intended to produce legal effects with regard to third parties in accordance with the requirements and procedures laid down by national law" (see Mitsilegas, 2020: 260). In addition, recital 88 of Council Regulation EU 2017/1939 affirms that when national courts review the legality of such acts, they may do so based on Union law, including this Regulation, and based on national law, which applies to the extent that a matter is not dealt with by this Regulation. As underlined in the case law of the Court of Justice, national courts should always refer preliminary questions to the Court of Justice when they entertain doubts about the validity of those acts against Union law as well as on the interpretation of EU law in case of courts of last resort. The national court may send preliminary questions to the Court of Justice, however, the EU Regulation 2017/1939 excludes questions on the validity of EPPO procedural acts concerning national procedural law or national measures transposing directives, even if the regulation refers to them (see Mitsilegas, 2020: 260). According to recital 88 of Council Regulation EU 2017/1939, this is, still, without prejudice to preliminary references concerning the interpretation of any provision of primary law, including the Treaties and the Charter, or the interpretation and validity of any provision of Union secondary law, including this Regulation and applicable Directives. In addition, this Regulation does not exclude the possibility for national courts to review the validity of the procedural acts of the EPPO which are intended to produce legal effects vis-à-vis third parties regarding the principle of proportionality as enshrined in national law (see Wade, 2021: 267). For these reasons, the role of the Court of Justice in holding the EPPO judicially accountable remains limited in the EPPO Regulation. The EPPO has no obligation to adopt such acts (see Mitsilegas, 2020: 260). Instead, the EPPO Regulation grants the Court of Justice jurisdiction to give preliminary rulings in three cases: (a) on the validity of procedural acts of the EPPO; (b) on the interpretation or validity of provisions of EU law, including the EPPO Regulation; (c) in relation to any conflict of competence between the EPPO and the national authorities (see Article 42, par. 2, Regulation EU 2017/1939). This demonstrates that the Court of Justice has a very limited role in actions for the annulment of EPPO acts under 263 TFEU, covering only decisions of the EPPO to dismiss a case. Furthermore, as the literature confirms, this means that key EPPO acts, including the decision to open an investigation or prosecution and decisions on conflicts of jurisdiction, are not subject to direct review by the Court of Justice (Bose, 2019: 195; Mitsilegas, 2020: 83). Such a limitation of the jurisdiction of the European Court of Justice is problematic in terms of control and accountability, since we have an EU agency with operational powers that are not accompanied by EU judicial scrutiny of several key decisions that directly affect the position of individuals. In addition to its limited jurisdiction under Article 263 TFEU, the Court of Justice has jurisdiction in disputes relating to compensation for damage caused by the EPPO under Article 268 TFEU. One more rule of law deficit emerges from the significant limits that the EPPO Regulation imposes on the Court of Justice under Article 263 TFUE. The Court of Justice has a very limited role in actions for annulment of EPPO acts under Article 263 TFEU, covering only decisions of the EPPO to dismiss a case in so far as they are contested directly because of EU law (see Article 42, par. 3, Regulation EU 2017/1939; Gohler, 2015: 102). Certain regulatory choices made by the European legislature have a significant impact on the legal position of the convenor, satisfying the legitimacy criteria of Article 263 TFEU, as their legal effects affect the interests of the plaintiff, resulting in a marked change in his or her legal position. For example, the EPPO Regulation does not give the Court of Justice jurisdiction over EPPO procedural acts at the decentralised level, even if such acts affect the legal position of the person concerned. In addition, Regulation EU 2017/1939 severely limits judicial review by the European courts and national courts of the vast majority of EPPO acts adopted at the centralised level. The Court of Justice has a very limited role in actions for annulment of acts of the EPPO under Article 263 TFEU, which concerns only its decisions to dismiss a case to the extent that they are challenged directly based on Union law (see Article 42(3), Regulation EU 2017/1939). However, the Court of Justice does not have jurisdiction under Article 263 TFEU over key EPPO decisions, including the initiation of an investigation and prosecution, bundling or reassignment of cases, and decisions on choice of court and conflicts of jurisdiction (see Mitsilegas, 2020: 261). By way of derogation from par. 1 of Article 42, Regulation EU 2017/1939, the decision of the EPPO to dismiss a case, in so far as they are contested directly because of Union law, shall be subject to review before the Court of Justice in accordance with the fourth paragraph of Article 263 TFEU. While leaning towards this interpretation, it should be noted that there is also a different interpretation on this last point. Part of the literature states, on the one hand, that the text of the regulation is silent on the question of a remedy against investigations as such and argues that such a remedy might be required by Article 19, par. 1, TEU (see Erbeznik, 2020: c72; Mitsilegas, 2020: 261). On the other, this doctrine argues that the EPPO's decision to open an investigation is not a procedural act intended to produce legal effects concerning third parties, but rather a preparatory act (see Herrnfeld et al., 2021: 231; Mitsilegas, 2020: 261).

However, the lack of a remedy before the Court of Justice undermines effective judicial protection and the role of advocacy, leaving key EPPO decisions without a sufficient level of judicial review and accountability. This is the case even though in general national courts can provide, together with the Court of Justice, a comprehensive system of legal remedies in EU law. Indeed, it is possible to question the action of national courts, to the extent that they are granted jurisdiction by the EPPO regulation, have the capacity and powers at the national level to provide effective judicial review of decisions made by the EPPO at the centralised level, including consideration of meaningful review of forum decisions (see Mitsilegas, 2020: 262; Panzavolta, 2018: 80). Furthermore, the literature states that it seems questionable that defence rights can be meaningfully upheld solely for the CJEU jurisdiction under Article 267 TFEU of the Court of Justice (see Mitsilegas, 2020: 262). Indeed, the main avenue for judicial review of EPPO acts is the preliminary reference mechanism under Article 267 TFEU (Mitsilegas, 2020: 83; Zivic et al., 2022: 409). Given the restricted jurisdiction of the CJEU in direct review of EPPO measures, the preliminary reference procedure will be crucial for national courts to guarantee effective judicial protection in the context of the EPPO's activities. National courts, including lower courts, must be stimulated to refer questions to the CJEU when issues relating to the operation of the EPPO at national level (notably in relation to the activities of the European Delegated Prosecutors) affect the protection of fundamental rights, the effective administration of justice and the rule of law (Mitsilegas, 2020: 83; Zivic et al., 2022: 409).

The narrow provisions for judicial review create a rule of law deficit that is exacerbated in forum decisions, where the position of the defendant is even more compromised. The EPPO Regulation essentially establishes "an EU agency without EU judicial review, a system of European investigation and prosecution without a European remedy" (see Mitsilegas, 2020: 262).

4 Conclusion

If initially it was thought to exploit the protection of the financial interest to protect the rule of law, the growth of the EU budget meant that the relationship was reversed. These changes suggest that rule of law is a useful tool to protect the EU's financial interest. Certainly, the protection of the EU financial interest has become central to the process of European integration. The safeguarding of this supranational objective relies mostly on cooperation, on the one hand, between EU and Member State levels. On the other, the coordination and effective action of EU bodies such as the EPPO and OLAF plays a crucial role. If these two bodies manage to have dialogue with each other and with national authorities, fraud against the financial interest will be circumscribed. If not, they will impair the success of the Next Generation EU and the European integration of administrative and criminal controls. However, the exponential growth in the importance of protecting the Union's financial interest is also reflected in the relationship between this principle and the rule of law.

Indeed, this process leads to the creation of a financial rule of law in the EU legal system (Sandulli & Nato, forthcoming). This seems obvious with the creation of the EU regulation 2020/2092 (see Hegedus and Christiansen in this volume). The close link between the EU's financial interests and the rule of law, or rather, the quasi-subordination of values to the objective of protecting the EU's financial interests, evidently arises from the conditions that activate the conditionality mechanism. Article 4 of EU Regulation 2020/2092 states that measures against Member States can only be taken if two conditions are met. First, there must be a violation of the principles of the rule of law. Secondly, such a breach must undermine, or pose a serious risk to, the sound financial management of the Union's budget or the protection of the Union's financial interests in a direct and tangible way (Tridimas, 2020). In essence, breaches of the rule of law principles must seriously undermine or risk undermining in a sufficiently direct way the sound financial management of the EU budget or the protection of the EU's financial interests. On this point, the Court of Justice clarified that the objective of Regulation 2020/2092 is to safeguard the EU budget from negative effects resulting directly from breaches of the rule of law in a Member State, rather than imposing penalties for such violations. Consequently, according to the relevant literature, the conditionality mechanism should no longer be classified only as a tool entrusted to the European Commission capable of protecting the rule of law, but it should be considered as a useful tool to protect the EU budget (Baraggia, 2022: 688; Łacny, 2021: 83; Staudinger, 2022: 730).

In particular, the EPPO case, however, shows that there are also sensitive profiles inherent in criminal law and the guarantee of effective judicial remedies that come to the fore. The CJEU recently intervened on these issues in the *G.K. and others (EPPO)* case law, C-281/22. In particular, the CJEU intervened with respect to the juridiciability of procedural acts that produce legal effects vis-à-vis third parties. It ruled that when the EPPO conducts an investigation in more than one EU Member State, the courts of the Member State of the prosecutor who is responsible for the investigation have jurisdiction to review the adoption and justification of the investigative measures. Judicial review of investigative measures in other Member States can only cover the elements related to the execution of such measures. In cases of serious interference with the rights of the person concerned guaranteed by the EU Charter of Fundamental Rights, investigative measures must be subject to prior judicial review carried out in the Member State of the prosecutor in charge of the investigation (see Bovend'Eerdt, 2024: 495). This jurisprudential intervention confirms how questions concerning the justiciability of EPPO acts is a very relevant issue linking the rule of law with the functioning of this EU body. Useful insights can be found in the Court of Justice's forthcoming interventions to clarify how the EPPO should function to be in line with the rule of law.

References

Baraggia, A. (2022). The "Conditionality" Regulation under the ECJ's Scrutiny: A Constitutional Analysis. *European Law Review, 47*(5), 687–698.

Bellacosa, M., & De Bellis, M. (2023). The Protection of the EU Financial Interests between Administrative and Criminal Tools: OLAF and EPPO. *Common Market Law Review, 60*(1), 15–50.

Benedetto, G. (2013). The EU Budget after Lisbon: Rigidity and Reduced Spending? *Journal of Public Policy, 33*(3), 345–369.

Berlin, D., Martucci, F., & Picod, F. (Eds.). (2017). *La fraude et le droit de l'Union européenne*. Bruylant.

Bose, M. (2019). Judicial Control of the European Public Prosecutor's Office. In T. Rafaraci & R. Belfiore (Eds.), *EU Criminal Justice: Fundamental Rights, Transnational Proceedings, and the European Public Prosecutor's Office* (p. 194). Springer.

Bovend'Eerdt, K. (2024). *The Protection of Fundamental Rights in OLAF Composite Enforcement Procedures*. Springer.

Cahn, O. (2023). Office de Lutte anti-fraude (OLAF). In K. Ambros & P. Rackow (Eds.), *The Cambridge Companion to European Criminal Law* (pp. 329–360). Cambridge University Press.

Council Regulation (EU) 2017/1939 of 12 October 2017 Implementing Enhanced Cooperation on the Establishment of the European Public Prosecutor's Office ('the EPPO').

Crijns, J., Haentjens, M., & Haentjens, R. (Eds.). (2022). *The Enforcement of EU Financial Law*. Hart.

De Amicis, G., & Kostoris, R. E. (2018). Vertical Cooperation. In R. E. Kostoris (Ed.), *Handbook of European Criminal Procedure* (pp. 202–244). Springer.

Directive (EU) 2017/1371 of the European Parliament and of the Council of 5 July 2017 on the Fight Against Fraud to the Union's Financial Interests by Means of Criminal Law.

Erbeznik, A. (2020). EU Criminal Law and the Way Forward in the Case of the Functions of the EPPO. *Croatian Annual of Criminal Sciences and Practice, 27*, 55–77.

Gohler, J. (2015). To Continue or Not: Who Shall Be in Control of the European Public Prosecutor's Dismissal Decisions? *New Journal of European Criminal Law, 6*(1), 102–125.

Groussot, X., & Popov, Z. (2010). What's Wrong with OLAF? Accountability, Due Process and Criminal Justice in European Anti-Fraud Policy Wrong with OLAF? *Common Market Law Review, 47*(3), 605–643.

Herrnfeld, H. H., et al. (Eds.). (2021). *European Public Prosecutor's Office: Article-by-Article Commentary*. Hart Publishing.

Izzi, S., & Jimenez Galli, A. L. (2016). *La lotta contro le attività illecite che ledono gli interessi finanziari europei. Dall'Uclaf alla procura europea, verso una più efficace protezione penale*. Aracne.

Klement, P. (2021). Reporting of Crime Mechanisms and the Interaction between the EPPO and OLAF as Key Future Challenges. *Eucrim: The European Criminal Law Associations Forum*, 51–52.

Kölling, M. (2022). The Role of (Rule of Law) Conditionality in MFF 2021–2027 and Next Generation EU, or the Stressed Budget. *Journal of Contemporary European Studies, 1*(9), 1–14.

Kratsas, G. (2012). A Case for OLAF: The Place and Role of the Anti-Fraud Office in the European Union Context. *European Public Law, 18*(1), 65–97.

Łacny, J. (2021). The Rule of Law Conditionality Under Regulation No 2092/2020—Is It All About the Money? *Hague Journal Rule of Law, 13*(1), 79–105.

Laffan, B. (1997). *The Finances of the European Union*. Palgrave Macmillan.

Ligeti, K. (2020). The Structure of the EPPO: Features and Challenges. *Croatian Annual of Criminal Sciences and Practice, 27*(1), 33–54.

Lopez, R. (2021). Riparto di giurisdizione e Procura europea. *Processo Penale e Giustizia, 3*, 700–717.

Mitsilegas, V., & Giuffrida, F. (2020). Judicial Review of EPPO Acts and Decisions. In K. Ligeti et al. (Eds.), *The European Public Prosecutor's Office at Launch* (p. 115). Wolters Kluwer CEDAM.

Mitsilegas, V. (2020). The European Public Prosecutor's Office between EU and National Law: The Challenge of Effective Judicial Protection. *Croatian Annual of Criminal Sciences and Practice, 27*(1), 79–88.

Oberg, J. (2021). The European Public Prosecutor: Quintessential Supranational Criminal Law? *Maastricht Journal of European and Comparative Law, 28*(2), 164–181.

Panzavolta, M. (2018). Choosing the National Forum for Proceedings Conducted by the EPPO: Who Is to Decide? In L. Bachmeier Winter (Ed.), *The European Public Prosecutor's Office. The Challenges Ahead* (p. 76). Springer.

Pizzolante, G. (2019). *Lotta alle frodi finanziarie nel diritto penale europeo. Tra protezione degli interessi economici dell'Unione Europea e nuove sfide poste da bitcoin e criptovalute*. Cacucci.

Regulation (EU, Euratom) No 883/2013 of the European Parliament and of the Council of 11 September 2013 Concerning Investigations Conducted by the European Anti-Fraud Office (OLAF) and repealing Regulation (EC) No 1073/1999 of the European Parliament and of the Council and Council Regulation (Euratom) No 1074/1999.

Sandulli, A., & Nato, A. (Forthcoming). EU Financial Interests Within the Financialisation Process of the European Legal Order.

Sicurella, R. (2023). The EPPO's Material Scope of Competence and Non-Conformity of National Implementations. *New Journal of European Criminal Law, 14*(1), 18–33.

Staudinger, I. (2022). The Rise and Fall of the Rule of Law Conditionality. *European Papers, 7*(2), 721–737.

Traversa, E. (2019). I tre principali aspetti istituzionali dell'attività della procura europea (EPPO): Legge applicabile, rimedi giurisdizionali e conflitti di competenza. *Archivio Penale, 3*, 1–72.

Tridimas, T. (2020). Editorial Note: Recovery Plan and Rule of Law Conditionality: A New Era Beckons? *Croatian Yearbook of European Law and Policy, 16*, VII–XXI.

Venegoni, A. (2018). *La protezione degli interessi finanziari dell'Unione Europea*. Key Editore.

Vervaele, J. A. E. (2018). The European Public Prosecutor's Office (EPPO): Introductory Remarks. In W. Geelhoed, L. H. Erkelens, & A. W. H. Meij (Eds.), *Shifting Perspectives on the European Public Prosecutor's Office* (pp. 11–19). T.M.C. Asser Press.

Wade, M. L. (2021). The EPPO and the Pitfalls of Actuarial Justice. *Maastricht Journal of European and Comparative Law, 28*(2), 265–280.

Weyembergh, A., & Brière, C. (2018). The Future Cooperation between OLAF and the European Public Prosecutor's Office. *New Journal European Criminal Law, 9*(1), 62–82.

White, S. (1998). *Protection of the Financial Interests of the European Communities: The Fight Against Fraud and Corruption*. Kluwer Law International.

Zivic, A., Zandstra, T., Pit, Q., & Vegt-Schouten, A. (2022). Who's Afraid of EU Primary Law? Judicial Review of the EPPO's Decision on Forum Choice. *New Journal of European Criminal Law, 13*(4), 398–419.

PART III

The Effectiveness of Soft Law Tools

CHAPTER 9

The Shortcomings of the Rule of Law Framework and Dialogue

Maciej Serowaniec

1 Introduction

Adherence to the values enshrined in Article 2 of the Treaty on European Union (TEU), namely respect for dignity, freedom, democracy, equality, the rule of law and human rights, which are common values between the Union and its Member States, is not only a condition for accession to the Union (Article 49 TEU), but also a permanent obligation for states after accession. It should be emphasised that the rule of law has been enshrined in EU primary law not only as one of the fundamental values, but also as an objective which the EU institutions have a clear mandate to achieve (Articles 3(1), 13(1) TEU). The EU institutions and the Member States have recognised the problem of the regular assessment of the continued observance of common values, including the rule of law. In order to achieve the objectives enshrined in Article 2 TEU, the instruments of Articles 258–260 TEU (proceedings for violation of treaty obligations by

M. Serowaniec (✉)
Nicolaus Copernicus University in Toruń, Toruń, Poland
e-mail: mserowaniec@umk.pl

C. Fasone et al. (eds.), *EU Rule of Law Procedures at the Test Bench*, Palgrave Studies in European Union Politics,
https://doi.org/10.1007/978-3-031-60008-1_9

a Member State, on which see Piccirilli in this Volume), the special procedure of Article 7 TEU (on which see Coman and Thinus in the Volume) and, since 2014, the European Commission tool defined as "A new EU Framework to strengthen the Rule of Law" and the Rule of Law Dialogue at the EU General Affairs Council, are used.

The mechanism presented by the European Commission in its communication of 11 March 2014, "A new EU Framework to strengthen the Rule of Law" (COM(2014) 158 final) was a response to the conclusions of the European Parliament and the Council in 2013 (Krygier, 2013), which called for the development of a new method and tools to protect the Union's fundamental values and the requirements of democracy, the rule of law and fundamental rights. The new mechanism aimed to ensure not only the effective and consistent protection of the rule of law in all Member States, but also the protection of the Union's fundamental values and to achieve a higher level of mutual trust and integration in the area of freedom, security and justice without internal borders. Indeed, under the mechanism established, the Commission monitors the situation in the Member States with regard to respect for the rule of law (adopting its own definition of the rule of law for the Communication) and seeks to prevent situations where the conditions for initiating the procedure under Article 7 TEU are met (Gormley, 2017). The aim is thus to avoid a clear risk of either a serious breach of the rule of law (Article 7(1) TEU) or a serious and persistent breach of the rule of law (Article 7(2) TEU).

2 Scope and Rationale of the Rule of Law Framework and Dialogue

The Communication refers to Member States' respect for the rule of law. Its scope therefore includes only one value among those indicated in Article 2 TEU, which in this context significantly limits the Commission's field of action (von Bogdandy et al., 2017). For the Communication, the Commission has adopted an autonomous definition of the rule of law and identified a core of constituent elements, considering the case law of the Court of Justice of the EU and the Council of Europe acquis. In the sense of Article 2 TEU, the rule of law includes, according to the Commission, legality—that is, a transparent, accountable, democratic and pluralistic law-making process—, legal certainty, prohibition of arbitrariness in the action of executive authorities, independent and impartial courts, effective judicial review, including a review of respect for fundamental rights and equality before the law (Kochenov, 2017).

The Communication creates a basis for examining the situation in a particular Member State in terms of compliance with the rule of law under Article 2 TEU and for providing information to the authorities of that state on the risks perceived (Kochenov & Pech, 2016). In this way, a framework enables the Commission to engage with the national authorities, who can present their views and exchange arguments with the Commission. Proceedings based on the Communication also enable the Commission to formulate allegations of a breach of the rule of law, which will form the basis of a proposal for an Article 7 TEU procedure. Even before the Article 7 TEU procedure is initiated, the exchange of arguments allows other Member States to observe the positions of the Commission and the Member State subject to proceedings under the Communication in the longer term. This increases the transparency and predictability of the Commission's proceedings and makes it possible to determine whether a perceived breach of the rule of law can be considered serious and persistent. Proceedings under the Communication have thus been presented as a separate mechanism to protect the rule of law. However, its main function is to monitor the situation in the Member States and prepare the Commission for proceedings under Article 7 TEU (Kochenov & Pech, 2015).

Proceedings under the Communication are intended to address future threats to the rule of law in Member States before the conditions for triggering the mechanisms under Article 7 TEU are met. In this regard, the Commission distinguishes between situations that fall within the scope of EU law and situations that do not fall within the scope of EU law (von Bogdandy et al., 2017). In doing so, it recognises that the Article 258 Treaty on the Functioning of the European Union (TFEU) mechanism can only be triggered within the scope of application of EU law. By contrast, the procedure under Article 7 TEU and the proceedings under the Communication can be applied irrespective of whether Member States' actions in breach of Article 2 TEU fall within the scope of the application of EU law (Kochenov, 2017). The initiation and conduct of proceedings under the Communication are not limited by the need for the Commission to demonstrate that there is an EU element to the alleged infringement that goes beyond a mere breach of the rule of law.

Proceedings under the Communication should be triggered when the Commission becomes aware of "clear indications" of a systemic threat to the rule of law in a Member State. For proceedings to be triggered, three conditions must be met:

1. Proceedings under the Communication are subsidiary to the measures available to individual Member States to address rule of law concerns. Proceedings will be implemented when Member State authorities adopt measures or tolerate situations that may have a systematic negative impact on the integrity, stability or proper functioning of institutions and protective mechanisms established at national level to ensure the rule of law. The mechanism contained in the Communication will be applied when national safeguards for the rule of law appear to be ineffective in countering these threats.
2. Proceedings under the Communication will be initiated if other mechanisms at Union level are unable to address threats to the rule of law. The Commission considers that existing instruments at EU level cannot in all circumstances effectively address a systemic threat to the rule of law. At the same time, the Commission mentions in this regard in particular the Article 7 TEU procedure. It states that the thresholds for its activation are very high, making it to be considered as a "last resort".
3. Proceedings under the Communication are triggered when there is a suspicion that there may be a systemic threat to the rule of law in a Member State. In this regard, the Commission recognises that a systemic threat to the rule of law and the functioning of the EU occurs in cases "where the mechanisms established at national level to ensure the rule of law cease to operate effectively". Thus, national mechanisms have a dual function: not only do they play a role in the context of the subsidiarity of proceedings under the Communication, but, if they cease to operate effectively, they are a premise for triggering proceedings under the Communication (Closa, 2019).

Furthermore, proceedings under the Communication cannot concern individual cases of fundamental rights violations or judicial errors, insofar as these cases can and should be dealt with by national judicial systems and in the context of the control mechanisms established under the ECHR, to which all EU Member States are parties. Thus, it is not a systemic threat if there are isolated violations of fundamental rights or errors in judicial decisions in a Member State (implicitly to be understood that these errors must be committed to the detriment of individuals). In principle, however, as protected under EU law, fundamental rights are not all part of the definition of the rule of law adopted for the Communication (apart from, for example, the principle of effective judicial protection). What seems to be at stake, therefore, is a situation where, irrespective of individual substantive errors, the legal mechanisms in a Member State are, in principle, working well and guarantee effective protection for individuals, as well as the chance that individual substantive breaches of the law can be remedied. Conversely, suppose there are massive violations of fundamental rights and jurisprudential errors that the national system is unable to neutralise. In that case, this will mean that the situation begins to threaten the rule of law as defined by the Commission. This understanding of a systemic threat to the rule of law is confirmed by the remainder of the Communication, according to which "the political, institutional or legal order of a Member State as such, the constitutional structure of that State, the separation of powers, the independence or impartiality of the judiciary or the system of judicial review, including constitutional justice where it exists—for example, as a result of the adoption of new measures or widespread practices by public authorities and the absence of legal remedies at national level—must be under threat" (Crabit & Bel, 2016).

Concerning the criteria adopted by the Commission as to the systemic nature of the threat to the rule of law, it should be noted that the situations arising from the Communication define systemic threats not by specifying what the threat is supposed to be, but mainly by specifying what is supposed to be at stake: the integrity, stability and proper functioning of institutions and protective mechanisms for the rule of law, as well as the threat to the political, legal and constitutional order, the separation of powers or the judiciary (Coman, 2022).

3 Procedural Aspects of the Rule of Law Framework and Dialogue

The Commission expressed its belief that proceeding under the Communication would allow it to respond quickly and effectively to threats to the rule of law in Member States. Proceedings are based on a number of principles: an emphasis on dialogue with the state under investigation, an objective and thorough assessment of the situation by the Commission, followed by an indication of swift and concrete steps that the Member State could take to address the signalled systemic threat to the rule of law and avoid triggering an Article 7 TEU procedure. The proceedings are also to be based on respect for the principle of equal treatment of Member States. This is an important Treaty principle stemming from Article 4(2) TEU, which is considered the constitutional basis for the principle of mutual trust between EU Member States.

Proceedings under the Communication essentially consist of three stages. During the proceedings, the Commission keeps the European Parliament and the Council of the EU informed and may also draw on the expertise of third parties. The Communication mentions in this respect, for example, the EU Agency for Fundamental Rights, the Network of Presidents of the Supreme Judicial Courts of the European Union, the Association of the Councils of State and Supreme Administrative Jurisdictions of the European Union or the European Network of Councils for the Judiciary, the Council of Europe and the Venice Commission. The Commission will coordinate its analysis with them for all cases that these bodies consider and analyse. The course of action under the Communication is shaped so that the Commission can have a soft impact on a Member State suspected of a breach of the rule of law. The first stage is initiated if there are "clear indications of a systemic threat to the rule of law". Such signals can come from any "available" sources and from recognised institutions, including in particular Council of Europe bodies or the EU Agency for Fundamental Rights. The first stage is for the Commission to assess the situation and establish a dialogue with the Member State. If the Commission considers the information received credible, it will initiate a dialogue on the matter. This will be made public. The dialogue will consist of, among other things, correspondence or meetings with the competent authorities of the Member State. This initial phase will culminate in a confidential Commission opinion on the rule of law addressed to the Member State in which the Commission sets out its concerns with reasons. Again, the public will only be informed that an opinion has been issued. The Member State has the right to respond to it. The Commission considers that from the first stage of the proceedings under the Communication, relations with the Member State concerned are covered by the principle of loyalty (Article 4(3) TEU). It therefore expects the Member State, firstly, to cooperate with the Commission in the exchange of information and arguments in the assessment process and, secondly, to refrain from adopting any irreversible measures in relation to the issues of concern raised by the Commission until the conclusion of the proceedings under the Communication. Failure to comply with the principle of loyalty will affect the assessment of the seriousness of the breach of the rule of law. The Communication therefore does not announce the initiation of more far-reaching consequences possible under the case law of the Court of Justice of the EU, i.e. the initiation of proceedings under Article 258 TFEU in case of a breach of the principle of loyalty. Such wording in the Communication may have certain consequences in assessing the legal status and the legal effects of the Communication and the documents (opinions, recommendations) issued on its basis (Taborowski, 2019).

The second stage will occur if the first stage does not produce a satisfactory result. Due to the emphasis on dialogue, there may be further exchanges of correspondence or meetings with Member State authorities each time, regardless of the stage. If these remain unsuccessful and the Commission considers that there is "objective evidence" of a systemic threat, a "recommendation on the rule of law" will be issued. The recommendation may provide guidance on how to remedy the situation and set a deadline for the Member State to comply with the recommendation.

The third stage consists of monitoring the Member State's action against the recommendation issued. If the measures taken in the framework of the established dialogue do not have an adequate effect, the Commission will propose to initiate the procedure under Article 7 TEU. Here, the Commission's role ends and the subsequent fate of the proposal is decided by the Member States within either the Council of the EU (Article 7(1)) or the European Council (Article 7(2) TEU). The Commission cannot propose the sanctions procedure (Article 7(3) TEU) (Kochenov & Bard, 2018).

Proceedings based on the Communication thus prepare the Commission for the potential initiation of an Article 7 TEU procedure (Pech, 2020). Recommendations on the rule of law contain the Commission's legal position vis-à-vis perceived irregularities. However, it should be noted that once a request has been made under either Article 7(1) TEU or Article 7(2) TEU, the Commission does not host further proceedings. This means that the legal assessments formulated by the Commission have no direct bearing on further proceedings by the Member States gathered in the Council of the EU or the European Council. From this perspective, states are free not to share the Commission's assessments, make their own findings and make separate recommendations to the Member State under procedure (Article 7(1) TEU). Member States also have the possibility to interpret for themselves the criteria underlying the triggering of an Article 7 TEU procedure (Pech et al., 2020). In this respect, documents produced based on the Communication can only influence further proceedings under their persuasive content, objective assessment and authority. Finally, the conduct of proceedings based on the Communication does not prevent the direct application of the mechanisms of Article 7 TEU if a sudden deterioration of the situation in a Member State requires a more decisive response from the EU (Nowak-Far, 2021).

On 13 January 2016, the European Commission activated the Rule of Law Framework against Poland. As this is the first time the Rule of Law Framework procedure has been launched, its course is important for possible similar decisions of the European Commission towards other Member States.

a. Evaluation of the Rule of Law Framework and Dialogue based on the Communication to Poland—A (De)Constructive Dialogue on the Rule of Law?

The procedural assumptions for the proceedings under the Communication are worth contrasting with the reality of the proceedings against Poland. In this case, the Commission used all three stages of the proceedings provided for in the Communication. The first stage, in which the Commission attempted to establish a dialogue and identify the problem in Poland, occurred in January 2016. This stage culminated in the Commission's confidential opinion on the rule of law addressed to Poland. As it turned out, the content of the (classified) opinion was subsequently disclosed, after the issuance of the first recommendation on the rule of law 2016/1374, following a request made by Professor L. Pech under the access to documents procedure. As the Polish government did not respond satisfactorily to the opinion, the Commission issued, in the second phase of the proceedings, four recommendations on the rule of law against Poland in succession: first recommendation 2016/1374 of 27.07.2016, second recommendation 2017/146 of 21.12.2016, third recommendation 2017/1520 of 26.07.2017 and fourth recommendation 2018/103 of 20.12.2017. The subsequent recommendations issued after the first recommendation 2016/1374 were structured to complement the earlier recommendations. This type of action was not foreseen in the

Communication (Kochenov & Pech, 2016). Moreover, while recommendations one 2016/1374 and two 2017/146 had the same subject matter (the Constitutional Tribunal, CT) and corresponded to the content of the earlier opinion addressed to Poland at the first stage of the proceedings, recommendations three 2017/1520 and four 2018/103 went beyond the issues concerning the CT. However, the Commission chose not to issue a new opinion to the Member State preceding the recommendation on these new areas. Thus, contrary to the Communication content, the first stage of the procedure was skipped, adopting the formula of a supplementary recommendation, not foreseen in the Communication, on issues that went beyond the matter of supplementary recommendations. Perhaps the Commission considered that the exchange of correspondence that had taken place with the Member State in the meantime was sufficient for the Member State to respond to the Commission's new allegations. In that case, issuing an opinion would not fundamentally change the assessment of the situation. Nevertheless, it should be noted that such a course of action, as adopted in relation to Poland, was not explicitly provided for in the Communication (Taborowski, 2019).

Contrary to the content of the Communication, the Commission not only disclosed the substantive content of the recommendations, but published them in full each time. The recommendations include a timeline of actions and events related to the subject of the assessment, as well as the related positions of national, EU and international institutions. The recommendations also include an extensive and detailed description of the risks that the Commission has identified, an explanation of why the risk that has arisen should be considered systemic and specific recommendations as to what steps should be taken by the Member State and by when. The content of the recommendations, modelled on the reasoned opinions in Article 258 TFEU proceedings, emphasises the legal dimension of the rule of law allegations to avoid a merely discretionary assessment of a political nature. In its recommendations, the Commission has taken into account the positions of other institutions at national and international level, such as the European Parliament, the Network of Presidents of the Supreme Judicial Courts of the European Union, the European Network of Councils for the Judiciary, the Venice Commission, the Commissioner for Human Rights of the Council of Europe, the UN Human Rights Committee, as well as numerous civil society organisations such as Amnesty International and the Network for Cooperation on

Human Rights and Democracy. This has given the Commission an additional strong legitimacy for its actions and assessments made during its proceedings based on the Communication. It also demonstrates that the issues raised by the Commission were of concern to many of the most important international organisations and actors and the international community (Taborowski, 2019).

The content of the recommendations on the rule of law concerning Poland covered important systemic issues. The first two recommendations contained reservations concerning the CT. These raised, among other things, defects concerning the publication of judgements of the CT, the appointment of the President of the CT, the composition of the CT and the changes made to it, as well as subsequent statutory solutions regulating the functioning of the CT. The Commission took the view that, in practice, a complete change in the composition of the CT was made outside the normal constitutional process of appointing judges (Wiącek, 2021). In its recommendations with regard to the CT, the Commission also emphasised that the legal solutions concerning the CT have created a situation in which there is no independent and effective control of the constitutionality of the law in the Polish legal system. Starting with the third recommendation 2017/5320, the Commission also pointed out threats to the independence of the ordinary judiciary and the Supreme Court (SC). The reservations concerned, among other things, the lowering of the age of retirement of SC judges, the procedure for extending the term of office of SC judges by the President of the Republic of Poland, the extraordinary complaint, disciplinary proceedings against judges of the SC and common courts, the National Judicial Council, the lowering of the age of retirement and the extension of the term of office of common court judges, the appointment and removal of presidents of common courts and the status of court assessors and prosecutors.

The European Commission found that in the two years since the commencement of the proceedings based on the Communication, more than a dozen laws had been adopted which affected the entire structure of the justice system in Poland. The common feature characterising all these legislative changes was that the executive or the legislature systematically gained the ability to significantly interfere with the composition, powers, administration and functioning of the said authorities and bodies. The legislative changes and their cumulative effects seriously threatened the independence of the judiciary and the independence of judges and the separation of powers in Poland, which are fundamental elements of the rule of law within the meaning of Article 2 TEU. The Commission also stressed that such intensified legislative activity was carried out without proper consultation with all stakeholders and without considering the opinions of numerous European and international organisations, and not in a spirit of loyal cooperation (Taborowski, 2019).

The subject matter of the recommendations reflected the Commission's position in the Communication that a breach of the rule of law under Article 2 TEU can occur through a Member State's actions both within the scope of the application of EU law (e.g. lowering the retirement age of judges may fall within the scope of the prohibition of age discrimination) and outside this scope (e.g. the question of the correctness of the appointment of the President of the CT).

Also noteworthy is how the Commission has set the limits of its dialogue with a Member State in its recommendations. In its third recommendation 2017/1520 on the rule of law, the Commission indicated that Poland's measures against the judges of the SC, including, for example, dismissing them or forcing them to retire, would cause such a significant threat to the rule of law that the Commission would have to "immediately" trigger the procedure under Article 7(1) TEU. This reservation by the Commission arose from the legislative solutions adopted at the time, which interrupted the terms of office of SC judges and gave the Minister of Justice the power to issue discretionary decisions regarding the continuation of SC judges in office. The President of Poland vetoed these solutions at the time. However, the Commission considered that the red line it had set had been crossed due to the law adopted on 8.12.2017 on the SC. This law was the subject of the fourth recommendation 2018/103 on the rule of law. It simultaneously became the direct cause for the Commission to submit a proposal under Article 7(1) TEU to the Council of the EU. According to the Commission, the new law on the SC raised doubts about the independence of judges due to the lowering of the retirement age of SC judges to 65, and due to the enlargement of the SC to at least 120 judges (nominated according to the new rules, by the parliamentary majority-dominated National Judiciary Council), which was expected to lead to a significant change in the composition of the SC within a short period. The First President of the SC was also to lose her post, contrary to the term reserved by the Constitution. Although judges could apply to the President of the Republic for the possibility to continue in office (extension could be granted for three years, no more than twice), the latter could refuse on a full discretionary basis and without any judicial review (Taborowski, 2019).

A certain hierarchy of violations detected by the Commission can be inferred from the Commission's action concerning the warning in its third recommendation 2017/1520 on the rule of law. From this perspective, the issue of the independence of the CT was not a reason for the Commission to set a limit to the dialogue (a specific warning to initiate proceedings under Article 7(1) TEU). Such a reason, on the other hand, was the threat to the independence of the Supreme Court, which under EU law is the so-called court of last instance, obliged to raise questions for a preliminary ruling under the third paragraph of Article 267 TFEU (Taborowski, 2019).

The Polish case clearly demonstrates that dialogue with "bad faith" actors who are *deliberately* undermining the rule of law does not work. National governments professing their attachment to the rule of law while still professing the need for dialogue or presenting dialogue as the way forward cannot and should not be taken seriously. National governments have also indeed learned they can beat the EU by creating new irreversible facts on the ground while pretending to be interested in further "dialogue" (Pech et al., 2021). So, instead of dialogue, we have dissensus. The core of this dissensus lies in the use of different meanings of the term "rule of law" by both sides, which is to a large extent politically motivated and therefore serves a particular, partisan purpose. Without prejudice to the importance of legal and political factors, there seems to be a real risk of a divergence between how the concept of the rule of law is interpreted by national authorities and by EU institutions. This is particularly the case in situations of conflict concerning the assessment of the actions of these authorities by supranational bodies. This divergence is related either to a deliberate restriction of the understanding of the rule of law to the purely formal sphere (extreme version) or to exclude from the scope of the concept of the rule of law essential substantive elements and including only those that fall within the narrowly interpreted rule of law clause (moderate version). Arguments questioning the validity and effectiveness of legal measures taken by EU authorities in response to allegations of rule of law violations by national authorities are examples of this type of narrowing, also in the extreme version. The dissensus over the rule of law is not only a question of competence. It also has an axiological dimension, which is reflected in the provisions of existing law and in the case law of the Court of Justice of the European Union.

b. Legal Nature of the Rule of Law Framework and Dialogue

The Commission points out that proceeding based on the Communication is primarily aimed at avoiding that the conditions for initiating proceedings under Article 7 TEU are met (preventive function). Undoubtedly, the Communication also has an explanatory purpose. It informs Member States on how the Commission intends to prepare for a request under Article 7(1) TEU and how it intends to respond to emerging signals of a systemic threat to the rule of law.

The same is true of the Commission's opinion on the rule of law, which concludes the first phase of the proceedings under the Communication. Considering, for example, the content of the opinion addressed to Poland, we will not find categorical formulations there. The result that the Commission expects is comments from the Government of the Republic of Poland to find a common solution. Although the Commission sets a deadline for submitting these comments and mentions that it would be good to solve the perceived problems within a reasonable time, non-compliance with this deadline can only result in the issuance of a recommendation. It can therefore be argued that the opinion is a preparatory document to the recommendation on the rule of law and serves primarily to allow the Member State to take a position on the objections raised by the Commission and the evidence gathered. It is also worth considering two judgements: in LM and C-619/18 European Commission v. Republic of Poland, in which the Court of Justice of the European Union (CJEU) gave a certain legal weight to the Commission's actions based on the Communication.

In the LM judgement, the CJEU held that the information contained by the Commission in its reasoned request to the Council of the EU under Article 7(1) TEU is of "particular relevance" to the assessment of how the judicial system is functioning in a Member State. This information must be considered when examining whether systemic irregularities have occurred in a Member State, resulting in a real risk of a breach of the right to a fair trial (Article 47 of the Charter of Fundamental Rights). As a result, information contained in a reasoned request under Article 7(1) TEU may lead to undermining confidence in the Member State's legal system (Taborowski, 2019).

In its order in Case C-619/18 European Commission v. The Republic of Poland, the Court held that the Commission documents produced in proceedings under the Communication affect the condition of urgency required for the grant of security (Article 279 TFEU) in proceedings under Article 258 TFEU. The Court considers the steps taken by the Commission in relation to the Republic of Poland to have protected the Commission from the allegation that the request for interim measures was made too late. The steps taken by the Commission based on the Communication found that the Commission did not delay bringing an action before the CJEU under Article 258 TFEU. The relevant factor for the CJEU was that the Commission had thus communicated its concerns about a breach of the rule of law, and the Member State should not have waited for a complaint to address those breaches adequately (Taborowski, 2019).

Nevertheless, the effects of proceedings under the Communication can only go beyond strict preparation for an Article 7 TEU procedure. The purpose of the procedure under the Communication is also to ensure that circumstances justifying the initiation of an Article 7 TEU procedure do not arise, and the legal significance of the information gathered during the procedure under the Communication is not limited to the Article 7 TEU procedure only. The Court considered that the information contained in the Commission's request under Article 7(1) TEU and in the recommendations made based on the Communication should be taken into account in the context of other judicial proceedings: both before the CJEU (the safeguard under Article 279 TFEU in proceedings under Article 258 TFEU) and before national courts (in the context of the principle of mutual trust and the stay of execution of the European Arrest Warrant).

4 Conclusion

Some authors have assumed that the procedure conducted by the Commission based on the Communication is only "medially troublesome" for the Member State concerned and "remains ineffective from a systemic point of view" (Würtenberg & Tkaczyński, 2017). Additionally, from the perspective of the application of the mechanism to Poland, it can be concluded that, contrary to the Commission's assumptions, the procedure was neither quick nor effective. The procedure is shaped in such a way that it allows the Commission to exert a shaming effect and soft pressure on the Member State, as well as an efficient substantive response to new developments, including a response to ongoing legal changes that, in the Commission's view, deepen the systemic threat to the rule of law. Additional pressure on the Member State is also generated by making the recommendations public at the second stage of the proceedings. Proceedings under the Communication appear to have the potential to provide a sound platform for resolving identified rule of law problems, provided that the Member State under investigation is willing to use such dialogue respecting the EU's principle of loyal cooperation. In the Polish case, the procedure was however essentially counterproductive. The Polish authorities have repeatedly demonstrated deep-rooted obstructionism, accompanied by numerous instances of bad faith and gross violations of the principle of loyal cooperation, in the context of the ongoing "dialogue". Thus, the Commission's faith in dialogue was naive. Any persistent attempts to engage in dialogue with authorities acting in bad faith are futile and doomed to fail when systematic violations of EU values are part of the government's plan to deliberately establish an "illiberal" system of governance (Pech et al., 2021). Then, instead of "dialogue", we have a source of increasing dissensus.

Regardless, the proceedings under the Communication against Poland have shown that it allows the Commission to gather the information and evidence necessary to propose the opening of Article 7 TEU procedures. Thanks to the proceedings under the Rule of Law Dialogue, the Commission's final proposal under Article 7(1) TEU contains a precise and detailed description of the perceived violations. Moreover, the procedure has enabled the Member State to take a position on each element of the materials gathered by the Commission.

References

Closa, C. (2019). The Politics of Guarding the Treaties: Commission Scrutiny of Rule of Law Compliance. *Journal of European Public Policy, 26*(5), 696–716. https://doi.org/10.1080/13501763.2018.1477822

Coman, R. (2022). *The Politics of the Rule of Law in the EU Polity Actors, Tools and Challenges*. Palgrave Studies in European Union Politics.

Communication from the Commission of 11 March 2014, A new EU Framework to Strengthen the Rule of Law, COM(2014) 158 Final.

Commission Recommendation of 27 July 2016 Regarding the Rule of Law in Poland (EU) 2016/1374.

Commission Recommendation of 21 December 2016 Regarding the Rule of Law in Poland Complementary to Commission Recommendation (EU) 2016/ 1374.

Commission Recommendation of 26 July 2017 Regarding the Rule of Law in Poland Complementary to Recommendations (EU) 2016/1374 and (EU) 2017/146.

Commission Recommendation of 20 December 2017 Regarding the Rule of Law in Poland Complementary to Commission Recommendations (EU) 2016/1374, (EU) 2017/146 and (EU) 2017/1520.

Crabit, E., & Bel, N. (2016). The Rule of Law Framework. In W. Schroeder (Ed.), *Strengthening the Rule of Law in Europe: From a Common Concept to Mechanisms of Implementation*. Hart Publishing House.

Gormley, L. W. (2017). Infringement Proceedings. In A. Jakab & D. Kochenov (Eds.), *The Enforcement of EU Law and Values: Ensuring Member States' Compliance* (pp. 65–78). Oxford University Press.

Kochenov, D., & Pech, L. (2015). Monitoring and Enforcement of the Rule of Law in the EU: Rhetoric and Reality. *European Constitutional Law Review, 3*, 512–540. https://doi.org/10.1017/S1574019615000358

Kochenov, D., & Bard, P. (2018). Rule of Law Crisis in the New Member States of the EU: The Pitfalls of Overemphasising Enforcement. Reconnect Working Papers. https://papers.ssrn.com/abstract=3221240

Kochenov, D., & Pech, L. (2016). Better Late than Never? On the European Commission's Rule of Law Framework and its First Activation. *Journal of Common Market Studies, 54*(5), 1062–1074. https://doi.org/10.1111/jcms.12401

Kochenov, D. (2017). The Acquis and Its Principles: The Enforcement of the 'Law' vs. the Enforcement of 'Values' in the European Union. In A. Jakab & D. Kochenov (Eds.), *The Enforcement of EU Law and Values: Ensuring Member States' Compliance*. Oxford University Press.

Krygier, M. (2013). Rule of Law (and Rechtsstaat). UNSW Law Research Paper No. 2013–52. https://papers.ssrn.com/sol3/papers.cfm?abstract_id=2311874

Nowak-Far, A. (2021). The Rule of Law Framework in the European Union: Its Rationale, Origins, Role and International Ramifications. In A. von Bogdandy, P. Bogdanowicz, I. Canor, C. Grabenwarter, M. Taborowski, & M. Schmidt (Eds.), *Defending Checks and Balances in EU Member States. Beiträge zum ausländischen öffentlichen Recht und Völkerrecht*. Springer.

Pech, L. (2020). The Rule of Law in the EU: The Evolution of the Treaty Framework and Rule of Law Toolbox. Reconnect Working Papers. https://www.ssrn.com/abstract=3608661

Pech, L. et al. (2020). Meaning and Scope of the EU Rule of Law. Reconnect Work Package 7, Deliverable 2.

Pech, L., Wachowiec, P., & Mazur, D. (2021). Poland's Rule of Law Breakdown: A Five-Year Assessment of EU's (In)Action. *Hague Journal on the Rule of Law, 13*, 1–43. https://doi.org/10.1007/s40803-021-00151-9

Taborowski, M. (2019). *Mechanizmy ochrony praworządności państw członkowskich w prawie Unii Europejskiej. Studium przebudzenia systemu ponadnarodowego [The European Union Law's Mechanisms for Protecting the Rule of Law in the Member States: A Study on the Awakening of the Supranational Systemta*. Wolters Kluwer Polska.

von Bogdandy, A., Antpöhler, A., & Ioannidis, M. (2017). Protecting EU Values: Reverse Solange and the Rule of Law Framework. In A. Jakab & D. Kochenov (Eds.), *The Enforcement of EU Law and Values: Ensuring Member States' Compliance*. Oxford University Press.

Wiącek, M. (2021). Constitutional Crisis in Poland 2015–2016 in the Light of the Rule of Law Principle. In A. von Bogdandy, P. Bogdanowicz, I. Canor, C. Grabenwarter, M. Taborowski, & M. Schmidt (eds.), *Defending Checks and Balances in EU Member States. Beiträge zum ausländischen öffentlichen Recht und Völkerrecht*. Springer.

Würtenberg, T., & Tkaczyński, J. W. (2017). Nowe ramy Unii Europejskiej na rzecz umocnienia praworządności (analiza krytyczna) [A New EU Framework to Strengthen the Rule of Law (Critical Analysis)]. *Państwo i Prawo, 9*, 16–29.

CHAPTER 10

Measuring Justice? The EU Justice Scoreboard in the Light of the Performance-Based Approach

Ylenia Guerra

1 Introduction: Notion, Scope and Genesis of the EU Justice Scoreboard

How does the EU Justice Scoreboard fit into the European system for protecting the rule of law?

The EU Justice Scoreboard (EUJS) is now part of the EU's Rule of Law toolbox and essentially provides an annual overview of indicators on "the performance of national judicial systems" (Dori, 2021: 281; Strelkov, 2019: 15). Since its creation in 2013, under the so-called consecutive leadership of José Manuel Barroso and Jean-Claude Junker (Strelkov, 2019: 15), the EUJS represents a quantitative and qualitative tool in the hands of the European Commission, added to the pool of EU policy instruments in the field of Justice and Home Affairs.

Y. Guerra (✉)
LUISS University, Rome, Italy
e-mail: yguerra@luiss.it

C. Fasone et al. (eds.), *EU Rule of Law Procedures at the Test Bench*, Palgrave Studies in European Union Politics,
https://doi.org/10.1007/978-3-031-60008-1_10

In line with the EU's rule of law instruments, the EUJS is a soft tool based on a modality that shapes behaviour through dialogue and persuasion (Coman, 2022: 13). As is well known, the instruments to protect the rule of law in the EU are both soft and hard. While Article 7 TEU (see Coman and Thinus in this book) is the coercive instrument, as is the infringement procedure, many new soft instruments have been created during the last decade: these are, for example, the EU Justice Scoreboard, the Rule of Law Framework (see Serowaniec in this book) and the Annual Rule of Law Report (see Citino in this book) (Coman, 2022: 13). Nowadays, the EUJS—not news at all as it is similar to a tool established by the European Commission for the Efficiency of Justice (CEPEJ)—is also one of the sources of information for the annual Rule of Law Report. Its results also inform the country-specific assessments within the European Semester, the EU's annual cycle of economic policy coordination within the Recovery and Resilience Facility (see Lupo in this book) and in the context of the application of the Rule of Law Conditionality Regulation (reg. EU 2020/2092, recitals 14, 16; Communication from the Commission "*on the application of Regulation (EU, Euratom) 2020/2092 of the European Parliament and of the Council of 16 December 2020 on a general regime of conditionality for the protection of the Union budget*", COM(2024) 17 final) (see Hegedűs and Christiansen in this book, also Fasone and Simoncini in this book). This shows the complex interrelationship and mutual influence between European instruments specifically designed to protect the rule of law and other instruments that address them laterally.

In the Communication "*The EU Justice Scoreboard. A tool to promote effective justice and growth*" (COM(2013) 160 final), in point 1, the Commission sets out the general scope of the EUJS:

> The objective of the EU Justice Scoreboard [...] is to assist the EU and the Member States to achieve more effective justice by providing objective, reliable and comparable data on the functioning of the justice systems of all Member States. Quality, independence and efficiency are the key components of an 'effective justice system'. Providing information on these components in all Member States contributes to identifying potential shortcomings and good examples and supports the development of justice policies at national and at EU level" (see also A. Dori, 2021, 281, nt. 5). In this way, through the EUJS, the EU pursues access to an effective justice system as an essential right "at the foundation of European democracies and enshrined in the constitutional traditions common to the

Member States" (Communication, COM(2013) 160 final) (Coman, 2016: 183; Velicogna, 2013).[1]

To evaluate the judiciary of Member States, the main indicators used in the EUJS are efficiency, independence and quality of justice systems.[2] The fields of focus are, in particular, civil, commercial and administrative litigation, "as well as, subject to availability of data, certain criminal cases (i.e. cases concerning money laundering at first instance courts)" (2023 EU Justice Scoreboard, COM(2023) 309 final, 2). Therefore the EUJS does not cover the entire sector of judiciary (Bárd et al., 2016: 8) meaning that several aspects of justice remained outside this form of comparative assessment.

The methodology applied in the Scoreboard looks at a range of information sources. The CEPEJ provides much of the quantitative data (2023 EU Justice Scoreboard, COM(2023) 309 final, 2). Data from other sources, such as the World Bank, the World Economic Forum and the World Justice Project, were also included in the first scenario (Communication, COM(2013) 160 final, 3; see also Alina Onţanu and Velicogna 2020: 250 and Pech, 2021: 322–323).

It is important to clarify two points from the outset: firstly, the EUJS is an evolving instrument that changes over time, mainly according to the needs emerging from the specific socio-political context (see also the survey on the effects of covid on the judicial system, in relation to the so-called digitalisation of justice); secondly, this instrument also takes into account civil society's perception of judiciaries, through the so-called Eurobarometer. Concerning the first observation, for instance, the 2023 EU Justice Scoreboard has been further developed to reflect the necessity for additional comparative data identified during the preparation of the 2022 Rule of Law Report comprising the area of the fight against corruption. Concerning the second point, the EU Commission has set

[1] See also Article 47 of the Charter of Fundamental Rights of the European Union.

[2] "The 2023 Scoreboard further develops the indicators for all three aspects, including on accessibility to justice for persons at risk of discrimination and older persons, and again on the digitalisation of justice, which has played a crucial role in keeping the courts functioning during the COVID-19 pandemic and supporting their recovery in its aftermath, as well as more generally, to promote efficient and accessible justice systems" (2023 EU Justice Scoreboard, COM(2023) 309 final, 1).

down a sort of statistical tool through which it is possible to ask EU citizens about their perception of the independence of the judiciary.

There are two main reasons for setting up this instrument: on the one hand, the economic crisis and the need to ensure an efficient judicial system in order to promote growth in the euro area; on the other hand, the promotion and protection of the rule of law, of which judicial independence is undoubtedly one of the essential elements. In particular, the genesis of the EUJS can be traced back to the EU economic and financial crisis of 2008, in which the EU institutions alleged that national justice systems could play a key role in the restoration of confidence and the return to growth (Jakab & Kirchmair, 2021: 3). In this regard, since 2012, the quality, independence and efficiency of national judicial systems have been one of the priorities of the EU's annual cycle of economic policy coordination, the "European Semester", to encourage structural reforms at the national level (Bárd et al., 2016: 7; Priebus, 2022: 1684).

Similarly, the EUJS is an essential instrument for the protection of the rule of law and this is not inconsistent with what has been written above with reference to the 2008 financial and economic crisis. Indeed, the introduction of the EUJS "was presented by EU Commissioner Viviane Reding (2013) as an answer to the so-called Copenhagen dilemma", i.e. insufficient control over Member States' compliance with EU founding values after the accession (Strelkov, 2019: 17; see also Bonelli, 2017: 189; Coman, 2022: 103; Pech, 2021: 322), in particular on the independence of the judiciary (Guazzarotti, 2022: 14; and, significantly, the so-called Tavares Report, on which see Scheppele, 2013). Essentially, and in this respect, it can be argued that the EU Scoreboard has a somewhat hybrid genesis in different contexts: the EU's economic and financial crisis, in particular the idea that an efficient justice system can contribute to economic development[3] and the protection of the Single Market (Coman, 2022: 108 ff.), and the rule of law crisis (Dori, 2023: 56).

Given the construction, the methodology used for the EUJS implied the collection of a large amount of data from three main categories of sources: data collected at the EU interinstitutional level, pilot exercises

[3] The justice system remains crucial as it determines Member States' ability to reduce litigation costs and ensure credible enforcement mechanisms in support of legal certainty. These elements are crucial to determining the competitiveness of economic institutions within a country (Dori, 2023: 57).

or field studies and EU external sources in line with the CEPEJ methodology (Dori, 2015: 24). The first category involves the cooperation of the ministerial and judicial offices of the Member States, with the result that there isn't any kind of verification mechanism on the reliability of such data. This is because the data does not come from an external and independent source, but rather from the Member States themselves. Also on this basis, the Commission proposes Country-Specific Recommendations (CSRs) in the European Semester[4] (see also Capati and Christiansen in this book). Scholars have clearly highlighted this close link through an empirical study that looked at CSRs: "Over time, the number of member states receiving CSRs concerning their justice systems increased. Looking at the 45 recommendations addressed to the 14 member states since 2011, it appears that in most cases, the Commission tends to focus its CSRs on the quality and efficiency of justice systems, while the more sensitive issue – independence – has been a matter of concern in Romania and Bulgaria (under the CVM), Malta, and Slovakia" (Coman, 2022: 1, 109).

2 EUJS' Follow-Up: Between Description and Performance

As a symbol of the "inevitable evolution of such tools, the dimensions covered by the Scoreboard have changed over time to focus on new and pressing issues" (Coman, 2022: 105), as happened, for example, in 2021 when the EUJS was used to provide an overview of the institutions involved in the appointment of judges to the Supreme Courts of the Member States (Coman, 2022: 105) or, nowadays, in 2023, in which the EUJS takes into account the constitutional jurisdiction (2023 EU Justice Scoreboard 78 ff.).

In terms of practice, the Commission has adopted 11 communications (2013–2023), from which some preliminary conclusions can be

[4] The 2023 EU Justice Scoreboard, page 3. In particular (see nt. 21 of the mentioned 2023 EU Justice Scoreboard), it is possible to know that the Council addressed country-specific recommendations on their judicial systems to seven Member States in 2019 (HR, IT, CY, HU, MT, PT and SK) and eight Member States in 2020 (HR, IT, CY, HU, MT, PL, PT and SK). The Commission is also following judicial reforms in BG and RO under the Cooperation and Verification Mechanism (see Dirri in this book). In 2022, there were two Member States (PL and HU) with country-specific recommendations related to the independence of the judiciary.

drawn, which will be used in the following analysis of the EUJS dissensus, looking particularly at its actors and themes. The first formal evidence is the increasing length of such communications: from 22 pages in 2013 to 84 pages in the 2023 Report. In terms of substance, a number of important steps have been taken to get to the current features of the EUJS. In the 2014 Report, the Commission tried to overcome the gap between the *perception* of judicial independence and *structural* judicial independence, through the provisions of several elements that strengthen the above mentioned independence (these are five indicators: the safeguards regarding the transfer of judges without their consent, the dismissal of judges, the allocation of incoming cases within a court, the withdrawal and recusal of judges and the threat against the independence of a judge, see Communication COM(2014) 155 final). One year later, in its 2015 Report, the European Commission underlined the importance of intensifying *dialogue* with Member States as a basis for structural cooperation aimed at improving the reform of the national judicial systems. This cooperation is backed up by financial support from the European Structural and Investment Funds (ESI Funds), which support the Member States' efforts to improve the functioning of their judicial systems. The year 2016 marks the transition from country-based data, which to a certain extent is not entirely impartial or complete, to a (cautious) *technicalisation* of the indicators and the sources. In this sense, in order to assess the quality of the justice systems, the Commission started to work with a group of contact persons on national justice systems specifically on the standards related to the functioning of justice systems (in particular, two contact persons, one from the judiciary and one from the ministry of justice). Indeed, in the 2017 Report, the first consideration was a quotation of President Barroso in which he emphasised the link between (the protection of) the EU Rule of Law and judicial independence: "The rule of law is not optional in the European Union. It is a must. The rule of law means that law and justice are upheld by an independent judiciary".[5] A further expansion occurred in 2018: the European Commission extended

[5] Not entirely new, the presentation of the second version of the EU Justice Scoreboard coincided with the adoption of a new Rule of Law Framework by the European Commission. Mr. Barroso stated that the aim of the framework was to provide a more appropriate instrument for responding to systemic threats to the rule of law in a particular Member State, thereby avoiding the more severe instrument of preventive or sanctioning measures under Article 7 of the Treaty (see Mak & Taekema, 2016: 32).

its monitoring of the judicial system through the News Indicators. This was achieved mainly by assessing the independence of the National Councils of the Judiciary, developing a section dedicated to criminal justice systems (in particular money laundering) and introducing some indicators on the organisation of prosecution services in the Member States. After 2018, the EU Justice Scoreboard became part of the EU's toolbox. The Communication on *Further strengthening the Rule of Law within the Union—State of play and possible further steps* (COM(2019) 163 final) identified the EU Justice Scoreboard as part of the EU's toolbox to strengthen the Rule of Law by contributing to supporting judicial reforms and rule of law standards (see also EU Justice Scoreboard Report on 2019).

Several years after its launch, the 2022 EUJS Report focuses on the implication of the Covid-19 pandemic on justice systems and the 2023 EUJS adds, for the first time, an analysis of the efficiency of first instance criminal courts in corruption cases, on the appointment of national supreme court judges and prosecutors general, as well as on the bodies involved in the prevention and repression of corruption.[6] The 2023 EUJS Report also focuses for the first time on constitutional courts, based on the consideration that "constitutional jurisdictions" are a central element of the system of checks and balances in a constitutional democracy and play a key role in the effective application of EU law, guaranteeing the integrity of the EU legal order and defining the fundamental principles of the rule of law. The data used in the report are purely descriptive and cover the type of constitutional body (such as a constitutional court, an ad hoc body, a supreme court, a supreme administrative court or a constitutional council) and the competences (such as the traditional review of legislation, the review of draft legislation or the constitutional complaint by natural or legal persons).

[6] In the context of the newly adopted proposal for a Directive on combating corruption. In particular, the 2023 EU Justice Scoreboard deals with data on "the bodies specialised in the prevention of corruption, giving an overview of the type of powers of such bodies and the rules on the appointment of these same bodies" (see page 47 of the 2023 EU Justice Scoreboard).

3 Contestation Surrounding the EU Justice Scoreboard's Evaluation and Performance

What form of contestation comes with the EU Justice Scoreboard? For the sake of clarity, it is useful to provide subcategories looking on *(i)* authors of contestations (such as Member States, members of the EU Parliament and scholars) and *(ii)* type of contestation (criticism, dissensus). This separation aims to give some summarised information, in order to elaborate preliminary conclusions on the use of EUJS in the light of the process of evaluation through the perform-based approach.

At the beginning of the established tool, as observed by Ramona Coman (2016, 2022), some Member States fearing the empowerment of the Commission "by stealth", opposed that, this type of quantitative and qualitative data (i.e. statistics and indicators) on the performance of the judiciary was already provided by other regional organisations, such as the Council of Europe and the Venice Commission, and therefore the Commission should not reproduce them[7] (Coman, 2016; cf. Velicogna, 2013, that emphasised the misunderstanding of Member States concerning the tool). It is possible to argue how, through this criticism, Member States have attempted to put the *measurement* of justice back at the centre of the protection of the rule of law, in the prism of the Council of Europe.

On the merits of data collected, most of the criticism comes from Member States. The most striking case is Poland. For instance, the latter Polish government uses EUJS data according to its needs claiming that the EUJS provides a positive assessment of the justice system. In doing so the government highlights the result in comparison with other Member States, even though it was condemned by the European Court of Human Rights for the excessive length of the procedure (see Rutkowski and Others v. Poland). On the contrary, when EUJS leads to a negative evaluation, as in the case of the above-average effectiveness of the Polish judicial

[7] On the denouncing of duplication see also the speech in the EP by Rebecca Taylor (ALDE): "Mr President, the oral amendment on behalf of the ALDE Group is as follows: 'Takes note of the EU Justice Scoreboard with great interest; calls on the Commission, in consultation with the European Parliament, to take this exercise forward in accordance with the Treaties with the engagement of the Member States, while bearing in mind the need to avoid unnecessary duplication of work with other bodies" (www.europarl.europa.eu/doceo/document/CRE-7-2014-02-04-INT-2-118-000_EN.html).

system "the Polish government merely suggested this could be due to unreliable statistics" (Pech, 2021: 323).

Another category that has criticised the EUJS is MEPs. In the European Parliament's report "On the EU Justice Scoreboard - Civil and administrative justice in the Member States (2013/2117(INI))", the rapporteur Zwiefka emphasised the importance of respecting certain fundamental criteria, such as equal treatment of Member States, objectivity and comparability of data.

Moreover, in its early days, the EUJS was criticised by (some) academics, looking at the construction of criteria and the use of that data. For Cappellina, the method by which the EU Commission selected the team of experts demonstrated the lack of socio-legal measurement and evaluation (in fact, most of the experts mentioned are lawyers with no experience in the specific field of socio-legal measurement and evaluation, cf. Cappellina, 2020: 148). This criticism could lead to the question of whether the EUJS is an appropriate instrument for assessing outputs consistent with indicators since the choice of the method, which implies the choice of indicators, directly affects final results. This point emerges evidently if one considers the specific indicators set out by the European Commission through which it measures the effectiveness of the judiciary. This problem also emerges in studies dealing with the measurement of the rule of law, although the question of what kind of definition of the rule of law one wants to assume ("thin" or "thick") must be considered. In particular, some scholars have highlighted how the "measurement strategy, rather than conceptualization, seems to be the dominant factor determining RoL indicators" (Versteeg & Ginsburg, 2017: 124).

Concerning the type of contestation, scholars mainly focus on methodology and data evaluation, dealing with how the result is processed and whether the process is capable of explaining the dimension of judicial effectiveness. "The way in which data is collected and reported at the national level for these European initiatives generates and perpetuates this difficulty in gathering comparable data sets" (Onţanu & Velicogna, 2021: 454). Another question of methodology looks, for instance, at the type of independence it must assess, e.g. perceived independence and formal independence. However, the European Network of Councils for the Judiciary distinguishes formal independence in terms of institutional safeguards (de jure independence) and perceived independence (de facto independence) and puts in evidence the link between de jure and de facto independence (van Dijk et al., 2016: 3 ff.).

A further category of challenge is related to the specific role of the EUJS in the rule of law framework. As highlighted by Dori, despite repeated appeals from the European Parliament to reorient the Scoreboard towards rule of law considerations and some criticism from the academic community regarding the scope of the EUJS in this matter, "the Commission did not tone down its economic reasoning and maintained the Scoreboard's focus on its role in fostering reforms that facilitate economic development" (Dori, 2023: 58; see also Mak & Taekema, 2016: 33).[8]

These considerations lead to a preliminary conclusion: a distinction must be made between general criticism and dissensus, whereby the essential difference is that dissensus is impossible to overcome within the political confrontation that marks democratic systems (Coman, 2022). However, looking at the EUJS, the type of contestation leads mostly to the constructive method of each indicator in relation to outputs. For this reason, it is useful to attempt an abstraction from the particular to the general, and thus from the particular objections raised against the tool, which are only summarised here, to the general problems facing the instrument. The future research question therefore focuses in particular on the teleological function entrusted to the instrument in the context of the method of setting the criteria chosen for the (performative) evaluation of the judicial systems of each Member State.

4 Conclusions: "In Data We Trust"?[9]

Focusing the examination of the EU Justice Scoreboard in the light of dissensus on EU instruments for the protection of the rule of law, there are two essential issues from which some concluding remarks can be made. The first point concerns the purpose of the instrument. In this sense, as explained above, the EU Justice Scoreboard is driven by the will to make justice systems more efficient in order to improve the (economic)

[8] EU funds also support the judiciary, see Article 3.1., reg. (EU) 2021/693 of the European Parliament and of the Council of 28 April 2021 establishing the Justice Programme and repealing Regulation (EU) No 1382/2013. This regulation sets out a programme in order to contribute to the further development of a European area of justice based on the rule of law including the independence and impartiality of the judiciary, mutual recognition and mutual trust and judicial cooperation thereby also strengthening democracy, the rule of law and the protection of fundamental rights.

[9] The expression is derived from the article written by Dori (2021).

competitiveness of Member States. This is not surprising, as the mechanism was born also out of the desire to overcome the 2008 financial crisis by restoring confidence in the efficiency of the justice system. Over time, however, the mechanism has also become an important element in measuring compliance with the principles underlying the rule of law, which necessarily intersect with the judicial system. These two different perspectives, whose discrepancies have already been pointed out in the literature, can be a first point of observation. Can an instrument that was created with the idea of measuring the efficiency of the judicial system be transformed to the point of effectively measuring compliance with the rule of law? Answering this question would also require, among other things, a statistical measurement of the use of the data aggregated in the EU Justice Scoreboard by the European institutions in their activities, which will require further (interdisciplinary) research.

The use of data, or rather the processing of data, is the second issue highlighted in the EU Justice Scoreboard study. The source of the data and its impartiality determine the quality of the aggregate data that appears on the Scoreboard. By the same token, the choice of data (e.g. length of civil proceedings) clearly influences the construction of the final result. This is well illustrated by Dori in a recent study published (Dori, 2023), in which he points out the contradictions in measuring the cost of justice, according to which a low expenditure of public resources is not always a good example of the efficiency of the justice system, because it could potentially lead to an increase in the costs paid by private parties, who would then see their right of access to justice restricted for economic reasons.

Hence the measurement of justice, which is understood as an essential dimension of the rule of law, needs a clearer teleological orientation of the data and opens the floor for a broader question dealing with the constitutional implications of the use of indicators in fields such as the rule of law.

Moreover, it seems possible to argue that the EUJS is an example of the EU's managerial approach, which evaluates Member States in a strict, performative way. It provides a method and approach by which the EU can measure the performance of member countries in particular areas. When such a method is combined with, and becomes a source of legitimacy for specific technical choices on the distribution of funds, it gives rise to issues relevant to legal science. These may be seen, for example, in the role of quantitative data in political choices or even in the way indicators are selected for the construction of the data to be evaluated.

References

Bárd, P. (2021). In Courts We Trust, or Should We? Judicial Independence as the Precondition for the Effectiveness of EU Law. *European Law Journal—Review of European Law in Context, 1–3*, 185–210.

Bárd, P., Carrera, S., Guild, E., & Kochenov, D. (2016). An EU Mechanism on Democracy, the Rule of Law and Fundamental Rights, with Thematic Contribution by Wim Marneffe. *CEPS Papers in Liberty and Security on Europe, 91*(2016), 1–234.

Beqiraj, J., & Moxham, L. (2022). Reconciling the Theory and the Practice of the Rule of Law in the European Union Measuring the Rule of Law. *Hague Journal on the Rule of Law, 14*, 139–164.

Besselink, L. (2017). The Bite, the Bark, and the Howl: Article 7 TEU and the Rule of Law Initiatives. In A. Jakab & D. Kochenov (Eds.), *The Enforcement of EU Law and Values: Ensuring Member States' Compliance* (pp. 128–144). Oxford University Press.

Bonelli, M. (2015). *The EU Justice Scoreboard: More Effective Justice in the EU?* Blog Maastricht University. www.maastrichtuniversity.nl/blog/2015/03/eu-justice-scoreboard-more-effective-justice-eu

Bonelli, M. (2017). Carrots, Sticks, and the Rule of Law: EU Political Conditionality Before and After Accession. *IANUS, 15–16*, 171–200.

Bustos Gisbert, R. (2022). Judicial Independence in European Constitutional Law. *European Constitutional Law Review, 4*, 591–620.

Cappellina, B. (2018). *Quand la gestion s'empare de la Justice: de la fabrique européenne aux tribunaux, Science politique. Université de Bordeaux, 2018* (Thèse doctorale). www.theses.hal.science/tel-02074161

Cappellina B. (2020). Legitimising EU Governance Through Performance Assessment Instruments European Indicators for a Judicial Administration Policy. *International Review of Public Policy, 2*, 141–158.

Coman, R. (2016). Strengthening the Rule of Law at the Supranational Level: The Rise and Consolidation of a European Network. *Journal of Contemporary European Studies, 1*, 171–188.

Coman, R. (2022). *The Politics of the Rule of Law in the EU Polity: Actors, Tools and Challenges*. Palgrave Studies in European Union Politics.

Communication from the Commission to the European Parliament, the Council, the European Central Bank, the European Economic and Social Committee and the Committee of the Regions, The EU Justice Scoreboard a Tool to Promote Effective Justice and Growth, in https://eur-lex.europa.eu/legal-content/EN/ALL/?uri=CELEX:52013DC0160

Communication from the Commission to the European Parliament, the European Council and The Council, Further Strengthening the Rule of Law within the Union State of Play and Possible Next Steps, in https://eur-lex.europa.eu/legal-content/EN/TXT/?uri=CELEX%3A52019DC0163

Dori, A. (2015). *The EU Justice Scoreboard—Judicial Evaluation as a New Governance Tool* (MPILux Working Paper, 2). www.mpi.lu

Dori, A. (2021). In Data We Trust? Quantifying the Costs of Adjudication in the EU Justice Scoreboard. *Erasmus Law Review, 4*, 281–297.

Dori, A. (2023). The Supply and Demand of Justice: What Policy Implications from the EU Justice Scoreboard? In E. Storskrubb (Ed.), *YSEC Yearbook of Socio-Economic Constitutions 2022 Eva Storskrubb Editor Funding of Justice* (pp. 53–86), e-book.

EU Justice Scoreboard 2013. https://eur-lex.europa.eu/legal-content/IT/TXT/?qid=1555419867264&uri=CELEX:52013DC0160

EU Justice Scoreboard 2014. https://eur-lex.europa.eu/legal-content/IT/TXT/?qid=1555419819123&uri=CELEX:52014DC0155

EU Justice Scoreboard 2015. https://eur-lex.europa.eu/legal-content/IT/TXT/?qid=1555419781140&uri=CELEX:52015DC0116

EU Justice Scoreboard 2016. https://eur-lex.europa.eu/legal-content/IT/TXT/?qid=1555419683920&uri=CELEX:52016DC0199

EU Justice Scoreboard 2017. https://eur-lex.europa.eu/legal-content/IT/TXT/?qid=1555419637816&uri=CELEX%3A52017DC0167

EU Justice Scoreboard 2018. https://eur-lex.europa.eu/legal-content/GA/TXT/?uri=CELEX:52018DC0364

EU Justice Scoreboard 2019. https://eur-lex.europa.eu/legal-content/IT/TXT/?qid=1562062740889&uri=CELEX:52019DC0198

EU Justice Scoreboard 2020. https://eur-lex.europa.eu/legal-content/IT/TXT/?uri=CELEX:52020DC0306

EU Justice Scoreboard 2021. https://eur-lex.europa.eu/legal-content/IT/TXT/?qid=1634640118533&uri=CELEX%3A52021DC0389

EU Justice Scoreboard 2022. https://commission.europa.eu/system/files/2022-05/eu_justice_scoreboard_2022.pdf

EU Justice Scoreboard 2023. https://eur-lex.europa.eu/legal-content/EN/TXT/PDF/?uri=CELEX:52023DC0309

Guazzarotti, A. (2022). Tutela dei valori e democrazie illiberali nell'UE: lo strabismo di una narrazione "costituzionalizzante". *costituzionalismo.it., 2*, 1–58.

Jakab, A., & Kirchmair, L. (2021). How to Develop the EU Justice Scoreboard into a Rule of Law Index: Using an Existing Tool in the EU Rule of Law Crisis in a More Efficient Way. *German Law Journal, 22*, 936–955.

Kmezić, M., & Bieber, F. (2020). *Protecting the Rule of Law in EU Member States and Candidate Countries*. SIEPS. www.sieps.se/globalassets/publikationer/2020/2020_12epa.pdf

Mak, E., & Taekema, S. (2016). The European Union's Rule of Law Agenda: Identifying Its Core and Contextualizing Its Application. *The Hague Journal on the Rule of Law, 8*, 25–50.

Moxham, L., & Stefanelli, J. (2013, November 15). *Safeguarding the Rule of Law, Democracy and Fundamental Rights: A Monitoring Model for the European Union* (Report). www.biicl.org/files/6758_main_report_15_11_2013_commission_consultation.pdf

Onţanu, E. A., & Velicogna, M. (2020). The Challenge of Comparing EU Member States Judicial Data. *Oñati Socio-Legal Series, 2*, 446–480.

Ontanu, E. A., Velicogna, M., & Contini, F. (2017, December). Something Good? In Search of New Practices to Improve the Quality of Justice in EU. In F. Contini (Eds.), *Handle with Care Assessing and Designing Methods for Evaluation and Development of the Quality of Justice*, p. 327 ff. IRSIG-CNR Bologna.

Pech, L. (2021). The Rule of Law. In P. Craig & G. De Búrca (Eds.), *The Evolution of EU Law* (3rd ed., pp. 322–324). Oxford University Press.

Pech, L., Wachowiec, P., & Mazur, D. (2021). Poland's Rule of Law Breakdown: A Five-Year Assessment of EU's (In)Action. *The Hague Journal on the Rule of Law, 1*, 1–43.

Priebus, S. (2022). The Commission's Approach to Rule of Law Backsliding: Managing Instead of Enforcing Democratic Values? *Journal of Common Market Studies, 6*, 1684–1700.

Scheppele, L., K. (2013, July 5). In Praise of the Tavares Report: Europe Finally Said No to Viktor Orbán. *Verfassungsblog*. www.verfassungsblog.de/in-praise-of-the-tavares-report-europe-finally-said-no-to-viktor-orban-2/

Strelkov, A. (2019). EU Justice Scoreboard: A New Policy Tool for "Deepening" European Integration? *Journal of Contemporary European Studies, 1*, 15–27.

van Dijk, F., van Tulder, F., & Lugten, Y. (2016, January). *Independence of Judges: Judicial Perceptions and Formal Safeguards*. www.rechtspraak.nl/SiteCollectionDocuments/Paper-independence-of-judges-160111.pdf

Velicogna, M. (2013). *The EU Justice Scoreboard and the Challenge of Investigating the Functioning of EU Justice Systems and Their Impact on the Economy of the Member States*. Paper presented at the SISP Conference, Florence. Last accessed July 5, 2024 from https://www.academia.edu/9860876/The_EU_Justice_Scoreboard_and_the_challenge_of_investigating_the_functioning_of_EU_justice_systems_and_their_impact_on_the_economy_of_the_Member_States

Versteeg, M., & Ginsburg, T. (2017). Measuring the Rule of Law: A Comparison of Indicators. *Law & Social Inquiry, 1*, 100–137.

von Bogdandy, A., & Ioannidis, M. (2014). Systemic Deficiency in the Rule of Law: What It Is, What Has Been Done, What Can Be Done? *Common Market Law Review, 51*(2014), 59–96.

CHAPTER 11

The Prospective Impact of the Rule of Law Reports: A Tool to Be Fine-Tuned

Ylenia Maria Citino

1 Introduction

Built as a response to growing fears about the erosion of democratic principles and the worrying trend of democratic backsliding, the EU Rule of Law Report (RoL Report) is a yearly publication edited by the European Commission to monitor and identify rule of law emerging trends in the Member States. Being the core commitment of the EU Rule of Law Mechanism, it provides insight into rising challenges, worrisome outcomes, or favourable developments. To achieve that, it encourages the involvement of national parliaments, national and local authorities, and other stakeholders in discussing emerging challenges and solutions. In this chapter, we examine the structure of the Report and its key features. We share a few words on the methodology used to compile the Report. Subsequently, we delve into the conditions that led to the establishment

Y. M. Citino (✉)
Sant'Anna School of Advanced Studies, Pisa, Italy
e-mail: ylenia.citino@santannapisa.it

C. Fasone et al. (eds.), *EU Rule of Law Procedures at the Test Bench*, Palgrave Studies in European Union Politics,
https://doi.org/10.1007/978-3-031-60008-1_11

of the Report, its evolution across the years, and the proposal of the European Parliament to reform it. Finally, after providing an assessment of the Report, to highlight both its advantages and its disadvantages, we put emphasis on the dissensus that the tool has triggered over the years and, accordingly, the future prospects of the instrument.

2 Structure of the Tool and Key Features

Since its first edition, dating back to 30 September 2020, the RoL Report has consisted of a synthetic communication on the overall situation across the Union as well as individual chapters on each of the 27 Member States assessing their country-specific situation. The report evaluates the quality of the rule of law compliance to ensuring better adherence to the EU Treaties, especially Article 2 TEU. It provides an insight on key topics such as judicial independence, corruption, and protection of basic rights. These topics shape the structure of the Report into four pillars: the national justice system, anti-corruption measures, media pluralism and freedom (for more insight on this, see Cseres in this Volume), and other institutional checks and balances, such as "the quality and inclusiveness of the national legislative process; the role of Constitutional Courts and independent authorities such as the Ombudsperson, equality bodies and national human rights institutions; and the role of civil society organisations in safeguarding the rule of law" (RoL Report 2023). These categories have been thoroughly evaluated by scholars with regard to their helpfulness in assessing the level of conformity with the RoL (Mannella et al., 2022: 30 ff.)

As a soft preventive mechanism, this annual publication differs from the other RoL toolbox instruments since it allows for early warning and timely information. It fosters interparliamentary cooperation meetings and debates, dialogue between the European Parliament and national parliaments and consultations within the Council. For instance, the LIBE Committee of the European Parliament (competent on Civil Liberties, Justice and Home Affairs) organised on 4 December 2023 an Interparliamentary Committee Meeting (ICM) on "The situation of the Rule of Law in the EU" to assess the fourth Commission's Rule of Law Report, focusing specifically on corruption (LIBE, 2023). This and other similar own initiatives provide meaningful exchanges of views and contribute to the advisory function of both parliaments at the national and the EU levels. Furthermore, they are supported by Thematic Digests, containing the most updated list of publications from the Parliament's Directorates-General for Internal Policies (IPOL) and the Parliamentary Research Service (EPRS), on the topics to be discussed.

In this vein, the RoL Report helps the EU institutions identify and address potential rule of law breaches before they become more serious or have a broader impact on the EU as a whole. In other words, it gives evidence of the EU's commitment to the rule of law as part of the wide-ranging set of procedures established by the European RoL Mechanism. According to the 2023 EP Resolution on the 2022 Rule of Law Report (European Parliament, 2023), the Report "represents a step towards a coherent mechanism to uphold the Union values enshrined in Article 2 TEU" and the key challenge now is "to make effective and consistent use of the existing toolbox in order to protect and enforce these values". In contrast, the practical follow-up of the Reports, according to many commentators (see below), is reportedly limp as they mainly foster further discussion. Although they cannot directly address breaches or violations of the rule of law, their main goal is to serve as an informative tool to raise awareness and call the Member States to take steps and remedy any problems highlighted by the Commission.

3 Current Methodology of the Report

The methodology of the report is based on a specific timetable involving a combination of written contributions by MS and non-governmental organisations, experts' opinions, and targeted stakeholders' consultation. Furthermore, the Commission organises country visits based on a network of national contact points and retrieves other information from publicly available documents. Recent studies suggest that this evidence-based and expert-led approach entails a depoliticisation strategy enacted when facing bottom-up political pressure (Bressanelli et al., 2020; Schimmelfennig, 2020).

After its publication, the annual Report is used, as said, to engage in and facilitate an exchange between the European Commission and those Member States where a problem is identified. This relies on recently introduced specific country recommendations, outlining steps that, according to the Commission, need to be taken in order to restore the rule of law.

As a follow-up to the Report, the Commission engages in further exchanges with the European Parliament and the Council to encourage them to continue addressing the Rule of Law Report issues in their initiatives. Additionally, the European Parliament and national parliaments are advised to establish dedicated interparliamentary cooperation and dialogue concerning rule of law matters.

Expanding the objectives of the tool could involve integrating the key elements of the methodology used in the annual Rule of Law reports into the assessment of all candidate and potential candidate countries for EU accession. Such integration would necessitate collaboration with the Commission, as called for in the 2023 EP Resolution (point 11).

4 Historical Context and Evolution of the Tool

The genesis of the report can be traced back to the EU's commitment to promoting and safeguarding the rule of law as a fundamental value of the EU, as enshrined in Article 2 of the Treaty on European Union (TEU). Since 2016, the European Parliament (EP) has firmly urged the Commission and the Council to sign by means of an interinstitutional agreement an EU Pact for Democracy including both anticipatory and remedial elements, called the Rule of Law and Fundamental Rights (DRF). This pledge is contained in a set of Resolutions (European Parliament, 2015, 2018).

The European Commission initially had some reservations about the EP's proposals, primarily due to concerns about their concrete and legal feasibility. However, in 2019, the Commission took a major step forward by launching the Rule of Law Review Cycle (RLRC), later renamed the Rule of Law Mechanism (RoLM). This initiative garnered support from the Council, who decided to strengthen the Annual Rule of Law Dialogue. In this sense, in the 2019 conclusions on the "Evaluation of the Annual Rule of Law Dialogue", the Council agreed that the effort "could be effectively furthered by undertaking a yearly stocktaking exercise concerning the state of play and key developments as regards the rule of law" (para. 8) and that the cyclical exercise "could make use of the Commission's annual rule of law reports, which would create synergies between the institutions" (para. 10) (Council of the European Union, 2019). However, in a comment issued before the note, the Council underlined how consensus on this document "could not be reached" on the conclusions, so that the text "was supported or not objected to by 26 delegations" (note that Hungary is suspected to have abstained: see the press statement from Hungarian Minister of Justice, Judith Varga [Varga, 2019]).

It is worth mentioning that in the 2023 Council conclusions on the "Evaluation of the Annual Rule of Law Dialogue", aimed at strengthening the political dialogue, less consensus was reached compared to a few years before, since the text was "supported or not objected by 25 delegations" (presumably Hungary and Poland) (Council of the European Union, 2023). However, these conclusions stand out as they contain the commitment to continue organising a general horizontal discussion, plus country-specific discussions three times a year concerning at least four Member States, based on the foundings of the RoL Report.

Since the RLRC was designed to be a set of actions informed by the paradigm of a "benevolent" and "compliant" Member State (Pech et al., 2019), concerns were expressed about the effectiveness of the exercise. Additional questions were raised about the use of local contact persons in the RLRC and the potential impact on the impartiality and accuracy of the reports produced, whether the contributors may have been "politically captured" (ibid.).

However, the Commission explained that the rejection of the EP proposal was caused by the need to include in the reporting exercise a panel of independent experts and to face concerns about "the legitimacy, balance of inputs, and accountability of results" (EU Commission, 2019a).

Moreover, despite its good intentions, the July 2019 communication (EU Commission, 2019b) failed to effectively tackle rule of law issues in deteriorating illiberal democracies (Kochenov, 2019). The blueprint was based on the establishment of constructive dialogue with "would-be" autocrats instead of imposing sanctions. This approach proved to be suboptimal, as leaders from so-called "illiberal democracies" were more likely to challenge the EU institutions than to cooperate with them (Varga, 2020; Pech et al., 2019).

Likewise, the reporting exercise, initially based on existing instruments such as the EU Justice scoreboard and the European semester, immediately triggered dissensus among scholars. It was doubted, in particular, whether the fact of associating in the same mechanism countries like Hungary and Poland next to Finland or the Netherlands would have given added value to the report. Using a standard set of parameters would have prevented identifying issues such as the "constitutional capture" of some MS (Kochenov, 2019: 432). This circumstance may, in the end, deviate attention from real problems. In other words, "an increase in the number of novel rule of law instruments is matched by further deterioration" in specific MS, instead of effectively restoring legal compliance (Priebus, 2022: 1685).

Dissensus was evident also in the Parliament's reaction to RLRC, since the resolution of 7 October 2020 (European Parliament, 2020) stressed how the annual assessment failed to incorporate the area of democracy and fundamental rights, including freedom of association and the rights of vulnerable groups. Following this failure, protracted breaches of Union values as set in Article 2(4) TEU by some MS went unnoticed. In particular, the RLRC was criticised for "excessively soft language, lack of context, and foreseeing no remedies for diagnosed problems" (Grabowska-Moroz, 2022). The way was paved for an imminent "densification of the rule of law toolbox" (Pech, 2020).

Announced in the State of the Union Address (European Commission, 2020), the publication of the first RoL Report dates back to 30 September 2020. It follows the demise of the EP's proposal for a DRF Mechanism. A study from the European Parliamentary Research Service (van Ballegooij, 2020) highlights key differences with the rejected EP's scheme, underlining that the scope of the RoL Report is more limited than Article 2 TEU. It does not entail any interinstitutional agreement, nor does it assign any official role to expert panels (2020: 8). Conversely, most scholars argue that the scope is too broad since the EU institutions can monitor developments and challenges in areas that fall outside the scope of EU legislation (Pech, 2022: 38). This generates a paradox, as the instrument is at the same time perceived as too narrow (since it does not comprise all Article 2 values and is limited to the rule of law) and too broad, (since it exceeds the EU's competencies touching upon national issues). Despite this, it should be noted that the RoL Report also aims at shaping key developments in the EU Member States.

5 Merits and Drawbacks of the RoL Report in the Present Context

The RoL Report has several positive features. Firstly, consistency and homogeneity. The topics and subtopics covered by the four pillars provide a clear understanding of the evolution of distinct issues over the years. A second positive feature is the pluralism of views: contributions from Member States and targeted stakeholders, including international organisations, national independent authorities, interested representatives, and civil society organisations, offer different perspectives than those highlighted by country visits. Thirdly, as welcomed by the European Parliament, the Commission's efforts to engage in dialogue and apply the same monitoring criteria to all EU countries are commendable. Its endeavour to monitor all Member States is to be further appreciated, according to the principle of equal treatment and proportionality. In general, the Commission's ability to produce a high-level reporting exercise is highly esteemed, even though the deadlines are always challenging. However, there are concerns that the Report falls short in assessing the effectiveness of changes made by each country (EP, 2021, recital E). As Pech argues (2020: 113), a further positive feature is that the Rule of Law Report "closely builds on the Commission's 2014 definitional efforts and offers a compelling definition of the core elements of the rule of law by codifying the key legal principles laid down in the EU Treaties, EU secondary legislation, the case-law of the Court of Justice as well as the case law of the European Court of Human Rights".

On the other side, starting from the 2020 Report, scholars highlight important pitfalls, arguing that the experience is "failing to give the necessary context, and to connect the dots" of a "devastating picture" (e.g. Bárd, 2020: 3). Likewise, weaknesses of the same kind have been detected in the two subsequent reports.

One major criticism is the Commission's reluctance to employ stronger remedial measures for serious breaches of the Rule of Law. Additionally, the use of mild expressions and "toothless" language (Kelemen, 2020), or even language that seems to condone worsening situations in autocratic states (Azmanova & Howard, 2021: 10), has been considered problematic. Consequently, the Report was judged as overly ambitious to function as a preventive tool.

In reality, the RoL Report fallout demonstrates that in some cases it failed to deter RoL breaches. A simple reporting cycle without express follow-up mechanisms cannot discourage Member States from acting in violation of RoL values. A more general concern is also underlined by Coman (2022: 14), emphasising that the whole set of RoL soft tools is "the result of one or many political battles" between EU institutions, jeopardising their respective effectiveness. Furthermore, specific shortcomings related to the four pillars have been identified (Pech & Bárd, 2022: 94) indicating untapped potential and ample room for improvement based on practical experiences.

Concerning the justice system pillar, among the many EP recommendations, they emphasise the need for the Commission to monitor the justice-enabling environment to broaden access to justice in specific States. They call for the inclusion of relevant information in both the Report and the country chapters to make the publication less static, such as the antecedents and the political context influencing judicial independence. The Parliament suggests integrating key elements from the Venice Commission's Rule of Law Checklist and incorporating detailed data on Member States' compliance with CJEU rulings (European Parliament, 2021, para. 16). Additionally, it is underlined how the Report shall perform a stricter monitoring of national court rulings, useful to assess whether to start infringement proceedings against national authorities not upholding the principle of primacy of the EU law.

As for the anti-corruption framework pillar, it is advised, for instance, that the Report be associated with the RoL Conditionality Regulation 2020/2092 in order to find synergies with the instrument and develop more insightful recommendations for countries' corruption offences and anti-corruption legislation (European Parliament and the Council of the European Union, 2020).

About the media freedom pillar, improvements include a closer monitoring of media freedom by associating the RoL Report with the tools provided by the revised AVMSD (Audiovisual Media Services Directive), also taking into account the prospects opened by the imminent approval of the EMFA (European Media Freedom Act). More topics should be included in the Commission's assessment, such as the degree of independence of private and public service media, as well as national regulatory bodies, while being careful that this does not overlap with the future monitoring tasks that the Commission will perform according to the EMFA (see Cseres in this Volume).

About the other checks and balances pillar, concerns of the Parliament include the little attention paid to civic spaces, national ombudsmen, and the exercise of political rights for EU citizens.

Further criticism comes from stakeholders, whose input documents offer valuable insight into how the Rule of Law Report shall be modified. Jakab puts forward the necessity to better quantify RoL either by developing a more sophisticated index than the EU Justice Scoreboard or by using a combination of the existing ones, such as the World Justice Project Rule of Law Index (Jakab, 2019: 3). Rohlfing and Wind underline that indexing issues are even more serious when indicators are "inattentive to and unable to account for a gradual legalist degradation of democracy" (2023: 2). Furthermore, another vision shared by a large coalition of civil society stakeholders is that an unfavourable evaluation ought to result in more than just suggestions and should entail automatic legal and/or financial repercussions in the Member State concerned. As argued in this Volume (Capati and Christiansen; Lupo), a desirable evolution of the instrument would involve enhancing the binding nature of Rule of Law Reports by linking them to both Country-Specific Recommendations (CSRs) within the European Semester and evaluations of National Recovery and Resilience Plans (NRRPs). The Commission tried to address the criticisms by providing some responses to EP, stakeholders and scholars' suggestions. For the first time, the 2022 RoL Report drew up specific country recommendations to support MS in planned or ongoing reforms or to address systemic challenges and identify improvements. The Commission clarified that they are now "sufficiently specific to allow the Member States to give a concrete and actionable follow-up, taking into account the national competences, legal systems and institutional context, as relevant" (para. 2). However, the Commission remains firm in its stance against the involvement of external experts, motivated by concerns about legitimacy, input balance, and accountability for results. As such, the RoL Report still reflects the institution's own evaluation, which will be the one answerable for.

6 East–West Dissensus and Future Prospects

After three cycles of reporting, another concerning kind of dissensus emerged. It can be referred to as the East–West dissensus and it describes the difficulties in managing specific rule of law issues stressed in the Report (Pech, 2022: 128; Waldron, 2021: 121). It is worth noting that this form of dissensus clearly affects the effectiveness of the EU's specific RoL policies, undermining their credibility and marking a contrast with the dialogue-based nature of the Report. It is significant, for example, that among the stakeholder's contributions to the 2022 report, neither Poland nor Hungary did submit any input. In the 2021 MS feedback documents, Hungary preliminarily stated that "based on the negative experience gained in relation to the Rule of Law Report 2020, this cooperation cannot be regarded as a commitment to the Commission's Rule of Law Mechanism" (Hungary, 2021). A detailed statement on Hungary's opposition to the instrument can be found in a very tense declaration released by the Hungarian Minister of Justice, underscoring how the Commission does not act upon any legal basis for the monitoring exercise nor it does rely on its own sources, thus resulting in a totally "arbitrary" report mainly based on external sources.

In perspective, a desirable development of the Report is its functioning in association with other "Euro-national" procedures, such as the European Semester and the implementation of the RRF. Although not directly related to the RoL, the combination of these frameworks could improve the soundness and efficacy of the recommendations contained in the RoL Report (Capati and Christiansen; Lupo in this Volume). Finally, another feature that could better be developed consists in the replacement of the cooperation and verification mechanism (CVM) by the ROLR as a permanent tool. This would enable continued surveillance of Bulgaria and Romania (as well as other possible countries) after the repeal of the CMV Commission Decisions in 2023, which ended the successful implementation of the measure (Dirri in this Volume).

In conclusion, since its inception, the EU's RoL report has undergone rapid and extensive changes, which can be interpreted from both a positive and negative perspective. On the one hand, it may be positively welcomed as an instrument fostering constructive dialogue and promoting harmonisation among the many notions surrounding the rule of law. It also allows the RoL value to be embodied in tangible actions and policies while at the same time underlining the relevance of contrasting potential and effective challenges to the credibility of the EU from RoL backsliding.

On the other hand, this transformation may be seen as a missed opportunity to directly confront those who intentionally contributed to weakening the rule of law in their countries (Closa, 2019: 696 ff.; Oxford Analytica, 2020), as the focus could have been directed to stronger action.

References

Azmanova, A., & Howard, B. (2021). *Binding the Guardian: On the European Commission's Failure to Safeguard the Rule of Law* (Project Report). European Parliament. https://kar.kent.ac.uk/id/eprint/92062

Bárd, P. (2020). *Diagnostic Autopsy: The Commission's 2020 Annual Rule of Law Report* (pp. 1–6). RECONNECT Blog. https://reconnect-europe.eu/blog/diagnostic-autopsy-the-commissions-2020-annual-rule-of-law-report/

Bressanelli, E., Koop, C., & Reh, C. (2020). EU Actors Under Pressure: Politicisation and Depoliticisation as Strategic Responses. *Journal of European Public Policy, 27*(3), 329–341.

Closa, C. (2019). The Politics of Guarding the Treaties: Commission Scrutiny of Rule of Law Compliance. *Journal of European Public Policy, 26*(5), 696–716.

Coman, R. (2022). *The Politics of the Rule of Law in the EU Polity: Actors, Tools and Challenges*. Palgrave Macmillan.

Council of the European Union. (2019). *Presidency Conclusions, Evaluation of the Annual Rule of Law Dialogue*. https://www.consilium.europa.eu/media/41394/st14173-en19.pdf

Council of the European Union. (2023). *Presidency Conclusions, Evaluation of the Annual Rule of Law Dialogue*. https://data.consilium.europa.eu/doc/document/ST-16547-2023-INIT/en/pdf

European Commission. (2019a). *Communication from the Commission on 'Further Strengthening the Rule of Law Within the Union', COM(2019) 163 Final*.

European Commission. (2019b). *Communication from the Commission on 'Strengthening the Rule of Law Within the Union. A Blueprint for Action', COM(2019) 343 Final*.

European Commission. (2020). *State of the Union Address by President von der Leyen at the European Parliament Plenary*. https://ec.europa.eu/commission/presscorner/detail/ov/SPEECH_20_1655

European Parliament. (2015). *Resolution of 25 October 2016 with Recommendations to the Commission on 'The Establishment of an EU Mechanism on Democracy, the Rule of Law and Fundamental Rights', 2015/2254(INL*).

European Parliament. (2018). *Resolution of 14 November 2018 on 'The Need for a Comprehensive Democracy, Rule of Law and Fundamental Rights Mechanism', 2018/2886(RSP)*. https://eur-lex.europa.eu/legal-content/EN/TXT/PDF/?uri=CELEX:52018IP0456&rid=2

European Parliament. (2020). *Resolution of 7 October 2020 on 'The Establishment of an EU Mechanism on Democracy, the Rule of Law and Fundamental Rights', 2020/2072(INI)*.

European Parliament. (2021). *Resolution of 24 June 2021 on 'The Commission's 2020 Rule of Law Report', 2021/2025(INI)*.

European Parliament. (2023). *Resolution of 30 March 20233 on the 2022 Rule of Law Report—The Rule of Law Situation in the European Union, 2022/2898(RSP)*. https://www.europarl.europa.eu/doceo/document/TA-9-2023-0094_EN.html

European Parliament and the Council of the European Union. (2020). Regulation (EU, Euratom) 2020/2092 of 16 December 2020 on a General Regime of Conditionality for the Protection of the Union Budget. *OJ L 433 I/1*.

Grabowska-Moroz, B. (2022). The Systemic Implications of the Supranational Legal Order for the Practice of the Rule of Law. *Hague Journal of Rule of Law, 14*(2–3), 331–347.

Hungary. (2021). *2021 Rule of Law Report—Input from Member States—Hungary—Addendum.* https://commission.europa.eu/system/files/2021-07/hu-additional_input.pdf

Jakab, A. (2019). *Stakeholder Contribution on Rule of Law—Prof. András Jakab.* https://commission.europa.eu/document/download/85ba7618-b76f-457e-8112-30587028991b_en?filename=stakeholder_contribution_on_rule_of_law_-_prof._dr._andras_jakab.pdf

Kelemen, R. D. (2020). *You Can't Fight Autocracy with Toothless Reports.* EU Law Live. https://eulawlive.com/op-ed-you-cant-fight-autocracy-with-toothless-reports-by-roger-daniel-kelemen/

Kochenov, D. (2019). Elephants in the Room: The European Commission's 2019 Communication on the Rule of Law. *Hague Journal of the Rule of Law, 11*(2–3), 423–438.

LIBE Committee. (2023). *Inter-Parliamentary Committee Meeting on 'The Situation of the Rule of Law in the EU' (LIBE), 4 December, Brussels.* https://www.europarl.europa.eu/relnatparl/en/upcoming-inter-parliamentary-committee-m/products-details/20231110CPU44261

Mannella, F., Paoletti, D., & Raspadori, F. (2022). The Rule of Law in Europe: Main Elements and Perspectives. In E. Carloni & D. Paoletti (Eds.), *Anti-Corruption Models and Experiences: The Case of the Western Balkans* (pp. 11–36) FrancoAngeli.

Oxford Analytica. (2020). EU's Rule of Law Report Will Have Little Effect. *Expert Briefings.* https://doi.org/10.1108/OXAN-ES256617

Pech, L. (2020). *The Rule of Law in the EU: The Evolution of the Treaty Framework and Rule of Law Toolbox* (RECONNECT Working Paper No. 7). https://reconnect-europe.eu/wp-content/uploads/2020/03/RECONNECT-WP7-2.pdf

Pech, L. (2022). The Rule of Law as a Well-Established and Well-Defined Principle of EU Law. *Hague Journal on the Rule of Law, 14*, 107–138. https://doi.org/10.1007/s40803-022-00176-8

Pech, L., & Bárd, P. (2022). *The Commission's Rule of Law Report and the EU Monitoring and Enforcement of Article 2 TEU Values.* European Parliamentary Research Service, PE 727.551.

Pech, L., Kochenov, D., Grabowska-Moroz, B., & Grogan, J. (2019). *The Commission's Rule of Law Blueprint for Action: A Missed Opportunity to Fully Confront Legal Hooliganism.* RECONNECT Blog. https://reconnect-europe.eu/blog/commission-rule-of-law-blueprint/

Priebus, S. (2022). The Commission's Approach to Rule of Law Backsliding: Managing Instead of Enforcing Democratic Values? *Journal of Common Market Studies, 60*(6), 1684–1700.

Rohlfing, R. H., & Wind, M. (2023). Death by a Thousand Cuts: Measuring Autocratic Legalism in the European Union's Rule of Law Conundrum. *Democratization, 30*(4), 551–568.

Schimmelfennig, F. (2020). Politicisation Management in the European Union. *Journal of European Public Policy, 27*(3), 342–361.

Van Ballegooij, W. (2020). *European Added Value of an EU Mechanism on Democracy, the Rule of Law and Fundamental Rights.* European Parliament Research Service, PE 642.831. http://www.europarl.europa.eu/RegData/etudes/BRIE/2020/642831/EPRS_BRI(2020)642831_EN.pdf

Varga, J. (2019). *Facts You Always Wanted to Know about Rule of Law but Never Dared to Ask.* Euronews.com. https://www.euronews.com/2019/11/19/judit-varga-facts-you-always-wanted-to-know-about-rule-of-law-hungary-view

Varga, J. (2020). *The EU Commission Rule-of-Law Report: Wrong in so Many Ways.* Euobserver.com. https://euobserver.com/opinion/149676

Waldron, J. (2021). The Rule of Law as an Essentially Contested Concept. In J. Meierhenrich & M. Loughlin (Eds.), *The Cambridge Companion to the Rule of Law* (pp. 121–136). Cambridge University Press.

Priebus, S. 2022b. The Commission's Approach to Rule of Law Backsliding: [illegible]

[illegible]

PART IV

The Economic and Fiscal Leverage

CHAPTER 12

Enforcing the European Union's Rule of Law Through Economic Governance Mechanisms: The Role of the European Semester

Andrea Capati and *Thomas Christiansen*

1 Introduction

Since its establishment in 2011, the European Semester has emerged as a key component of the Economic and Monetary Union (EMU) and the main institutional architecture for the coordination of Member States' fiscal and macro-economic policies in the EU (Verdun & Zeitlin, 2018). If anything, the two economic crises the EU has experienced over the last decade—the global financial crisis and the COVID-19 pandemic—have further consolidated the European Semester as the instrument through which national macro-economic policies are negotiated and possibly enforced, especially for euro area countries (Vanhercke & Verdun,

A. Capati (✉) · T. Christiansen
Luiss University, Rome, Italy
e-mail: acapati@luiss.it

C. Fasone et al. (eds.), *EU Rule of Law Procedures at the Test Bench*, Palgrave Studies in European Union Politics,
https://doi.org/10.1007/978-3-031-60008-1_12

2022). The European Semester mainly comes with a set of soft-law tools, including communications, opinions, reports, and recommendations. These are intended to facilitate a constructive dialogue between the European Commission and the Member States regarding the timely alignment of national socio-economic policies with EU benchmarks.

Due to the apparent weakness of other instruments dedicated to the protection of fundamental values in the Union, EU institutions have increasingly relied on economic governance mechanisms to safeguard rule of law principles in the Member States (European Commission, 2013). In particular, the European Semester has arguably become one of the European Commission's preferred institutional frameworks to advance its rule of law agenda. This chapter focuses on the role of the European Semester in EU rule of law surveillance, it examines the specific economic governance tools adopted for rule of law guidance and monitoring within the European Semester and discusses their advantages and limitations. To do so, the chapter is structured as follows. Section 2 provides an overview of the European Semester, shedding light on its functioning and the configuration of institutional actors and powers. Section 3 illustrates how the European Semester developed into a rule of law tool based on economic governance mechanisms. Section 4 discusses the advantages and limitations of enforcing rule of law principles through the European Semester, with a focus on the 'soft law' nature of its tools, and provides possible explanations for that. Section 5 explores institutional developments following the COVID-19 pandemic and the Russian invasion of Ukraine. Finally, the concluding section revisits the main findings in the context of ongoing developments in the early 2020s.

2 The Functioning of the European Semester

The European Semester, an institutional framework for the coordination of macro-economic policies of EU Member States, has a fixed timetable. The annual cycle of the European Semester starts off in November with an Autumn Package where the European Commission sets out comprehensive policy priorities and provides the Member States with policy guidance for the following fiscal year. The Autumn Package consists of the Annual Sustainable Growth Survey (ASGS) on the EU's medium-term economic policy agenda, which the Member States need to observe when devising their budgetary plans for the coming year; the Alert Mechanism Report (AMR), which reviews macro-economic credentials in individual Member

States with a view to identifying the existence of potential imbalances under the Macroeconomic Imbalance Procedure (MIP); and a Euro area recommendation to address economic policy issues in the currency union and foster convergence (Council of the EU, 2023).

In May, with the Spring Package, the European Commission elaborates a country report for all Member States, taking stock of their national reform programmes (NRPs) and stability and convergence programmes (SCPs). The country reports also include in-depth reviews addressed to Member States where (risks of) macro-economic imbalances exist, and may suggest corrective action under the excessive imbalance procedure (EIP). Drawing on advice from expert committees, the European Commission then issues a series of country-specific recommendations (CSRs) for each Member State, providing tailored guidance on national budgetary and socio-economic policy measures. While country reports are issued by the European Commission alone, CSRs are proposed by the European Commission and adopted by the Council by qualified majority voting (QMV) after unanimous endorsement by the European Council. At the end of the annual cycle, and by 15 October each year, the Member States submit their national draft budgetary plans, which are then evaluated by the European Commission based on the criteria of the Stability and Growth Pact (SGP) and the CSRs (see Fig. 1).

Due to the link between the European Semester and the SGP, the long-standing debate about the reform of the latter is also relevant for the present discussion. Under the revised SGP, proposed by the European Commission in April 2023 and approved by the European Parliament and Council in April 2024 (Council of the EU, 2024), Member States' NRPs and SCPs will be replaced by national medium-term fiscal-structural plans, bringing together their fiscal trajectories, structural reforms, and investment programmes. Such plans will follow a technical dialogue between the Commission and the Member States aimed at ensuring national compliance with the EU fiscal framework. Moreover, in the elaboration of its CSRs, the European Commission will base its assessment of debt sustainability on a single indicator, which is nationally financed net primary expenditure (i.e. government expenditure net of interest expenditure), so as to simplify the economic governance rulebook and increase the transparency of fiscal surveillance. In terms of corrective action, Member States facing public debt challenges that deviate from the net expenditure path will be automatically subjected to a debt-based

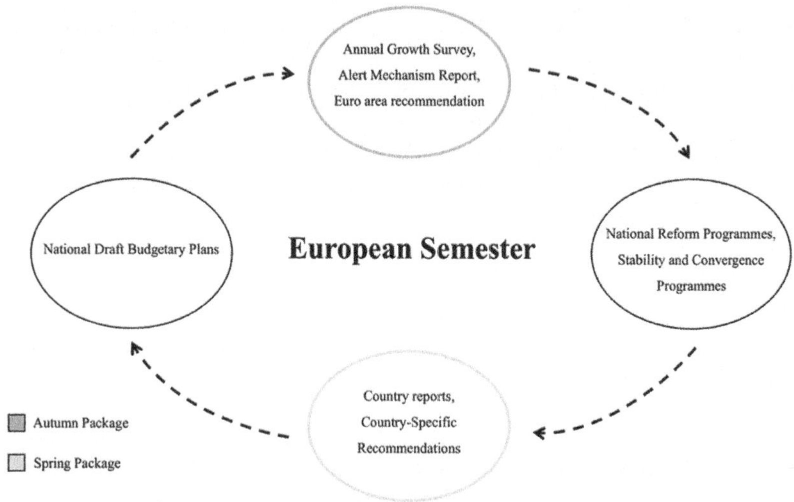

Fig. 1 Visual representation of the European Semester economic coordination cycle (*Source* Authors' own elaboration based on Council of the EU [2023])

excessive deficit procedure (EDP), requiring adjustments to their national medium-term fiscal plans until their deficit no longer exceeds 3% of GDP.

Overall, beyond a formal distribution of powers, in practice it is the European Commission that calls the shots throughout the European Semester (Crum, 2018; Zeilinger, 2021). The ASGS, which is arguably the Autumn Package's key policy measure, is generally endorsed by the European Council meeting of March each year without a substantive discussion by the Heads of State and Government of the fiscal and socio-economic priorities identified by the Commission for the budgetary year ahead. Similarly, while the ECOFIN formally adopts the CSRs by QMV, it is expected to approve the Commission's proposal or to publicly explain its position based on the so-called 'comply-or-explain' principle (Zeitlin & Vanhercke, 2018). Furthermore, the possibility to impose sanctions to non-compliant member states under the EDP has assumed a quasi-automatic character in the European Semester, meaning that they are proposed by the Commission and are deemed to be adopted unless the ECOFIN rejects them by reversed qualified majority voting (RQMV) (European Commission, 2014a). In sum, by virtue of its 'political autonomy' and 'technical expertise', the European Commission steers the policy coordination cycle of the European Semester and acts as the de facto economic government of the EU (Coman, 2022).

3 The European Semester as a Rule of Law Tool

Since the European Semester was first launched in 2011, EU Member States have systemically criticised the European Commission for encroaching on domestic economic policies and national legislation through its CSRs (Crespy & Menz, 2015). While accepting in principle the idea of institutionalised policy coordination at the EU level, Member States have generally seen in the European Semester a tool that provides the Commission with 'a tremendous amount of political discretion to make decisions' with implications for national policymaking (Schmidt, 2020: 179), a discretionary power that fed into the political rhetoric of domestic populist and Eurosceptic actors pointing to a hollowing out of national sovereignty (Carrieri & Vittori, 2021; Fabbrini & Zgaga, 2023). This is all the more relevant as one of the most overlooked aspects of the European Semester in the scholarly literature concerns its gradual development into an institutional framework for the guidance, monitoring, and enforcement of rule of law principles across the EU, a policy domain traditionally close to the core of national sovereignty (Fabbrini & Sajó, 2019; Kelemen & Pech, 2019).

In the absence of a single comprehensive rule of law mechanism, EU institutions have extensively relied on the Spring Package of the European Semester to provide advice on, and monitor compliance with, rule of law principles and the fundamental values of the Union. Indeed, following its 2014 communication entitled 'A new EU Framework to Strengthen the Rule of Law', the European Commission set out to use the existing architecture of economic policy coordination to address rule of law challenges, arguing that the European Semester would provide a unique opportunity to promote the rule of law at the national level (European Commission, 2014b). Since 2016, in both country reports and CSRs addressed to the Member States, the European Commission has in fact made systematic reference to the quality of institutions (including the separation of powers and judicial independence), transparency (including access to public information and the quality of the anti-corruption framework), media freedom, political pluralism (including civic oversight, social dialogue, and stakeholder engagement) and respect for the primacy of

EU law (European Commission, 2022a). Especially in the case of countries with low or deteriorating rule of law credentials—like Hungary and Poland (Pech & Scheppele, 2017)—such economic governance instruments have over time become key for EU institutions to place rule of law concerns at the top of national political agendas while avoiding the more controversial options related to Article 7 TEU or the infringement procedure.

To this effect, country reports take stock of a country's performance in terms of respect for the rule of law and the fundamental values following the submission of NRPs and the SCPs by the Member States in April each year. Country reports thus pave the way for specific advice by the Commission and Council in the form of CSRs on the steps that the Member States need to take to make progress on outstanding rule of law issues. To be sure, references to the rule of law in country reports and CSRs, as an integral part of the European Semester, are always associated with macro-economic considerations (Fromont & van Waeyenberge, 2022). In its 2022 CSRs to Hungary and Poland, for instance, the European Commission made clear that 'the independence, efficiency and quality of the justice system are crucial to attracting business and enabling economic growth', as they contribute to 'a stable and predictable business environment and a friendly investment climate' (European Commission, 2022a, 2022b). This arguably led to a gradual 'economisation' of EU justice systems, intended as the inclusion of rule of law issues and justice reform considerations into an institutional framework primarily devoted to macro-economic and budgetary policy coordination.

Because of the largely intergovernmental character of its governance, the European Semester has dealt with rule of law issues in a predominantly consensual manner, providing institutionalised channels of dialogue, consultation, and debate between the European Commission and national authorities (Eeva, 2021) as well as framing policy recommendations in terms of economic efficiency and legal certainty. However, when Member State governments perceived their national independence was called into question, conflicts about the scope and legitimacy of the European Semester did not take long to surface. After the European Commission published a country report in 2017 stating that the rule of law crisis in Poland had started undermining trust in the Polish legal system, Polish authorities soon claimed that 'the rule of law was not a matter to be discussed in the framework of the Semester' (Coman, 2022: 113), calling on the Economic Policy Committee and COREPER to take care of such a 'political issue'. The attempt proved unsuccessful as Poland's request, lacking sufficient support at the ambassadorial level, did not make it onto the Council's political agenda. The European Commission thus carried on with its rule of law recommendations in the framework of the European Semester thereafter.

4 The Challenge of Enforcing Rule of Law Principles Through the European Semester: Advantages, Limitations, and Explanations

The practice of enforcing rule of law principles by means of economic governance instruments under the European Semester has its advantages and limitations, largely stemming from their nature as soft-law tools. Soft law refers to 'rules of conduct which, in principle, have no legally binding force but which nevertheless may have practical effects' (Snyder, 1993). EU rule of law monitoring under the European Semester is thus non-binding and takes place along the lines of the Open Method of Coordination (OMC), a form of intergovernmental governance based on benchmarking, peer pressure, and naming and shaming (Heritier & Rhodes, 2010). It starts with setting EU-level standards, which are addressed by the Member States in their NRPs, which are then in turn assessed in the country reports and CSRs by EU institutions, notably the European Commission and Council, with nothing but the expectation that the Member States will work towards meeting those standards. Differently from the CSRs targeting national macro-economic policies under the European Semester, those concerning rule of law issues do not fall within the 'corrective arm' of the SGP, the so-called 'Excessive Deficit Procedure' (Bekker, 2021). In other words, in case of non-compliance, no further procedure is activated, thus ruling out the use of sanctions.

On the one hand, soft-law instruments of a non-binding nature such as country reports and CSRs targeting rule of law issues can also induce changes in the institutions and practices of the Member States in the medium- to long-term. Non-binding tools 'can gradually become politically, socially, and morally binding for the actors involved' (Jacobsson, 2004: 359) due to the intervention of factors beyond the legal force of an act, such as knowledge and meaning-making (Stefan, 2017). To this effect, soft-law instruments can foster a common understanding of the challenges and policy goals of the Union across the Member States, thus increasing the scope for voluntary cooperation. In a recent study, for instance, Zeitlin and Vanhercke (2018) have found that the implementation of CSRs at the national level is increasingly facilitated by the emergence of peer review, deliberation, and consensus-seeking practices among Member State governments at the EU level. On the other hand, due to the lack of legally binding force, any type of coercion to enforce soft-law mechanisms is excluded, leaving negotiations as the only game in town (Chinkin, 2000). Without coercive means, most notably the use of sanctions, EU institutions are deprived of a crucial deterrent against potential non-compliance by individual Member States, which by itself makes free-riding on rule of law issues inexpensive. This may well explain why, while most CSRs are followed by at least 'some progress' in terms of implementation at the national level, full or substantial implementation levels remain low and the European Commission's monitoring is itself not always complete (European Court of Auditors, 2020; see also Darvas & Leandro, 2015). As recent research observed, the application of CSRs by the Member States has even worsened over time, raising doubts about both the efficiency and the legitimacy of the European Semester (Efstathiou & Wolff, 2018).

There are several explanations for the European Commission's increased tendency to rely on the European Semester to enforce rule of law principles across the EU rather than on hard-law tools, such as Article 7 or the rule of law conditionality mechanism. First, the literature has shown that the Commission seeks to anticipate the effects of its decisions (Closa, 2019). Because of the long-standing reluctance of Member State governments to intrude in each other's domestic politics, and the unanimity requirement for activating the 'nuclear option' of Article 7, the risk that the Council and the European Council overrule the Commission's initiatives in this respect is high (Kelemen, 2017; Wilms, 2017). The European Commission may thus refrain from adopting hard-law mechanisms to enforce rule of law norms if it anticipates that Member State governments will not support its proposals, and favour instruments involving engagement and dialogue with national actors instead (Kochenov & Pech, 2016). Along these lines, the Commission may also act on the calculation that its hard-law initiatives could backfire. More and less recent research has shown that the threat of sanctions might trigger a nationalist response from national governments and constituencies, and that such a rally-round-the-flag effect is very likely to emerge if the EU activates Article 7 (Allen, 2008; Grauvogel & von Soest, 2014; Schlipphak & Treib, 2016). To this effect, the Commission's enforcement of the rule of law might paradoxically increase the domestic support for those national actors that the policy decision is meant to weaken and further alienate that Member State and its citizens from the EU and its institutions (Bieber & Maiani, 2014; Wilms, 2017).

The scholarly literature has then emphasised how, in its enforcement of rule of law principles, the European Commission tries to avoid compliance obstacles. Expectations about Member States' compliance with EU decisions heavily influence the behaviour of those actors to which enforcement is delegated. In particular, on the assumption that compliance with EU law is ultimately voluntary, the European Commission has used hard-law mechanisms very rarely (Batory, 2016). According to Grabbe (2014: 46), 'if a Member States defies the Commission or ignores a ruling by the CJEU, it undermines the community of law that underpins European integration'. In fear of undermining its own credibility and the legitimacy of European integration, the European Commission has shied away from hard-law tools involving potential confrontation with the Member States, prioritising persuasion and structured dialogue in the framework of the European Semester (Börzel, 2001; Checkel, 2001; Hartlapp, 2007). The 'compliance dilemma' has thus affected the European Commission's rule of law enforcement policy, and has made negotiation and dialogue in the European Semester prevail over the controversial arsenal of hard-law tools, such as the use of sanctions and the suspension of a Member State's voting rights as provided by Article 7.

This explanation is in line with Kelemen and Pavone's (2023) observation that the European Commission has, since the mid-2000s, engaged in the so-called 'politics of supranational forbearance', that is the intentional and revocable under-enforcement—or outright non-enforcement—of law by the supranational executive body (see also Holland, 2016). Following the hypothesised shift from 'permissive consensus' to 'constraining dissensus' in European integration dynamics (Hooghe & Marks, 2009), with a steady decrease in national government and popular comfort with supranational integration, the Commission has seemed to realise that its rule of law enforcement practice risked antagonising national constituencies and undermining its policymaking role as well as support for the EU as a whole. Identifying declining consensus for European integration and supranational policymaking as a serious problem, the

European Commission has thus adopted a political strategy of forbearance for rule of law violations in the Member States, shielding the EU from increasing national contestation to the detriment of effective law enforcement. According to Kelemen and Pavone's argument, 'privileging conciliatory political dialogue over rigorous law enforcement, the Commission worked to safeguard its political role as the engine of integration by partially sacrificing its legal role as the guardian of the Treaties' (2023: 781). In this vein, the European Semester has arguably offered the Commission an incredibly suitable institutional framework to pursue its politics of supranational forbearance, contributing to the promotion of structured dialogue and to the renunciation of sanctions as a primary tool to resolve rule of law conflicts.

5 The Impact of the Global Pandemic and the Russian Invasion of Ukraine

Following the outbreak of the pandemic crisis, the European Semester became the governance framework for the assessment of the National Recovery and Resilience Plans (NRRPs) presented by the Member States under the Recovery and Resilience Facility (RRF). To be approved, the NRRPs need to be in line with the economic policy objectives of the EU as well as the CSRs (Crum, 2020). In this respect, the RRF provides the European Commission and Council within the European Semester with the additional power to suspend the disbursement of financial assistance to individual Member States in case of persistent macro-economic imbalances or failure to take the recommended corrective action (Capati, 2024). In and of itself, the RRF regulation does not explicitly include rule of law issues among the grounds for triggering the suspension of funds. However, it makes the disbursement of financial assistance conditional on the protection of the 'financial interests of the Union', including through measures relating to 'the prevention, detection, correction and investigation of fraud, corruption and conflicts of interests' (RRF Regulation, 2021: 74). This implicitly allows the European Commission to protect rule of law principles in its assessment of Member States' NRRPs.

In the wake of COVID-19, the EU has thus seemed to consolidate the practice of fighting rule of law violations by means of economic and budgetary tools, most notably the European Semester, in the name of the 'financial interests' of the Union. The EU's different prioritisation between economic and rule of law values has become even more apparent, and the trend towards economisation of rule of law principles has further evolved into an outright 'hierarchisation' (Fromont & van Waeyenberge, 2022: 143). This strategy may result in a tacit disregard for democracy, separation of powers, and fundamental rights enforcement by the European Commission, and imply that rule of law norms can only be addressed when they are likely to have a direct bearing on the economic and budgetary objectives of the Union (Fromont & van Waeyenberge, 2022). At the same time, as part of its response to the pandemic crisis, the EU has established the new general regime of conditionality based on the protection of the rule of law. Although the conditionality system is also formally geared towards the 'protection of the Union's budget' (GRC Regulation, 2021), it is nonetheless expected to provide the EU with the capacity to enforce respect for the rule of law and the fundamental principles of the Union as such.

The application of the general regime of conditionality in lieu of the European Semester became even more salient when, after the Russian-Ukrainian war broke out in February 2022, several scholars and observers pointed out that the European Commission could use this crisis as an excuse to further renege on rule of law enforcement in the Union (Kelemen, 2022). Soon after the invasion started, the Commission was perceived as postponing the application of the rule of law regulation in an attempt to foster unity and cohesion among the Member States at a time of unprecedented and existential crisis (Krukowska & Bodoni, 2022). As Bárd and Kochenov argued, the Russian invasion of Ukraine worked 'as a pretext for putting aside internal discussions about the rule of law, and provided additional political rationales for inaction against Member State governments responsible for the violation of European values' (2021: 39). However, recent research has detected a change in the Commission's attitudes, with the supranational executive adopting a tougher approach against Hungary as the war dragged on, while remaining relatively more accommodating vis-à-vis Poland. This, as has been argued, may depend on the different positions adopted by Warsaw and Budapest in the definition of the EU's response to the Russian unprovoked aggression (Hernández & Closa, 2023). While the Polish government condemned Putin's war and fully supported the EU's sanctions policy, Hungary's Orbán aligned with Moscow and threatened to veto political action by the European Council.

To this effect, in Kelemen's words, 'with Poland now hosting two million refugees from Ukraine, the Commission will likely be wary of the optics of suspending any EU funds flowing to the government in Warsaw' (2022: 181). Thus, while the European Commission has decided to activate the general regime of conditionality against Hungary, rule of law violations in Poland continued being addressed through soft-law instruments within the framework of the European Semester until the change of government in December 2023, which—thanks to the leadership of new Prime Minister Donald Tusk—gave hope for a return of Poland towards the path of compliance with the EU's fundamental values.

The change of government in Poland and the expected radical shift regarding its attitudes to both the rule of law and the process of European integration more generally also mean that as of early 2024 Hungary remains the main challenge in the EU's attempts to uphold the respect for fundamental values among its member states (see also Hegedus & Christiansen in this volume). Here, despite more concerted EU action through a variety of instruments, the situation remains highly problematic given Viktor Orban's autocratic tendencies and his control of a sizeable majority in parliament. Based on the past trajectory, it remains doubtful whether any combination of internal and external political pressure, as well as of legal and financial sanctions, can achieve the kind of compliance with the rule of law, both in principle and in practice, that the EU hopes to achieve.

6 Conclusion

The present analysis of the EU's use of the European Semester as a tool to defend the rule of law in the Union has demonstrated the complexity of the task. On the one hand, it is evident that the large amounts of fiscal resources involved make the European Semester a potentially meaningful instrument to achieve compliance with the EU fundamental values, especially if the more dedicated mechanisms have proven ineffective. On the other hand, the reliance on largely soft law and non-binding provisions and the consensual nature of decision-making in this field hinder an effective application. The apparent unwillingness of the European Commission to make full use of the opportunities that the European Semester and the surveillance of national spending under the RRF provide has further weakened the potential of this instrument, as has the ability of the Hungarian government to leverage the need for its support of unanimous decisions in the context of the Russian war of aggression against Ukraine.

The European Semester, despite its massively enlarged scope after the agreement on the RRF, does therefore not constitute a silver bullet in the EU's cumbersome efforts to uphold its fundamental values and protect the rule of law. Yet, this is not to say that it has no effects—overcoming the rule of law crisis clearly requires a range of different tools, none of which on its own appears to be able to achieve the desired results, but which in combination with one another can have an effect. The introduction of a more comprehensive regime with the rule of law conditionality regulation has added further to this array of tools, even if this dedicated instrument has not emerged as a game changer.

Ultimately, the response to the rule of law crisis in the European Union requires not only a range of legal instruments, fiscal sanctions, and financial incentives, but also the political will by the European Commission and Member State governments to actually apply these aggressively—something that has been lacking in the earlier stages of the crisis (what Kelemen [2019] termed the 'peril of passivity') and that has become even more problematic more recently as the need for unanimity in the EU's support for Ukraine could be utilised by a delinquent state such as Hungary to extort exemptions from the financial penalties that ought to be imposed under the rules. The defence of the rule of law, also through the opportunities provided by the European Semester, thus remains work in progress.

References

Allen, S. (2008). The Domestic Political Costs of Economic Sanctions. *Journal of Conflict Resolution, 52*(6), 916–944.

Bárd, P., & Kochenov, D. V. (2021). War as a Pretext to Wave the Rule of Law Goodbye? The Case for an EU Constitutional Awakening. *European Law Journal, 27*, 39–39.

Batory, A. (2016). Defying the Commission: Creative Compliance and Respect for the Rule of Law in the EU. *Public Administration, 94*(3), 685–699.

Bekker, S. (2021). Hardening and Softening of Country-Specific Recommendations in the European Semester. *West European Politics, 44*(1), 114–133.

Bieber, R., & Maiani, F. (2014). Enhancing Centralised Enforcement of EU Law: Pandora's Toolbox? *Common Market Law Review, 51*, 1057–1092.

Börzel, T. A. (2001). Non-compliance in the European Union: Pathology or Statistical Artefact? *Journal of European Public Policy, 8*, 803–824.

Capati, A. (2024). The COVID-19 pandemic and institutional change in the EU's financial assistance regime: The governance of the Recovery and Resilience Facility (RRF). *Journal of European Integration, 46*(3), 341–363.

Carrieri, L., & Vittori, D. (2021). Defying Europe? The Euroscepticism of Radical Right and Radical Left Voters in Western Europe. *Journal of European Integration, 43*(8), 955–971.

Checkel, J. T. (2001). Why Comply? Social Learning and European Identity Change. *International Organization, 55*, 553–588.

Chinkin, C. (2000). Normative Development in the International Legal System. In D. Shelton (Ed.), *Commitment and Compliance: The Role of Non-Binding Norms in the International Legal System* (pp. 21–42). Oxford University Press.

Closa, C. (2019). The Politics of Guarding the Treaties: Commission Scrutiny of Rule of Law Compliance. *Journal of European Public Policy, 26*(5), 696–716.

Coman, R. (2022). *The Politics of the Rule of Law in the EU Polity: Actors, Tools and Challenges*. Palgrave Macmillan.

Council of the EU. (2023). *How the European Semester Works*. https://www.consilium.europa.eu/en/policies/european-semester/how-european-semester-works/

Council of the EU. (2024). *Regulation of the European Parliament and of the Council on the Effective Coordination of Economic Policies and Multilateral Budgetary Surveillance and Repealing Council Regulation (EC) No 1466/97*. https://www.consilium.europa.eu/media/70386/st06645-re01-en24.pdf.

Crespy, A., & Menz, G. (2015). Commission Entrepreneurship and the Debasing of Social Europe Before and After the Eurocrisis. *Journal of Common Market Studies, 53*(4), 753–768.

Crum, B. (2018). Parliamentary Accountability in Multilevel Governance: What Role for Parliaments in Post-Crisis EU Economic Governance? *Journal of European Public Policy, 25*(2), 268–286.

Crum, B. (2020). How to Provide Political Guidance to the Recovery and Resilience Facility? *European Parliament*. https://doi.org/10.2861/108171

Darvas, Z., & Leandro, Á. (2015). *The Limitations of Policy Coordination in the Euro Area Under the European Semester*. Bruegel Policy Contribution, n. 19. https://www.bruegel.org/policy-brief/limitations-policy-coordination-euro-area-under-european-semester#:~:text=The%20European%20Semester%20is%20not,recommendations%20issued%20to%20member%20states

Eeva, K. (2021). Governing Through Consensus? The European Semester, Soft Power and Education Governance in the EU. *European Educational Research Journal*. https://doi.org/10.1177/14749041211055601

Efstathiou, K., & Wolff, G. B. (2018, June 13). *Is the European Semester Effective and Useful?* Bruegel Policy Contribution. https://www.bruegel.org/policy-brief/european-semester-effective-and-useful

European Commission. (2013, April 22). *Safeguarding the Rule of Law and Solving the "Copenhagen Dilemma": Towards a New EU-Mechanism.* Speech by Vice-President of the European Commission, EU Justice Commissioner. https://cursdeguvernare.ro/wp-content/uploads/2013/04/SPEECH-13-348_EN1.pdf

European Commission. (2014a, November 28). *The EU's Economic Governance Explained.* https://ec.europa.eu/commission/presscorner/detail/en/MEMO_14_2180

European Commission. (2014b, March 11). *Communication from the Commission to the European Parliament and the Council: A New EU Framework to Strengthen the Rule of Law.* Brussels. https://eur-lex.europa.eu/legal-content/EN/TXT/PDF/?uri=CELEX:52014DC0158

European Commission. (2022a, May 23). *Country-Specific Recommendation to Hungary.* Brussels. https://commission.europa.eu/system/files/2022-05/2022-european-semester-csr-hungary_en.pdf

European Commission. (2022b, May 23). *Country-Specific Recommendation to Poland.* Brussels. https://commission.europa.eu/system/files/2022-05/2022-european-semester-csr-poland_en.pdf.

European Court of Auditors. (2020). *The European Semester—Country Specific Recommendations Address Important Issues but Need Better Implementation* (Special Report). https://www.eca.europa.eu/Lists/ECADocuments/SR20_16/SR_european-semester-2_EN.pdf

Fabbrini, F., & Sajó, A. (2019). The Dangers of Constitutional Identity. *European Law Journal, 25*(4), 457–473.

Fabbrini, S., & Zgaga, T. (2023). Right-Wing Sovereignism in the European Union: Definition, Features and Implications. *Journal of Common Market Studies*. https://doi.org/10.1111/jcms.13497

Fromont, L., & van Waeyenberge, A. (2022). Trading Rule of Law for Recovery? The New EU Strategy in the Post-Covid Era. *European Law Journal, 27*, 132–147.

GRC Regulation. (2020, December 16). *Regulation of the European Parliament and of the Council on a General Regime of Conditionality for the Protection of the Union Budget.* Brussels. https://eur-lex.europa.eu/legal-content/EN/TXT/PDF/?uri=CELEX:32020R2092

Grabbe, H. (2014). Six Lessons of Enlargement Ten Years on: The EU's Transformative Power in Retrospect and Prospect. *Journal of Common Market Studies, 52*(Annual Review), 40–56.

Grauvogel, J., & von Soest, C. (2014). Claims to Legitimacy Count: Why Sanctions Fail to Instigate Democratization in Authoritarian Regimes. *European Journal of Political Research, 53*, 635–653.

Hartlapp, M. (2007). On Enforcement, Management and Persuasion: Different Logics of Implementation Policy in the EU and the ILO. *Journal of Common Market Studies, 45*(3), 653–674.

Heritier, A., & Rhodes, M. (Eds.). (2010). *New Modes of Governance in Europe: Governing in the Shadow of Hierarchy*. Palgrave Macmillan.

Hernández, G., & Closa, C. (2023). Turning Assertive? EU Rule of Law Enforcement in the Aftermath of the War in Ukraine. *West European Politics*. https://doi.org/10.1080/01402382.2023.2268492

Holland, A. (2016). Forbearance. *American Political Science Review, 110*(2), 232–246.

Hooghe, L., & Marks, G. (2009). A Postfunctionalist Theory of European Integration: From Permissive Consensus to Constraining Dissensus. *British Journal of Political Science, 39*(1), 1–23.

Jacobsson, K. (2004). Between Deliberation and Discipline: Soft Governance in the EU Employment Policy. In U. Mörth (Ed.), *Soft Law in Governance and Regulation: An Interdisciplinary Analysis*. Edward Elgar.

Kelemen, R. D. (2022). Appeasement, Ad Infinitum. *Maastricht Journal of European and Comparative Law, 29*(2), 177–181.

Kelemen, R. D. (2019, November 26). *The Perils of Passivity in the Rule of Law Crisis: A Response to von Bogdandy*. Verfassungsblog. https://verfassungsblog.de/the-perils-of-passivity-in-the-rule-of-law-crisis-a-response-to-von-bogdandy/

Kelemen, R. D. (2017). Europe's Other Democratic Deficit: National Authoritarianism in Europe's Democratic Union. *Government and Opposition, 52*(2), 211–238.

Kelemen, R. D., & Pavone, T. (2023). Where Have the Guardians Gone? Law Enforcement and the Politics of Supranational Forbearance in the European Union. *World Politics, 75*(4), 779–825.

Kelemen, R. D., & Pech, L. (2019). The Uses and Abuses of Constitutional Pluralism: Undermining the Rule of Law in the Name of Constitutional Identity in Hungary and Poland. *Cambridge Yearbook of European Legal Studies, 21*, 59–74.

Kochenov, D., & Pech, L. (2016). Better Late Than Never? On the European Commission's Rule of Law Framework and Its First Activation. *Journal of Common Market Studies, 54*(5), 1062–1074.

Krukowska, E., & Bodoni, S. (2022, March 14). *Ukraine War Adds to EU Doubts Over Pursuing Poland, Hungary*. Bloomberg News. https://financialpost.com/pmn/business-pmn/eu-to-hold-back-on-rule-of-law-budget-fight-amid-war-in-ukraine

Pech, L., & Scheppele, K. L. (2017). Illiberalism Within: Rule of Law Backsliding in the EU. *Cambridge Yearbook of European Legal Studies, 19*, 3–47.

RRF Regulation. (2021, February 12). *Regulation of the European Parliament and of the Council Establishing the Recovery and Resilience Facility*. Brussels. https://eur-lex.europa.eu/legal-content/EN/TXT/PDF/?uri=CELEX:32021R0241&from=EN

Schlipphak, B., & Treib, O. (2016). Playing the Blame Game on Brussels: The Domestic Political Effects of EU Interventions Against Democratic Backsliding. *Journal of European Public Policy, 24*(3), 352–365.

Schmidt, V. A. (2020). *Europe's Crisis of Legitimacy: Governing by Rules and Ruling by Numbers in the Eurozone*. Oxford University Press.

Snyder, F. (1993). The Effectiveness of European Community Law: Institutions, Processes, Tools and Techniques. *The Modern Law Review, 56*(1), 19–54.

Stefan, O. (2017). Soft Law and the Enforcement of EU Law. In A. Jakab & D. Kochenov (Eds.), *The Enforcement of EU Law and Values: Ensuring Member States' Compliance*. Oxford University Press.

Vanhercke, B., & Verdun, A. (2022). The European Semester as Gridlocks: Macroeconomic Policy Coordination and the Recovery and Resilience Facility. *Journal of Common Market Studies, 60*(1), 204–223.

Verdun, A., & Zeitlin, J. (2018). Introduction: The European Semester as a New Architecture of EU Socioeconomic Governance in Theory and Practice. *Journal of European Public Policy, 25*(2), 137–148.

Wilms, G. (2017). *Protecting Fundamental Values in the European Union Through the Rule of Law Articles 2 and 7 TEU from a Legal, Historical and Comparative Angle*. RSCAS. http://cadmus.eui.eu/handle/1814/44987.10.2870/083300

Zeilinger, B. (2021). The European Commission as a Policy Entrepreneur Under the European Semester. *Politics and Governance, 9*(3), 63–73.

Zeitlin, J., & Vanhercke, B. (2018). Socializing the European Semester: EU Social and Economic Policy Co-ordination in Crisis and Beyond. *Journal of European Public Policy, 25*(2), 149–174.

CHAPTER 13

Recent Trends and Ambiguities of Conditionality as an Instrument of the EU Internal Governance

Cristina Fasone and Marta Simoncini

1 Conditionality in Multilevel Governance and the Rule of Law: The Case of the EU

Conditionality is a typical instrument of multilevel governance. Yet, the design and functioning of conditions change considerably depending on the context where they are implemented and the structure and organisation of the executive powers. For decades conditionality has been used in international law as an instrument of financial assistance and development aids, for example by the World Bank and the International Monetary Fund (IMF). These experiences widely practice forms of strict conditionality, where the relationships between the international organisation lending money and the recipient states show little consideration for the

C. Fasone (✉) · M. Simoncini
Luiss University, Rome, Italy
e-mail: cfasone@luiss.it

C. Fasone et al. (eds.), *EU Rule of Law Procedures at the Test Bench*, Palgrave Studies in European Union Politics,
https://doi.org/10.1007/978-3-031-60008-1_13

domestic constitutional impact of the measures adopted in exchange for money (Jeanne et al., 2008).

By contrast, in fully fledged federations conditional spending protects constitutional interests and serves three main purposes: to deal with vertical fiscal imbalances between the federal level and the sub-national units; to address horizontal fiscal imbalances between sub-national units and arising from decentralisation; to redirect the expenditures of the sub-national authorities towards federal objectives, like efficiency, equity, and equality in the living conditions (see Boadway & Watts, 2004).

In the EU, conditional spending stands halfway between the international model and consolidated systems of fiscal federalism. In particular, during the Eurozone crisis the EU granted financial assistance by adopting the strict conditionality approach vis-à-vis the Member States. This approach, however, contributed to a rule of law backlash in Europe and attracted significant criticism in terms of the scope of the EU action and the protection of fundamental rights at national levels. With the design and implementation of the Next Generation EU (NGEU) and the 2021 revision of the Common Provisions Regulation (Regulation 2021/1060/EU) the EU embraced a more federal model and deployed a variety of conditionality regimes for the fulfilment of supranational regulatory priorities and for the enforcement of EU law.

However, conditionality instruments have often paved the way to challenges and dissensus in the recipient countries. Their alleged interference with national competences, the broad discretion left to executive actors in the enforcement and monitoring of the various conditions, and the weak accountability instruments have made the EU internal governance by conditionality increasingly complex.

This chapter reconstructs and assesses the ambiguous use of conditionality by the EU considering the rule of law both as a policy objective and as a standard of conduct in the allocation of funding. Firstly, it offers an overview of the pros and cons of conditional spending (Sect. 2) and engages with the evolution of conditionality as an instrument of EU governance (Sect. 3). The chapter then analyses the use of conditionality during the Eurozone crisis as a critical turning point from the rule of law perspective (Sect. 4). The NGEU package will be characterised as the "game changer" in EU conditional spending (Sect. 5), before delving into conditional spending and EU funds instrumental to safeguard the rule of law as important, yet often neglected, tools to combat the rule of law backsliding (Sect. 6). Section 7 concludes on these recent trends and the EU's inconsistent approach in managing conditionality in support of the rule of law.

2 Pros and Cons of Conditionality and Its Constitutional Ramifications

Scholars highlighted a series of advantages and disadvantages in the use of conditionality (Vita, 2018), which contributed to polarising the debate on its implementation. Among the advantages, EU conditional spending ensures: minimum standards of unity and uniformity in the supply of public services, in the guarantee of rights and in the enjoyment of public goods; cooperative, negotiated, and generally shared solutions to problems of an economic and institutional nature, without applying the traditional command-and-control scheme of action; the effective management of some critical issues, such as interdependencies, externalities, and free-riding; as well as forms of vertical and horizontal solidarity and participation. Conversely, conditionality can lead to an encroachment of competences by the central (EU) level of government towards the local, national, or sub-national ones; undermine the quality and transparency of decision-making; diminish or alter the value of democratic accountability channels, by shifting the responsibility on local levels of government that do not make the substantive choices and decisions; surreptitiously limit or modify the enjoyment and distribution of rights and goods among citizens.

After all, conditionality always assumes a certain level of mistrust or limited trust on the subject in which the conditions are placed. In all the cases where conditionality has been applied there was a degree of asymmetry between the parties: the actor requiring conditions had the final say on both setting the conditions and on the monitoring of their implementation. This inner asymmetry can even lead to question, in the most extreme cases, the compliance of conditional spending with rule of law principles, particularly when it entails an exercise of too broad discretion without any effective judicial remedy against the decision of the "condition-maker" (Kilpatrick, 2015). It is not by chance that in the landmark rulings on the rule of law conditionality regulation the Court of Justice clarified that conditional spending in the EU shall be instrumental to build mutual trust between the Member States and with EU institutions and to ensure a shared and responsible use of common resources (Case C-156/21, para. 129).

It follows that various accounts have been confronted on the nature of conditionality, well-exemplifying the level of scholarly dissensus that surrounds the tool. Some consider conditionality an instrument of "reinforcement by reward" (Schimmelfennig et al., 2003: 496); others view conditionality as a coercive tool (Salmoni, 2021) or as a tool of "colonization" (Smilov, 2006: 331), yet implemented with no legally binding prescriptions; for others, eventually, conditionality can be hardly differentiated by the idea of sanctions, considering that a certain conduct by the State triggers a financial benefit or a punishment (Montaldo et al., 2021).

According to the scope of application and the effects, scholars have identified different types of conditionality (see, extensively, Coman, 2023: 7 ff.). Firstly, positive conditionality provides incentives to meet the conditions, while negative conditionality produces punitive effects (Fierro, 2002). The Recovery and Resilience Facility (RRF) Regulation (2021/241/EU) covers both cases. The positive conditionality applies to the satisfactory fulfilment of milestones and targets foreseen in the national recovery and resilience plans (Article 24), thus entailing the disbursement of the relevant instalment. However, as further clarified by the Commission's RRF Communication of 21 February 2023 (COM (2023) 99 final, Annex II), funding can also be suspended (as happened vis-à-vis Lithuania and Romania) or withdrawn. The methodology devised by the Commission is based on coefficients assigned to reforms and investments out of the overall system of milestones and targets envisaged by the plan and particularly penalises the missed realisation of reforms.

Secondly, conditionality can operate either *ex ante* or *ex post* (Vita, 2018: 18). *Ex ante* conditionality requires the Member States to meet the conditions before the disbursement of the funds. This is the case of structural funds. The macroeconomic conditionality under the European Semester, instead, works ex post, as compliance is verified and monitored during the financial period under review or after the fiscal year.

Thirdly, input-oriented conditionality is based on inputs provided when the actions and steps to be followed are predetermined in detail (according to the so-called "check list method"). This applies to all structural and investment funds, which are cost-based instruments. In contrast, output-oriented conditionality applies to the RRF and creates a performance-based mechanism, insofar as it fixes not only the general policy objectives, but also the concrete results (Vita, 2018: 19).

Fourthly, conditionality may be designed to affect the same sector in which the expenditure is made as for the Common Provisions

Regulation's requirement (Annex IV) for structural Funds' investment expenditure in the waste sector to comply with the provisions of the Waste Framework Directive 2008/98/EC. Instead, examples of horizontal conditions are those demanding the respect of the Charter of Fundamental Rights in all the actions of the structural and investment funds (see Common Provision Regulation, Annex IV and Sect. 6 below).

Finally, conditionality can also be "diagonal", where macroeconomic conditions make the possibility of spending structural funds contingent on the compliance with the criteria set for the financial assistance at the EU and at the international level (Article 19, para. 8, lit. d, Common Provisions Regulation) (Bieber & Maiani, 2014).

3 Conditional Spending in the EU: From External Action to Internal Governance

Inspired by the practice of other international organisations (e.g. Council of Europe, International Monetary Fund, World Bank) (Coman, 2022: 88), the EU has firstly used conditionality to govern its external action. For instance, in bilateral agreements with third countries the EU has made financial assistance or development aid contingent upon the respect of human rights (de Búrca, 2011: 685). Subsequently, conditionality has been used to control the accession of new States to the EU, thus in between EU external and internal governance. Conditional access was meant to not only adapt the domestic legal system to the *acquis communautaire* in a timely manner, but also to introduce, practice, and develop the democratic and rule of law principles in the candidate countries during the latest accession processes (Coman, 2022; Cremona, 2002; Pinelli, 2004). Conditionality could in fact ensure a "*win–win*" solution, allowing, on the one hand, the Eastern European countries to proceed in parallel with the democratic transition and with the accession and, on the other hand, the Union to oversee the transition process on its own terms with a view to avoid disruptions to the integration process (Bartole, 2020).

The conclusions of the Luxembourg European Council in 1997 (para. 25) established a sort of "hierarchy" among the Copenhagen criteria and introduced a major change in the Union's interpretation of conditionality (Kochenov, 2008). The fulfilment of the "block of political criteria became a priority requirement for the opening of accession negotiations" (Tucny, 2000). This has led to contestation and enforcement problems, the consequences of which are perhaps still being faced today. The European Commission, entrusted with monitoring the progress of countries towards the Copenhagen criteria, had no problem setting technical standards for the implementation of the *acquis communautaire*, but it could not define clear guidelines on the overarching political criteria, which were found to be even more vague than those developed, for instance, by the Venice Commission (Kochenov, 2008). Given the very sensitive nature of such criteria, the Commission's approach was however instrumental in not to interfere (too much) with national constitutional discretion by imposing "specific institutional solutions and devices" (Sadurski, 2006: 31).

The weakness of conditionality in accession policies is linked to the dilemma that traps the instrument. To prevent allegations of *ultra vires* action, supranational institutions setting the conditions shall be cautious to avoid any direct violation of national sovereignty and not to affect national constitutional architecture. Normally, conditions are not imposed but negotiated between the parties (Bartole, 2020: 21–24). However, asymmetric bargaining powers can cross the line between negotiation and imposition. Such blurred line also emerged in the use of conditionality as an instrument of internal governance during the Eurozone crisis.

4 Rule of Law Concerns on the Use of Conditionality During the Eurozone Crisis

The strict conditionality practised on financial assistance programmes during the Eurozone crisis has shown that when domestic institutions lack effective margins of manoeuvre in the negotiations, the governance by conditionality can become a severe constraint on national autonomy (Kilpatrick, 2015; Markakis, 2020). During the Eurozone crisis conditionality resembled the approach adopted by international organisations, like the IMF, which was also involved in some rescue funds and notably in the European Stability Mechanism (ESM).

This was the first time that conditionality was intensively used as an instrument of internal governance beyond the domain of cohesion policy, where it has been applied since the 1990s (Bachtler et al., 2017). Compared to the use of conditionality in the frameworks of the European external action and of cohesion funds, the 2010 financial crisis has somehow led to an *upgrade* in the use of emergency conditionality as a tool to respond to asymmetric shocks in the absence of clear legal bases in the Treaties (Leino-Sandberg & Ruffert, 2022). The Eurozone crisis paved the way to a transformation in the understanding of conditionality in the EU.

In general terms, the strict application of conditions does not create special conditionality arrangements. The specificity rather rests upon the tight enforcement, and it served to accept that public financial assistance could be offered to Eurozone countries in need (Ioannidis, 2016). For instance, the various *Memoranda of Understanding* (MoU) concluded between the Government of the rescued country (i.e. Greece, Portugal, Ireland, Spain, Cyprus), the Board of Governors of the ESM and the European Commission detailed the reforms needed in exchange for financial assistance to a degree that was never envisaged before, and it concerned issues that were not necessarily linked to EU matters (e.g. wage and pension reforms, in particular in the public sector) (Faraguna et al., 2019). In addition, to benefit from the loans, targets, and reforms were often to be achieved within very tight deadlines, with review missions on the territory of the beneficiary States at least every six months (the well-known Troika missions, composed of representatives of the IMF, the ECB, and the Commission). The conditions set were not the result of an arbitrary imposition by the Troika. They were proposed by the requesting country, carefully examined by those who managed the funds and by the EU institutions, revised if necessary, and finally co-determined in the MoU. The legal nature of the MoU also divided scholars between those arguing for their binding force (Correia Baptista, 2011) and those defending their soft law nature (Katrougalos, 2013). However, it cannot be neglected that the negotiating capacity of a bailout country is quite limited, and it may be inclined to accept demanding conditions under the risk of economic and financial collapse. The conditions of the rescue package also extended well beyond the loan period to the *ex post* surveillance phase, which could last for decades, until at least 75% of the debt incurred (and the interests on the debt) has been paid off (Article 14, Regulation no. 472/2013).

5 Conditional Spending in the NGEU Era: A Primer

The backlash on the implementation of strict conditionality regimes during the Eurozone crisis triggered the reconsideration of conditions and procedures in the new funding instruments adopted to tackle the

Covid-19 multiple crises. The NGEU package and particularly the RRF mixed positive and negative conditions in the negotiation scheme serving specific EU law and policy goals and protecting the EU financial interests. Access to funding is remarkably based on a range of conditionality regimes, which for the first time have been used to devise what has been described as a new method of government in the EU based on the accommodation of EU-wide and national priorities, a performance-based approach, and a constant bilateral dialogue between the Commission and national governments (Lupo, 2022; Fasone & Lupo, 2023).

In particular, the RRF provides intertwining regimes of conditions whose interplay shapes Member States' investments and reforms financed through the EU common borrowing (Lupo in this Volume). Scholars have provided different taxonomies to define the several conditions that govern access to funding under the RRF (Domorenok & Guardiancich, 2022: 192; Pisani-Ferry, 2020: 6–7). Three main kinds of spending conditions can be identified in the RRF. Firstly, thematic conditions aim at the implementation of EU public goods in fields like green, digital, intergenerational, and gender policies (Article 18, Regulation 2021/241/EU; points 2.5 and 2.6, Annex V, Regulation 2021/241/EU) and, after the REPowerEU reform of the RRF regulation, the security of energy supply (Regulation 2023/435/EU). Under this regime, environmental goals assume specific relevance, as the principle of "do no significant harm" applies as a stringent limit to any economic activity pursued under the programme (Article 5 (2), Regulation 2021/241/EU) and prioritises environmental protection over other relevant public interests. Only the need to meet immediate security of gas supply allows for derogation from the principle, under the control of the Commission (Recital 13, Regulation 2023/435/EU). In addition, macroeconomic conditions exist with the aim of implementing the Countries Specific Recommendations (CSRs) adopted in the European Semester (Article 17 (3) and 18 (4) b), Regulation 2021/241/EU; point 2.2., Annex V, Regulation 2021/241/EU), some of which have started targeting more and more often the rule of law deficiencies in the Member States (see Capati and Christiansen in this Volume). On top of these conditions, Regulation 2020/2092/EU assists the implementation of the RRF as well as any other EU fund. Such conditionality regime applies horizontally to all EU funding and combats the infringement of the rule of law principles resulting in the *vulnus* of the EU financial interests (Hegedus and Christiansen in the Volume).

The co-existence of these different conditions shall guide national reforms and investments towards specific goals fostering EU environmental, fiscal, and democratic sustainability. Yet, the mixture of conditionality regimes under various NGEU legal instruments may become problematic and prone to dissensus for at least three distinct reasons.

Firstly, the wide scope of the national recovery and resilience plans (NRRPs) and of spending conditions favours the competence-creep between the EU and the Member States. National plans covering the entire spectrum of public policies save for CFSP and CDSP and the broad design of the conditions—ranging from the digital transition to social policies, macroeconomic standards to the rule of law principles—prompt the EU action to go beyond its conferred powers, while deferring to national authorities the choice of how to spend large scale EU resources (Leino-Sandberg & Raunio, 2023; Leino-Sandberg & Ruffert, 2022).

Secondly, the enforcement of conditionality by EU institutions is largely discretionary and at times can become arbitrary. Alongside the attempts to clarify the methodology for the assessment of the NRRPs' implementation, the Commission applied double-standards in the enforcement of the rule of law conditionality vis-à-vis Hungary and Poland in 2022 and showed the relevance of the wider political context in the partial lift of the funds' suspension in favour of Hungary in December 2023 to tame veto powers against the Council decision to open accession negotiations with Ukraine and the mid-term review of the Multiannual financial framework. The allegation that conditional spending and payments are heavily influenced by politics rather than by the application of the law has resurfaced in the aftermath of the appointment of the new Tusk government in Poland. Unlike the previous right-wing government, as soon as in office and without carrying out new reforms and investments, particularly on the "supermilestones" (Pech et al., 2023: 37), the government has immediately asked for the payment of the first instalment of the NRRP.

Thirdly, accountability problems arise from the lack of sufficient democratic oversight and ownership by domestic institutions and citizens in the governance of the NGEU (Dani et al., 2021: 326; Rittberger, 2023), as well as from the little involvement of Parliaments, sub-national authorities and stakeholders in the design and implementation of the NRRPs, which has become increasingly bureaucratic (Leino-Sandberg & Raunio, 2023; Zeitlin et al., 2023).

6 Conditional Spending Beyond the NGEU: The Case of the Charter Enabling Condition

If conditionality under the NGEU has attracted significant criticism on the way it is implemented and on its effectiveness, scholars have neglected the prospective impact of additional EU conditional spending tools on the rule of law, with some notable exceptions (Fisicaro, 2022; Hegedus, 2023; Pech et al., 2023). Unlike the RRF, administered through the direct management system according to a performance-based approach, the shared management between the Commission and the Member States of most funds under the Common Provisions Regulation entails the reimbursement of the eligible costs, based on the "receipts" provided, although since the previous programming period 2014–2020 some performance indicators have been added (Zeitlin et al., 2023).

The Regulation 2021/1060/EU introduces a series of 20 enabling conditions to be fulfilled by the Member States to get the reimbursement of expenditure operations for the European Structural and Investment Funds (ESI Funds) and for other funds in the field of migration (Article 15 and Annexes III and IV). There are 16 thematic conditions—some of which are relevant for the protection of the rule of law as related to the implementation of the European Pillar of Social Rights, ranging from the protection of gender equality to anti-discrimination measures for vulnerable groups—applicable to the European Regional Development Fund, the European Social Fund Plus, and the Cohesion Fund specifically. The remaining four conditions are horizontally enforced in all ESI Funds and for all policy objectives and cover public procurement, state aid, compliance with the EU Charter of Fundamental Rights, and the enforcement of the UN Convention on Persons with Disabilities. The requirement to implement the programmes selected for funding and agreed with the Commission in line with the Charters' provisions during the entire programming period is of great significance for the protection of the rule of law (Rubio et al., 2023: 40–45). The introduction of a Charter-based enabling condition responds to the long-advocated need to enhance the effectiveness of the Charter to address the rule of law backsliding (Jakab, 2016; see also Cecchetti in this Volume). In addition, it eventually seconds the view of those who claimed that the leverage of cohesion funds should be used against the European autocrats practising patronage and securing their positions at the domestic level through EU funds (Halmai, 2018; Kelemen & Scheppele, 2018).

Although the previous Common Provision Regulation 1303/2013/EU envisaged *ex ante* conditions in cohesion funds, "[un]fortunately, the Commission adopted a very narrow interpretation of its powers (...) and understood it as precluding any ex-ante suspensions" (Pech et al., 2023: 27; see also Scheppele & Morijn, 2023). For example, the fulfilment of *ex ante* conditions had to be guaranteed only before the disbursement of the fund or, at the latest, before 31 December 2016, and not for the entire programming period (ending in 2020). Moreover, the Commission had largely relied on voluntary compliance by the Member States that had to certify the respect of the conditions (Fisicaro, 2022: 706). Only in two cases has the Commission suspended payments, well after the deadline of December 2016 had expired, against Spain in 2018, and Italy in 2019 (ECA Special Report 24/2021, paras. 33–34). Moreover, under the previous financial cycle the enabling conditions related to the Charter did not trigger any payment suspension (Vita & Podstawa, 2017). The Commission's interpretation of the scope of application of the Charter followed the narrow reading of Article 51(1) provided by the Court of Justice, thereby limiting the potential of the Charter in steering conditional spending (Fisicaro, 2022: 707; drawing on the 2016 Commission Guidance on ensuring the respect for the Charter when implementing the European Structural and Investment Funds).

The 2021 Common Provision Regulation does not confine any longer the Charter-based horizontal condition to the EU funding instruments in the field of home affairs but applies it to all ESI Funds and shall be checked during the entire period 2021–2027 in all stages of deployment of the funds and in every type of operation. As a result, since 2022 the Commission has endorsed an encouraging use of the Charter condition. This shift in the Commission's approach was anticipated by the "Strategy to strengthen the application of the Charter of Fundamental Rights in the EU" (COM (2020) 711 final, para. 1.2) and by the decision to reject the funding applications of Polish cities under the Twinning programme (thus beyond the ESI Funds), due to the patent discriminatory effort against LGBTIQ+.

In December 2022, the Commission held that Hungary had not fulfilled the Charter enabling condition in four areas related to judicial independence (Article 47 of the Charter): the powers of the President of the National Office of the Judiciary; the autonomy of the judges sitting in the Supreme Court vis-à-vis its President; the Supreme Court's review of the preliminary ruling request to the European Court of

Justice by lower courts; and the possibility for administrative authorities to appeal judgments of ordinary courts before the (politically captured) Constitutional Court. As a result, all Cohesion Policy, the Maritime and Fisheries funds, and Home Affairs funds but those for the technical assistance (21.9 billion Euros), were suspended. After Hungary managed to introduce substantive reforms in these four critical areas and reinforced the independence of the judiciary, on 13 December 2023 funds were partly unblocked, but with no immediate payment. Once payment claims are submitted, Hungary will receive the reimbursement from the Commission for the expenditures incurred under the Cohesion Policy, the Maritime and Fisheries funds, and Home Affairs funds for up to 10.2 billion Euros. The remaining funds (more than 11 billion Euros) are still suspended in part for further problems in complying with the Charter enabling condition.[1] The Commission has indeed raised new concerns regarding the safeguarding of academic freedom (Article 13), the right to asylum (Article 18), and the protection of LGBTIQ+ against discrimination perpetrated by the so-called "child protection law" (Article 21), on which an infringement proceeding is pending.

The enabling conditions of the Common Provision Regulation have also been used against Poland, the largest beneficiary of EU funds. As reported by Scheppele and Morjin (2023: 31), "at least €100 billion have been withheld from Poland without the Conditionality Regulation ever being invoked".[2] This is an estimate because the exact amount of funds suspended and the grounds for the breach of the Charter enabling condition have not been formally disclosed. Neither official documents nor implementing decisions have been made public on the matter with regard to Poland, but the suspension may be due to problems with judicial independence.[3] A variety of sources—in particular the Report from the Commission to the European Parliament and the Council of 28 June

[1] Hungary has been also found in breach of some thematic enabling conditions of the Common Provision Regulation, and for 6.3 billion Euros out of 11.7 there is still in operation the rule of law conditionality suspension (see Hegedus and Christiansen in this Volume).

[2] That amount refers to the ESI Funds expected by Poland under the Partnership Agreement with the Commission for the period 2021–2027 (75.6 billion Euros) plus the funds available to Poland under the RRF, 35.4 billion Euros, not yet paid at the time of writing with the new Tusk Government asking for the first instalment in December 2023.

[3] Quoted in A. Krzysztoszek, European Commission to freeze Poland's cohesion money, Euractiv.com, 18 October 2022.

2023 on the follow-up to the discharge for the 2021 financial year (COM (2023) 384, para. 2.b.)—confirmed the suspension of the reimbursement to Poland due to the lack of fulfilment of the Charter enabling condition, but none revealed further details on its legal basis and rationale. The silence of the Polish authorities and of the Commission has been harshly criticised for prompting serious accountability problems (Scheppele & Morijn, 2023: 44 ff.). As highlighted by Pech et al. (2023: 51), "this could for instance result in this funding suspension being lifted for reasons of political expediency regardless of whether meaningful legal changes have been adopted and implemented as regards compliance with, inter alia, the right to an effective remedy (Article 47(1)) and the right to a fair trial by an independent and impartial tribunal established by law (Article 47 (2))" of the Charter.

Similar transparency problems occurred with regard to the suspension of the funding of the Asylum, Migration and Integration Fund (AMIF) and of the Instrument for Financial Support for Border Management and Visa Policy (BMVI) for Cyprus, Hungary, and Poland—most likely in breach of the right to asylum (Article 18)—for a total of around 1 billion Euros (PICUM and ECRE 2023: 5). The relevant implementing acts are not systematically published nor are the assessments of the Directorate-General for Justice and Consumers (DG JUST) on the compliance of national programmes with the Charter made available.

To tackle rule of law problems, the Commission has clearly started to use the Charter enabling condition extensively. In the case of Hungary, it seems to have brought some changes, but the inference is not conclusive also because on the same critical issues of judicial independence the Commission has unblocked part of the ESI funds under the Charter enabling condition but has kept the suspension under the rule of law conditionality Regulation (Hegedus, 2023). One may wonder whether the lack of access to detailed information on the Commission's justifications to unblock Hungary's reimbursement on the part of the ESI Funds is due to political reasons beyond the alleged redress of the Charter's violations, perhaps connected to the gridlock of other crucial EU dossiers on which the country threatened the veto. This is more evident in the case of Poland where the lack of activation of the rule of law conditionality mechanism has been widely contested, but the suspension in the reimbursement of other EU funds has also been overlooked due to the semi-secrecy of the Commission decision and the negotiations.

7 Conclusions

The EU has strongly intensified the use of the conditionality instruments. Spending conditions have increasingly become intrusive tools of internal governance and have been employed to exert pressure on the compliance with the rule of law principles by the Member States. The mixture of positive and negative, input and output, conditionality regimes intersect the EU need to ensure the proper functioning of domestic institutions as a guarantee for the protection of the EU financial interests and the reach of EU policy goals. The complex mechanisms of governance by conditionality depart from the problematic experience of strict conditionality during the Eurozone crisis, which in some cases worsened the rule of law standards in the rescued countries. However, a pondered reflection on the actual constitutional shortcomings has not yet consolidated (Baraggia & Bonelli, 2022).

The rule of law conditionality is probably the most debated conditionality tool of the last decade, whose enforcement has been delayed and diluted over time. The RRF has also been criticised as its conditionality regimes intrude on the division of competence between the EU and the Member States, confer broad discretion on the Commission accompanied by weak accountability instruments in the decisions on access to funding, suspension in the payments, and its lift. It cannot be denied, however, that the number of resources available and the performance-based scheme make the RRF and the "rule of law-oriented milestones and targets" a formidable leverage to combat the consolidation of autocracies in the EU.

In addition, since 2022 the Commission has enforced as never before and under limited media coverage the Charter enabling condition under the Common Provisions Regulation 2021/1060 to limit the access of illiberal regimes like Hungary and Poland to EU funds. While this has become the preferential negative conditionality regime used by the Commission, its enforcement has been problematic due to the lack of transparency surrounding the Commission's decisions, their rationales, and legal basis in the Charter. There is also very limited access to information on the suitability of the remedies put in place by the targeted countries and the grounds to lift the suspension. To date these questions remain unanswered and may affect the credibility of the Charter enabling condition and the predictability of its procedures, largely deficient from the perspective of accountability and transparency.

References

Bachtler, J., Berkowitz, P., Hardy, S., & Muravska, T. (2017). Introduction: Reassessing the Performance and Direction of EU Cohesion Policy in 2014–20. In J. Bachtler et al. (Eds.), *EU Cohesion Policy: Reassessing Performance and Direction*. Routledge.

Baraggia, A., & Bonelli, M. (2022). Linking Money to Values: The New Rule of Law Conditionality Regulation and Its Constitutional Challenges. *German Law Journal, 23*(2), 131–156.

Bartole, S. (2020). *The Internationalization of Constitutional Law: A View from the Venice Commission*. Hart.

Bieber, R., & Maiani, F. (2014). Enhancing Centralized Enforcement of EU Law: Pandora's Toolbox? *Common Market Law Review, 51*(4), 1057–1092.

Boadway, R., & Watts, R. L. (2004). *Fiscal Federalism in Canada, the US and Germany* (Institute of Intergovernmental Relations Working Paper 6). Queen's University.

Coman, R. (2022). *The Politics of the Rule of Law in the EU Polity: Actors, Tools and Challenges*. Palgrave Macmillan.

Coman, R. (2023). *Increasing the Policy Effectiveness Through Renewed Conditionality Mechanisms* (Final Report for the High Level-Group of Specialists on the Future of Cohesion Policy). Brussels, European Commission.

Correia Baptista, E. (2011). Natureza Jurídica dos Memorandos com or IMF and com at União Europeia. *Revista da Ordem dos Advogados*, 477–488.

Cremona, M. (2002). Accession to the European Union: Membership Conditionality and Accession Criteria. *Polish Yearbook of International Law, 25*, 219–240.

Dani, M., Chiti, E., Mendes, J., Menéndez, A. J., Schepel, H., & Wilkinson, M. A. (2021). It's the political economy ...!" A Moment of Truth for the Eurozone and the EU. *International Journal of Constitutional Law, 19*(1), 309–327.

De Búrca, G. (2011). The Road Not Taken: The European Union as a Global Human Right Actor. *American Journal of International Law, 105*(4), 649–693.

Domorenok, E., & Guardiancich, I. (2022). The Italian National Recovery and Resilience Plan: Coordination and Conditionality. *Contemporary Italian Politics, 14*(2), 191–206.

European Commission, Communication on Recovery and Resilience Facility: Two Years on. A Unique Instrument at the Heart of the EU's Green and Digital Transformation, COM (2023) 99 final, 21.2.2023.

European Court of Auditors (ECA) (2021), Special Report 24/2021, 'Performance-Based Financing in Cohesion Policy: Worthy Ambitions, but Obstacles Remained in the 2014–2020 Period'.

Faraguna, P., Fasone, C., & Tega, D. (2019). Greece, Ireland, Portugal and Spain Ten Years Later: Introduction to a Study of the Eurocrisis in the Constitutional Perspective. *Quaderni Costituzionali, 1*, 199–214.

Fasone, C., & Lupo, N. (2023). Learning from the Euro-Crisis: A New Method of Government for the EU's Economic Policy Coordination After the Pandemic? *STALS Research Paper Series, 4*, 3–25.

Fierro, E. (2002). *The EU's Approach to Human Rights Conditionality in Practice*. Brill.

Fisicaro, M. (2022). Beyond the Rule of Law Conditionality: Exploiting the EU Spending Power to Foster the Union's Values. *European Papers, 7*(2), 697–719.

Halmai, G. (2018). *The Possibility and Desirability of Economic Sanction: Rule of Law Conditionality Requirements Against Illiberal EU Member States* (EUI Department of Law Research Paper 2018/06).

Hegedus, D. (2023, December 21). *Same, Same but Different? The Pitfalls in Unfreezing EU Funds*. VerfBlog. https://verfassungsblog.de/same-same-but-different/; https://doi.org/10.59704/90a6c60ebafa2c61.

Ioannidis, M. (2016). Europe's New Transformations: How the EU Economic Constitution Changed During the Eurozone Crisis. *Common Market Law Review, 53*(3), 1237–1282.

Jakab, A. (2016). The EU Charter of Fundamental Rights as the Most Promising Way of Enforcing the Rule of Law Against EU Member States. In C. Closa & D. Kochenov (Eds.), *Reinforcing Rule of Law Oversight in the European Union* (pp. 1187–1205). Cambridge University Press.

Jeanne, O., Ostry, J., & Zettelmeyer, J. (2008). *A Theory of International Crisis Lending and IMF Conditionality*. IMF.

Katrougalos, G. (2013, January 29). *The Greek Austerity Measures: Violations of Socio-Economic Rights*. International Journal of Constitutional Law Blog.

Kelemen, R. D., & Scheppele, K. L. (2018, September 10). How to Stop Funding Autocracy in the EU. *VerfBlog*. https://verfassungsblog.de/how-to-stop-funding-autocracy-in-the-eu/

Kilpatrick, C. (2015). On the Rule of Law and Economic Emergency: The Degradation of Basic Legal Values in Europe's Bailouts. *Oxford Journal of Legal Studies, 35*(2), 325–353.

Kochenov, D. (2008). *EU Enlargement and the Failure of Conditionality: Pre-Accession Conditionality in the Field of Democracy and Rule of Law*. Kluwer Law International.

Leino-Sandberg, P., & Raunio, T. (2023). From Bad to Worse: The Continuous Dilemma Facing Parliaments in European Economic and Fiscal Governance. *Government and Opposition*, early view, 1–18.

Leino-Sandberg, P., & Ruffert, M. (2022). Next Generation EU and Its Constitutional Ramifications: A Critical Assessment. *Common Market Law Review, 59*(2), 433–472.

Lupo, N. (2022). Next Generation EU e sviluppi costituzionali dell'integrazione europea: verso un nuovo metodo di governo. *Diritto pubblico, 3*, 729–755.

Markakis, M. (2020). *Accountability in the Economic and Monetary Union: Foundations, Policy, and Governance*. Oxford University Press.

Montaldo, S., Costamagna, F., & Miglio, A. (Eds.). (2021). *EU Law Enforcement—The Evolution of Sanctioning Powers*. Routledge.

Pech, L., Wójcik, A., & Wachowiec, P. (2023). *The Case for Activating the Rule of Law Conditionality Regulation in Respect of Poland*. Study for the Greens/EFA Group, European Parliament.

Pinelli, C. (2004). Conditionality and Enlargement in Light of EU Constitutional Developments. *European Law Journal, 10*(3), 354–362.

Pisani-Ferry, J. (2020). European Union Recovery Funds: Strings Attached, but Not Tied Up in Knots. *Bruegel Policy Contribution, 19*, 1–10.

Platform for International Cooperation on Undocumented Migrants (PICUM) and European Council on Refugees and Exiles (ECRE). (2023). *Fundamental Rights Compliance of Funding Supporting Migrants, Asylum Applicants and Refugees Inside the European Union*. Policy Note.

Rittberger, B. (2023). *Democratic control and legitimacy in the evolving EU economic governance framework*. Study prepared for the Economic Governance and EMU Scrutiny Unit (EGOV) Directorate-General for Internal Policies. (pp. 733–742).

Rubio, E., et al. (2023, April). *The Tools for Protecting the EU Budget from Breaches of the Rule of Law: The Conditionality Regulation in Context*. Study requested by the BUDG committee, PE 747.469.

Sadurski, W. (2006). EU Enlargement and Democracy in New Member States. In W. Sadurski, A. Czarnota, & M. Krygier (Eds.), *Spreading Democracy and the Rule of Law? The Impact of EU Enlargement on the Rule of Law, Democracy and Constitutionalism in Post-Communist Legal Orders* (pp. 27–49). Springer.

Salmoni, F. (2021). *Recovery Fund, Condizionalità e Debito Pubblico*. CEDAM.

Scheppele, K. L., & Morijn, J. (2023). What Price Rule of Law. In A. Södersten & E. Hercock (Eds.), *The Rule of Law in the EU: Crisis and Solutions* (pp. 39–54). SIEPS, April 2023:1.

Schimmelfennig, F., Engert, S., & Knobel, H. (2003). Cost, Commitment and Compliance: The Impact of EU Democratic Conditionality on Latvia, Slovakia and Turkey. *Journal of Common Market Studies, 41*(3), 495–518.

Smilov, D. (2006). EU Enlargement and the Constitutional Principle of Judicial Independence. In W. Sadruski, A. Czarnota, & M. Krygier (Eds.), *Spreading Democracy and the Rule of Law? The Impact of EU Enlargemente for the Rule of Law, Democracy and Constitutionalism in Post-Communist Legal Orders* (pp. 313–334). Springer.

Tucny, E. (2000). *L'élargissement de l'union européenne aux pays d'Europe centrale et orientale: La conditionnalité politique*. L'Harmattan.

Vita, V. (2018). *Research for REGI Committee—Conditionalities in Cohesion Policy*. European Parliament

Vita, V., & Podstawa, K. (2017). *When the EU Funds Meet the Charter of Fundamental Rights: On the Applicability of the Charter of Fundamental Rights to EU Funds Implemented at the National Level* (Global Campus Working Paper 1/17).

Zeitlin, J., Bokhorst, D., & Eihmanis, E. (2023, June). *Governing the RRF: Drafting, Implementing, and Monitoring National Recovery and Resilience Plans as an Interactive Multi-Level Process*. Foundation for European Progressive Studies (FEPS) Policy Study.

CHAPTER 14

Contesting the Rule of Law in the European Union: The Creation and Implementation of the Rule of Law Conditionality Regulation

Dora Hegedus and Thomas Christiansen

1 Introduction

In the context of a series of interacting crises (Caporaso, 2018), also labelled as polycrisis (Zeitlin et al., 2019) that have engulfed the European Union (EU) over the past decade, the rule of law (RoL) crisis stands out as a particular occurrence, resulting from internal decay rather than an external shock. It is also an existential threat to the Union, given that the decline of RoL standards cuts into the very fabric of EU integration, jeopardising mutual trust, and mutual recognition among member

D. Hegedus (✉) · T. Christiansen
Luiss University, Rome, Italy
e-mail: dhegedus@luiss.it

T. Christiansen
e-mail: tchristiansen@luiss.it

C. Fasone et al. (eds.), *EU Rule of Law Procedures at the Test Bench*, Palgrave Studies in European Union Politics,
https://doi.org/10.1007/978-3-031-60008-1_14

states (Müller, 2015). The EU of course has a range of well-established tools to address such issues, be it of a soft law nature (see the chapters by Serowaniec, Guerra, and Citino in this Volume) or with more serious material and legal effects (see the chapters by Coman and Thinus and by Piccirilli in this Volume). Yet, as none of these appeared to bring this corrosive trend to a halt, the Commission proposed in 2018 a new regulation for the "protection of the Union's budget" in case of generalised RoL deficiencies, linking member states' normative performance explicitly to the financial disbursements they could expect to receive (European Commission, 2018). This chapter provides a brief review of the adoption and early implementation of this new regulation, indicating the degree to which action to protect the rule of law in the EU has been contested.

The massive increase in the EU's spending that came with the 2021–2027 Multiannual Financial Framework and the NextGenerationEU (NGEU) financial support package, provided new impetus in the quest to better protect EU funds. However, the idea of a new instrument giving the Union the power to intervene in the internal workings of member states by using financial sanctions was controversial (de Mesquita, 2018; Sedelmeier, 2016; Vita, 2017). Further fault lines emerged between supporters and critics of such a "RoL Conditionality Regulation" in the course of the negotiation, adoption, and eventual implementation of the new mechanism. There have been inter-institutional battles throughout this process, most recently in 2023 when the EU struck what some critics referred to as a "Faustian bargain" (Pavone, 2023) with Viktor Orbán, Prime Minister of Hungary as the Commission authorised the unblocking of 10.2 billion EUR of previously frozen cohesion funds to Hungary (European Commission, 2023). Ostensibly, the Commission's aim was to avoid Hungary's veto on initiating EU membership talks with Ukraine and on channelling aid to the war-torn country from the EU's MFF. However, the Commission's decision inadvertently drew attention to another contentious issue regarding conditionality attached to the RoL, namely that Hungary's funds were not exclusively suspended via the novel RoL conditionality Regulation, but via two different, parallel tools (Hegedus, 2023; Scheppele & Morijn, 2023). It will be argued that the parallel, inconsistent implementation of diverse tools not only makes the unblocking mechanism of frozen funds highly obscure, but also it might weaken the position of the novel RoL mechanism.

2 The Conditionality Regulation in the Academic Debate

EU inaction and incompetence when it comes to safeguarding the RoL in recalcitrant member states, has long been criticised by academics. Despite the broad consensus over the necessity of reforms in the EU's RoL toolkit, the introduction of a new conditionality regime did not enjoy unequivocal support. Disputes emerged whether financial sanctions were the right way ahead, and if so, in what form should they be employed. Sedelmeier argued that conditionality could function when a highly valued prize is at stake (such as joining the EU), nonetheless, "material sanctions have limits as an instrument to rein in breaches of liberal democracy" (Sedelmeier, 2016: 340). According to him, the stronger the illiberal grip gets, the more difficult it becomes to advance changes against the backdrop of financial sanctions. He equally drew attention to unintended negative consequences, such as politicians making a scapegoat of the EU, and mobilising support for demagogue, illiberal governments (Sedelmeier, 2016: 343), in case funds are withheld. Therefore, Sedelmeier attributed greater potential to the naming and shaming element of the Commission's 2014 consultative RoL Framework. However, in hindsight it is clear that consultative tools have not been utilised wisely. The Council was adamant to engage in an inter-institutional competition with the Commission to reinstate its status via drawing up similar, parallel, and highly ineffective tools (Christiansen & Hegedus, 2023; Kochenov & Pech, 2015), such as the yearly Council dialogues (Council, 2014) and later the peer review mechanism (Germany's Presidency of the Council, 2020).

Regardless of the above criticism, the vast majority of scholars have been urging a more resolute reaction from the EU (Halmai, 2018; Kelemen, 2020; Kirst, 2021; Müller, 2015; Scheppele, 2016; Scheppele et al., 2021; von Bogdandy et al., 2012). Yet, accord has been sparse, when it comes to the exact form and nature of an alternative RoL tool. Questions emerged whether the solution should be political or legal, and whether it should consist in creating a new legislation such as Müller's Copenhagen Commission (Müller, 2015), or reforming some existing ones as proposed in Scheppele's systematic infringement actions (Scheppele, 2016), or von Bogdandy et al.'s Reverse Solange doctrine (von Bogdandy et al., 2012). Reflecting briefly on the wider academic debate is vital to illustrate that financial conditionality was not a simple, straightforward choice to provide a remedy to Europe's internal RoL problems.

The Commission's 2018 proposal was the first practical manifestation of the EU's solid commitment to introduce a new tool to protect the RoL. The legislation underwent substantive changes until it reached its final form in December 2020. During the process, the academic debate shifted the focus more succinctly on the specific tool itself, its practical features, and the alterations implemented in the original proposal. Three different viewpoints have emerged in the scholarly community: one, which believes that the Commission proposal was watered down to a weak, toothless instrument (Kirst, 2021; Scheppele, Pech & Platon, 2020; Staudinger, 2022); a second one, which interprets changes as a necessary evil (Baraggia & Bonelli, 2022); and a third one, which describes alterations as utmost desirable (Łacny, 2021; von Bogdandy & Łacny, 2020). Critics, who belong to the first group, labelled the transformation of the tool as a transition from a RoL-focussed, procedurally robust instrument, to a weak, "mere budgetary conditionality mechanism" (Staudinger, 2022: 737). In fact, the text of the Regulation reiterates, that the mechanism might be triggered only in case the Commission demonstrates "a sufficient and direct link between detected RoL violations and the sound financial management of the Union" (Staudinger, 2022: 737). Furthermore, the application of the tool became restricted to a "closed list of homogenous elements" instead of detecting "generalised RoL deficiencies" (Scheppele, Pech & Platon, 2020). In a similar vein, the title of Regulation 2020/2092 tellingly omits the reference to the "Rule of Law" altogether, as opposed to the initial Commission proposal title, which was also interpreted as a diversion from the original goal of the instrument (Baraggia & Bonelli, 2022). Lastly, critics were equally ready to lambast some substantive changes in the process of implementing the conditionality mechanism. Originally, the Commission's suggestion to freeze a member state's EU funds were supposed to pass by reverse QMV in the Council, which was altered to simple QMV in July 2020 by the EUCO (2020b). According to Kirst, keeping reverse QMV[1] arrangements would have created an even more robust tool, "since it would have put the burden of proof upon the accused member state" (Kirst, 2021: 106).

[1] The Commission's proposal is adopted unless a qualified majority of member states reject the proposal in the Council.

Thus, simple QMV was interpreted as another blow on the efficiency of the new RoL instrument.

To the contrary, Łacny (2021) welcomed the reformed, restricted scope of the conditionality mechanism, which according to her, should increase the probability of deploying the tool, as opposed to already existing, often vague RoL instruments. In another publication together with von Bogdandy (von Bogdandy & Łacny, 2020), they expressed that reforms were utmost necessary for the legitimate application of the RoL Mechanism. Von Bogdandy and Łacny (2020) found reverse QMV incompatible with EU treaties, as "no legal provision under EU primary law authorises reverse QMV arrangements in the Council" (von Bogdandy & Łacny, 2020:9). Therefore, in sharp contrast to the previous group of scholars, they saw strong merits in the alterations and sticking to simple QMV. Likewise, even though Baraggia and Bonelli recognised certain limitations in the Regulation's final version, they did not consider all changes to be "watered-down compromises" (Baraggia & Bonelli, 2022: 131). Not only did they agree with von Bogdandy and Łacny's interpretation of reverse QMV in the Council, but also, they echoed the Council's Legal Service (2018) on the inevitable need to draw a clear distinction between Article 7 TEU and the RoL Conditionality Mechanism, to avoid producing parallel tools. The Council's Legal Service report, which expressed some concerns about the new instrument's legality, was published swiftly after the Commission's original proposal (Council of the European Union, 2018). It argued that the new mechanism should be firmly anchored in Article 322 TFEU, and must focus on protecting EU funds. In agreement with the Council's Legal Service, Baraggia and Bonelli hailed the alteration in the Regulation, which compels the Commission to justify a clear link between RoL violations and protecting the EU's budget (Baraggia & Bonelli, 2022), in order to trigger the tool. In conclusion, scholarly contestation has manifested along remarkably clear fault lines regarding the evaluation of the new RoL Conditionality Mechanism's content. The two sides encompass those on the one hand, who wished to see the establishment of a widely applicable tool to counter RoL breaches against the backdrop of EU funds, versus those on the other hand, who intended to place greater emphasis on protecting the EU's budget should it be negatively affected due to RoL breaches, in the framework of a narrower, budget-oriented instrument (Fig. 1).

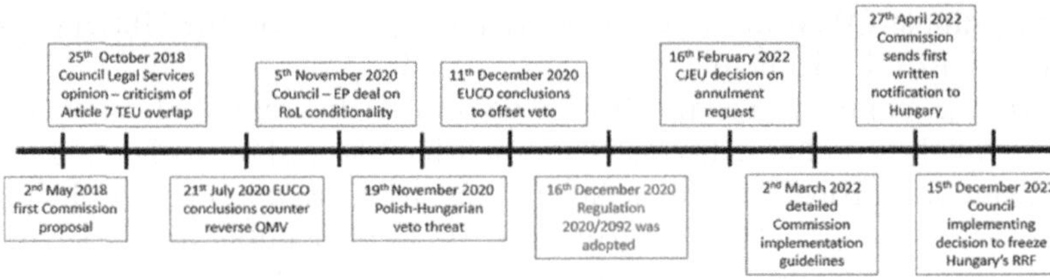

Fig. 1 Timeline of negotiating and implementing the "RoL Conditionality Regulation" (*Source* Author's own elaboration)

3 Inter-Institutional Contestation About the Conditionality Regulation

Inter-institutional contestation was equally palpable, especially during the course of adapting and implementing the RoL mechanism, owing to the Polish and Hungarian veto threat, which was offset with a controversial compromise. The conditionality mechanism could have been adopted in the absence of full consensus; yet, due to issue linkage with the EU's MFF and the own resources regulation (Schramm & Wessels, 2022: 9), it became indirectly susceptible to veto threats, and subject to quasi-unanimity decision. The EUCO in its December 2020 conclusions (European Council, 2020a) presented a deal, which attached two time-consuming conditions to the implementation of the new regulation. First, it was expressly acknowledged that an action for annulment should be brought in front of the CJEU, even though on a general level this is an implicit option with regard to any Union legal act (Article 263 TFEU). Secondly, after the CJEU's judgement, the Commission was asked to establish detailed implementation guidelines (European Council, 2020a). Thus, the Commission was compelled to delay the triggering of the new tool until April 2022, when all conditions set out in the EUCO conclusions were met, even though the conditionality instrument to protect the budget of the EU was created in December 2020.

In response, the EP promptly accepted a stiff resolution, in which the institution scolded the EUCO for overstepping its treaty functions, and reminded the EUCO that its conclusions should be regarded as a political declaration instead of binding, legislative rules (European Parliament, 2020c: 2). The EP already saw as problematic the EUCO's actions, when in July 2020 the EUCO altered reverse QMV to simple QMV in its conclusions on a whim, without proper institutional deliberation (European Parliament, 2020a, 2020b). Even if necessary inter-institutional bargaining took place at a later stage, the EP was not able to reinstate reverse QMV. The disputes, reached a peak when the EP took the Commission to court due to the unduly delayed triggering of the new mechanism against recalcitrant member states. Although, it should be noted that the case has been dropped in May 2022, when the Commission bowed to pressure and agreed to launch the mechanism against Hungary at the end of April 2022 (Hanke Vela, 2022).

An additional linchpin of inter-institutional debates was a questionable point in the December 2020 EUCO conclusions (European Council, 2020a). Practically, the EUCO attempted to reinstate its role in the activation mechanism of the RoL conditionality, via point 2(j). Notably, point 2(j) reiterates the importance of a final life-line or emergency brake to countries, whose funds are about to be suspended, pursuant to recital 26 of Regulation 2020/2092. Via this measure presumably, an affected member state could escalate the case to EUCO level provided "the principles of objectivity, non-discrimination and equal treatment" were disrespected in the process of triggering the RoL mechanism by relevant EU institutions (such as the Commission). Hypothetically, the activation of the emergency brake can result in a 3-month delay in rubberstamping the freezing of EU funds, or even the overall suspension of the case (Scheppele et al., 2020). The European Parliament during the trilogues firmly stood by rejecting the inclusion of the so-called emergency brake also dubbed as 'Orbán loop' (Scheppele et al., 2020; Pech & Bárd, 2022: 124), as part of the legally binding articles of Regulation 2020/2092, hence its incorporation only in the recital section. Moreover, the CJEU in the opinion of Advocate General Campos Sánchez-Bordona reasserted that "the preamble to an EU act has no binding legal force and cannot be validly relied on either as a ground for derogating from the actual provisions of the act in question or for interpreting those provisions in a manner clearly contrary to their wording" (Opinion of Advocate General, 2021). In this light, nor recital 26 in the Regulation, neither point 2(j) of the EUCO conclusions have a legal effect—see paragraph 133 and 134 in the Opinion of the Advocate General. The Court's publication was hailed by those scholars, who view the emergency brake as an attempt to create an additional, unnecessary loophole in the regulation (Scheppele et al., 2020; Pech, 2022). In hindsight, it is known that Hungary so far decided not to appeal to recital 26, which quelled inter-institutional contestation and scholarly discontent. However, it cannot be excluded that disputes might resurface (Coman, 2022), should a member state opt for triggering this legally antagonistic provision during the future application of the RoL Regulation.

4 Implementing the Regulation: Continued Contestation

The December 2020 EUCO compromise fuelled scholarly discontent too, especially among those, who would have liked to see in the first place the creation of a wider RoL instrument. They drew attention to an unfair institutional imbalance echoing the EP's criticism (Scheppele, Pech, & Platon, 2020; Schramm & Wessels, 2022), according to which the EUCO embraced a quasi-legislator role in its December 2020 conclusions. Scheppele, Kelemen, and Morijn went as far as requesting the European Commission to trigger the conditionality mechanism immediately (Scheppele et al., 2021: 6). While Alemanno and Chamon (2020) declared that the EUCO acted ultra vires (Alemanno & Chamon, 2020). Provided their appeal was published prior to the CJEU's judgements of Hungary's and Poland's requests for annulment, it essentially encouraged the Commission to disregard the EUCO's conclusions.

Lastly, those who view the December 2020 EUCO conclusions as a linchpin of contestation highlight that the document prescribes certain guidelines for the implementation of the instrument. Thus, the EUCO conclusions can be viewed as an interpretative declaration (Coman, 2022: 230), which not only recalls some legislative tenets in Regulation 2020/2092, but also at times it stipulates additional 'terms and conditions' for its application. For instance, point 2(d) of the conclusion emphasises the mere "subsidiary" nature (Hillion, 2021: 271) of the RoL conditionality mechanism, recalling Article 6(1) of the Regulation with the following statement: "Measures under the mechanism will be considered only where other procedures set out in Union law, including under the Common Provisions Regulation, the Financial Regulation or infringement procedures under the Treaty, would not allow to protect the Union budget more effectively" (European Council, 2020a). Thus, the EUCO conclusions re-emphasise the sheer "last resort" character of the Regulation (Coman, 2022: 231; Kirst, 2021: 108), and hint at the presumption that infringement proceedings still remain the primary tool of dealing with RoL breaches by explicitly listing the instrument (Hillion, 2021).

On a different note, point 2(k) demands that the Regulation should be applicable only under the new Multiannual Financial Framework (MFF) 2021–2027, including Next Generation EU (Łacny, 2021: 80), which is not mentioned in the actual text of Regulation 2020/2092 per se. Again, since the Commission effectively abided by this decision via not touching Hungary's resources from the previous budget cycle when initiating the RoL mechanism, contestation was less apparent about this issue. Nevertheless, it adds further ground to criticising the EUCO for overstepping its treaty role and becoming a quasi-legislator.

Once the CJEU's decisions were delivered (C-156/21 and C-157/21), scholarly discontent somewhat abated. Fisicaro praised the CJEU for delivering a rigorous judgement, and coming to the "rescue of EU political institutions in the RoL battlefield" (Fisicaro, 2022: 352). He equally praised the Court for compartmentalising in well-delineated boxes the EU's RoL tools to dispel any doubts of overlaps especially with Article 7 (Fisicaro, 2022). Albeit, he also pointed out that the Court was too zealous to root the RoL mechanism in Article 322 TFEU, and as a result, the CJEU diminished the Regulation's RoL element to an insignificant component, stating that sanctions "must be lifted where the impact on the implementation of the budget ceases, even though the breaches of the principles of the rule of law may persist" (Fisicaro, 2022: 347). Lastly, Baraggia and Bonelli (2022) emphasised the unintended positive normative consequences of the judgement, such as reaffirming the EU's competences in ensuring judicial independence in its member states, pursuant to Article 19 TEU (Fisicaro, 2022: 147). Furthermore, the case was also an opportunity for the CJEU to "reflect more broadly on the legitimacy of conditionality tools", which was severely neglected during the Eurocrisis (Fisicaro, 2022: 145).

5 Practical Challenges in Applying the New Regulation: The Case of Hungary

The final part of this chapter discusses developments up to December 2023 in the practical application of the RoL conditionality mechanism. It will particularly address the case of Hungary, this being the only member state against which the Commission had at this point chosen to trigger the process. As a result of the Council implementing decision on 15 December 2022 (Council implementing decision 2022), Hungary's portion of the Recovery and Resilience Facility (5.8 billion

EUR in grants) was blocked (see also chapter 5.4)., as well as part of its cohesion funds (6.3 billion EUR). During the necessary consultative phase which was initiated by the Commission on 27 April 2022—also documented in the recital section of the Council implementing act—the relevant Hungarian authorities drew up a reform package with 17 remedial measures to please the Commission and to avoid penalties. The reform plan was quickly condemned as insufficient not only by those who advocate a stiff approach towards RoL breaches (Mészáros & Scheppele, 2022; Scheppele et al., 2022), but also in a letter signed by four members of the EP (MEPs) representing the EPP, the S&D, the Renew and the Greens/EFA party groups (Sarvamaa et al., 2022). Hence, it was widely welcomed when the Commission issued recommendations to the Council on 30 November 2022 to suspend Hungary's RRF funds up until appropriate guarantees are presented to protect the EU's budget. In addition, the Commission also recommended to incorporate 27 super milestones in Hungary's national Resilience and Recovery Plan to improve anti-corruption safeguards, to reform public tenders, to reinforce the prevention and detection of fraud, and to preserve the independence of the judiciary (Schwarcz, 2023 – see Annex 1).

Simultaneously, a few days after the publication of the Council implementing decision, on 22 December the Commission also decided to block the funding of Hungary's programmes under the Cohesion Policy, the Maritime and Fisheries funds, and Home Affairs funds (22 billion EUR) (European Commission, 2023) citing Hungary's incomplete adherence to some horizontal and thematic enabling conditions listed as ex-ante conditionality in Regulation 2021/1060. Ex-ante conditionality which extends to the above-mentioned funds is not unknown, as it was already attached to the previous MFF cycle (Łacny, 2021: 83). Nonetheless, the current budget has been supplemented with some brand-new elements. While academic and media attention concentrated mostly on the widely publicised "drama around the Conditionality Regulation", other RoL-related conditionality mechanisms "were quietly embedded throughout EU law" (Scheppele & Morijn, 2023), for instance through the new Common Provisions Regulation. In particular, when the Commission decided to withhold all of Hungary's cohesion and other funds, its justification invoked a horizontal enabling condition under Regulation 2021/1060. Hungary was criticised for not complying with the EU Charter of Fundamental Rights owing to breaches of judicial freedom, the so-called child-protection law, abuses of academic freedom, and the curtailed rights to seek asylum in the country's territory (Commission, 2023). It should be pointed out that there are some notable overlaps between the reform demands of the Commission in exchange for unfreezing Hungary's cohesion funds, and the above-mentioned 27 super milestones, which govern the unblocking process of Hungary's RRF funds. However, the simultaneous, overlapping implementation of double-conditionality didn't ignite scholarly discussions, apart from some notable exceptions (Kölling, 2022; Scheppele & Morijn, 2023).

The issue regained relevance when Viktor Orbán, Hungary's PM threatened to veto the initiation of Ukraine's official EU membership negotiations, and a novel aid package to the war-ravaged country, which were discussed during the 14–15th December 2023 EUCO summit. Notwithstanding the Hungarian PM's suspected blackmail attempt in the prelude to the gathering (Uitz, 2023), the country's portion of the RRF remained sealed. To the contrary, on 13 December the Commission fostered the unblocking of 10.2 billion EUR worth of cohesion funds, which has already generated an outburst of scholarly criticism (Pavone, 2023; Uitz, 2023). Moreover, inter-institutional calamity between the EP and the Commission is equally again on the horizon, provided MEPs of various political groups were prompt to label the decision as a serious mistake (Bayer, 2023). Besides, the deal wasn't successful, provided Orbán pursued a veto on the aid package, and abstained during the first vote on Ukraine's membership talks. As of now, it is difficult to predict the practical implications of the Commission's lucrative gesture, and the theoretical debates, which may emerge in the scholarly arena as a result of this decision. Nevertheless, some pitfalls in RoL-related conditionality are already visible. Concerns about judicial autonomy were the central pillar of suspending Hungary's RRF, as well as cohesion funds. Therefore, reforms pertaining to restore judicial freedom were extensively mentioned both among the 27 super milestones of the national recovery and resilience plan (see Lupo's chapter in this Volume), and the Commission's demands to respect the horizontal enabling conditions listed under the Common Provisions Regulation (Hegedus, 2023; see also Fasone and Simoncini's chapter in this Volume). The Commission's latest review, which prompted the release of 10.2 billion EUR claims that Hungary has managed to accomplish reforms exactly in the area of overlap between the two criteria (European Commission, 2023). Hence, it can be perceived that the decision to unblock one funding channel, but not the other was at the discretion of the Commission. This and similar ambiguities in the unblocking process together with the peculiar timing of the decision's publication might convey the impression that the Commission indeed gave in to blackmailing. Thus, it can be concluded that the future of the RoL conditionality mechanism is uncertain, provided political games can easily resurface due to issue linkage and unanimity vote.

6 Conclusion

This chapter has provided an overview of both the scholarly debate and the inter-institutional contestation which emerged during the creation and implementation of the RoL conditionality Regulation. In conclusion, a number of findings should be highlighted: first, it is evident that observers do not consider financial conditionality as a panacea in resolving the RoL crisis. As a complementary tool to the structurally weak Article 7, several alternative proposals advocating a variety of RoL instruments have been put forward to address the crisis. Second, the significant discrepancies between the Commission's original proposal and the final shape of the RoL conditionality mechanism ignited fierce academic and institutional debates. The main fault line lay between those who wished to see the creation of a broad RoL instrument with the primary aim of using budgetary sanctions to penalise RoL breach, and those who only wished to see a narrow focus on the protection of the EU's budget. Third, the expansion of the European Council's role both during the decision-making and implementation stages of the Regulation also fuelled some scholarly disagreement.

Finally, even though sanctions had been imposed on Hungary in December 2022—at the time of writing in December 2023 the only case so far—this action has not delivered unequivocally the expected results. Political and academic debate has centred on the—allegedly insufficient—remedy measures proposed by Hungary. Overall, the experience of the drafting, adoption, and implementation of the Conditionality Regulation has divided opinions about the effectiveness of the new mechanism, demonstrating that the use of financial conditionality in the defence of the Rule of Law in the European Union continues to be susceptible to political interference and potential 'blackmail'.

References

Alemanno, A., & Chamon, M. (2020, December 11). To Save the Rule of Law You Must Apparently Break It. *Verfassungsblog*. https://verfassungsblog.de/to-save-the-rule-of-law-you-must-apparently-break-it/. Last Accessed: 22 December 2023.

Baraggia, A., & Bonelli, M. (2022). Linking Money to Values: The New Rule of Law Conditionality Regulation and Its Constitutional Challenges. *German Law Journal, 23*, 131–156.

Bayer, L. (2023, December 13). European Commission Unlocks €10bn for Hungary Despite Criticism from MEPs—As it Happened. *The Guardian*. https://www.theguardian.com/world/live/2023/dec/13/european-union-viktor-orban-ukraine-europe-live. Last Accessed: 22 December 2023.

Caporaso, J. A. (2018). Europe's Triple Crisis and the Uneven Role of Institutions: The Euro, Refugees and Brexit. *Journal of Common Market Studies, 56*(6), 1345–1361.

Christiansen, T., & Hegedus, D. (2023). The Institutional Politics of the European Union's Rule of Law Crisis. In M. Belov (Ed.), *Rule of Law in Crisis* (pp. 131–151). Routledge.

Coman, R. (2022). *The Politics of the Rule of Law in the EU Polity*. Palgrave Macmillan.

Council Implementing Decision 2022/2506 on Measures for the Protection of the Union Budget Against Breaches of the Principles of the Rule of Law in Hungary (2022, December 15). *Official Journal*, L 325/94.

Council of the European Union. (2014, December 16). 3362nd Council Meeting General Affairs (Press release). *PRESSE 652 PR CO 74*. https://www.consilium.europa.eu/media/24763/146348.pdf. Last Accessed: 13 March 2023.

Council of the European Union. (2018, October 25). Opinion of the Legal Services on the Proposal for a Regulation of the European Parliament and of the Council on the Protection of the Union's Budget in Case of Generalised Deficiencies as Regards the rule of Law in the Member States, *13593/18, 2018/0136(COD).*

de Búrca, G. (2022). Poland and Hungary's EU Membership: On Not Confronting Authoritarian Governments. *International Journal of Constitutional Law, 20*(1), 13–34.

de Mesquita, M. J. (2018). European Union values, Rule of Law and the Multiannual Financial Framework 2021–2027. In *ERA Forum* (Vol. 19, pp. 287–294.

European Commission. (2018, May 2). Proposal for a Regulation of the European Parliament and of the Council on the Protection of the Union's Budget in Case of Generalised Deficiencies as Regards the Rule of Law in the Member States, *324 final, 2018/0136 (COD).*

European Commission. (2023, December 13). Commission considers that Hungary's judicial reform addressed deficiencies in judicial independence, but maintains measures on budget conditionality (Press release). https://ec.europa.eu/commission/presscorner/detail/en/ip_23_6465. Last Accessed: 21 December 2023.

European Council. (2020a, December 11). European Council meeting, EUCO 22/20.

European Council. (2020b, July 21). Special meeting of the European Council EUCO 10/20.

European Parliament. (2016). EU Mechanism on Democracy, the Rule of Law and Fundamental Rights P8_TA(2016)0409. https://www.europarl.europa.eu/doceo/document/TA-8-2016-0409_EN.html. Last Accessed: 21 December 2023.

European Parliament. (2020a, July 23). European Parliament Resolution of 23 July 2020 on the Conclusions of the Extraordinary European Council Meeting of 17–21 July 2020, *P9_TA(2020)0206*. https://www.europarl.europa.eu/doceo/document/TA-9-2020-0206_EN.html. Last Accessed: 16 February 2023.

European Parliament. (2020b, October 7). The Establishment of an EU Mechanism on Democracy, The Rule of Law and Fundamental Rights, *P9_TA(2020)0251*. https://eur-lex.europa.eu/legal-content/EN/TXT/?uri=CELEX:52020IP0251. Last Accessed: 13 March 2023.

European Parliament. (2020c, December 17). European Parliament Resolution of 17 December 2020 on the Multiannual Financial Framework 2021–2027, The Interinstitutional Agreement, the EU Recovery Instrument and the Rule of Law Regulation, *P9_TA(2020)0360*. https://eur-lex.europa.eu/legal-content/EN/TXT/?uri=CELEX:52020IP0360. Last Accessed: 16 February 2023.

European Parliament and Council Regulation 2020/2092 on a general regime of conditionality for the protection of the Union budget (2020, December 16). *Official Journal* LI 433/1.

European Parliament and Council Regulation 2021/1060 laying down common provisions on the European Regional Development Fund, the European Social Fund Plus, the Cohesion Fund, the Just Transition Fund and the European Maritime, Fisheries and Aquaculture Fund and financial rules for those and for the Asylum, Migration and Integration Fund, the Internal Security Fund and the Instrument for Financial Support for Border Management and Visa Policy (2022). Official Journal (2021). *Official Journal* L 231/159, 24 June.

Fisicaro, M. (2022). Protection of the Rule of Law and 'Competence Creep' via the Budget: The Court of Justice on the Legality of the Conditionality Regulation. *European Constitutional Law Review, 18*, 334–356.

Germany's Presidency of the Council of the European Union, (2020, October 2). Germany: Working to Promote the Rule of Law in Europe. *Federal Foreign Office*. https://www.auswaertiges-amt.de/en/aussenpolitik/europe/rule-of-law-europe/2341072. Last Accessed: 13 March 2023.

Halmai, G. (2018). The Possibility and Desirability of Rule of Law Conditionality. *Hague Journal Rule of Law, 11*, 171–188.

Hanke Vela, J. (2022, August 2). European Parliament Drops Bid to Force EU Action on Rule-of-law. *Politico*. https://www.politico.eu/article/european-parliament-drop-rule-law-case-against-eu-commission/. Last Accessed: 16 February 2023.

Hegedus, D. (2023, December 21). Same, Same but Different? The Pitfalls in Unfreezing EU Funds. *Verfassungsblog*. https://verfassungsblog.de/same-same-but-different/

Hillion, C. (2021). Compromising (On) the General Conditionality Mechanism and the Rule of Law. *Common Market Law Review, 58*(2), 267–284.

Hungary v Parliament and Council. (2022, February 16). Case no. C-156/21, Judgement of the Court. https://eur-lex.europa.eu/legal-content/EN/TXT/PDF/?uri=CELEX:62021CJ0156&from=EN. Last Accessed: 18 February 2023.

Kelemen, D. (2020). The European Union's Authoritarian Equilibrium. *Journal of European Public Policy, 27*(3), 481–499.

Kirst, N. (2021). Rule of Law Conditionality: The Long-Awaited Step Towards a Solution of the Rule of Law Crisis in the European Union? *European Papers, 6*(1), 101–110.

Kochenov, V. D. (2017). Busting the Myths Nuclear: A Commentary on Article 7 TEU. *EUI Working Papers*, LAW2017/10.

Kochenov V. D., & Pech L. (2015, January 20). From Bad to Worse? On the Commission and the Council's Rule of Law Initiatives. *Verfassungsblog*. https://verfassungsblog.de/bad-worse-commission-councils-rule-law-initiatives/. Last Accessed: 16 February 2023.

Kölling, M. (2022). The Role of (Rule of Law) Conditionality in MFF 2021–2027 and Next Generation EU, or the Stressed Budget. *Journal of Contemporary European Studies*. https://doi.org/10.1080/14782804.2022.2059654?scroll=top&needAccess=true. Last Accessed: 22 December 2023.

Łacny, J. (2021). The Rule of Law Conditionality Under Regulation No 2092/2020—Is it all About the Money? *Hague Journal Rule of Law, 13*, 79–105.

Mészáros, G., & Scheppele, K. L. (October 6, 2022). How NOT to Be an Independent Agency The Hungarian Integrity Authority. *Verfassungsblog*. https://verfassungsblog.de/how-not-to-be-an-independent-agency/. Last Accessed: 22 December 2023.

Müller, J.-W. (2015). Should the EU Protect Democracy and The Rule of Law Inside Member States? *European Law Journal, 21*(2), 141–160.

Opinion of Advocate General. (2021, December 2). Case no. C-156/21, Sánchez-Bordona. https://curia.europa.eu/juris/document/document.jsf?docid=250424&doclang=EN. Last Accessed: 21 December 2023.

Pavone, T. (2023, December 17). The EU's Faustian Bargain. *Verfassungsblog*. https://verfassungsblog.de/the-eus-faustian-bargain/. Last Accessed: 21 December 2023.

Pech, L. (2022, February 16). No More Excuses. *Verfassungsblog*. https://verfassungsblog.de/no-more-excuses/. Last Accessed: 22 December 2023.

Pech, L., & Bárd P. (2022). The Commission's Rule of Law Report and The EU Monitoring and Enforcement of Article 2 TEU Values, EP Study Requested by the LIBE and AFCO Committees. https://www.europarl.europa.eu/RegData/etudes/STUD/2022/727551/IPOL_STU(2022)727551_EN.pdf. Last Accessed: 22 December 2023.

Pech, L., Wachowiec, P., & Mazur, D. (2021). Poland's Rule of Law Breakdown: A Five-Year Assessment of EU's (In)Action. *Hague Journal of the Rule of Law, 13*, 1–34.

Poland v Parliament and Council. (2022, February 16). Case no. C-157/21, Judgement of the Court. https://eur-lex.europa.eu/legal-content/EN/TXT/PDF/?uri=CELEX:62021CJ0157&from=EN. Last Accessed: 18 February 2023.

Sarvamaa, P., Gardiazabal, E., Körner, M., & Freund, D. (2022, November 17). The 7.5 Billion Euro Question: Did the Hungarian Government Implement the Necessary Reforms to Avoid Rule of Law Sanctions?, EP Open Letter. https://www.politico.eu/wp-content/uploads/2022/11/17/17-assessment-final.pdf. Last Accessed: 22 December 2022.

Scheppele, K. L. (2016). Enforcing the Basic Principles of EU Law Through Systemic Infringement Actions. In C. Closa & D. V. Kochenov (Eds.), *Reinforcing Rule of Law Oversight in the European Union* (pp. 105–130). Cambridge University Press.

Scheppele, K. L., Kelemen, D., & Morijn, J. (2021, July 7). The EU Commission has to Cut Funding to Hungary: The Legal Case. *Study funded by the Greens/EFA Group of the EP*. https://www.greens-efa.eu/en/article/document/the-eu-commission-has-to-cut-funding-to-hungary-the-legal-case. Last Accessed: 16 February 2023.

Scheppele, K. L., Kochenov, D. V., & Grabowska-Moroz, B. (2020). EU Values Are Law, After All: Enforcing EU Values Through Systemic Infringement Actions by the European Commission and the Member States of the European Union. *Yearbook of European Law, 39*(1), 3–121.

Scheppele, K. L., Mészáros, G., & Bárd, P. (2022, October 26). Useless and Maybe Unconstitutional: Hungary's Proposed Judicial Review of the Prosecutorial Decisions. *Verfassungsblog*. https://verfassungsblog.de/useless-and-maybe-unconstitutional/. Last Accessed: 22 December 2023.

Scheppele, K. L., & Morijn, J. (2023, June) What Price Rule of Law? *The Rule of Law in the EU: Crisis and Solutions SIEPS Report*, June. https://www.sieps.se/en/publications/2023/the-rule-of-law-in-the-eu-crisis-and-solutions/. Last Accessed: 22 December 2023.

Scheppele, K. L., Pech, L., & Platon, S. (2020, December 13). Compromising the Rule of Law While Compromising on the Rule of Law. *Verfassungsblog*. https://verfassungsblog.de/compromising-the-rule-of-law-while-compromising-on-the-rule-of-law/. Last Accessed: 16 February 2023.

Schramm, L., & W. Wessels. (2022). The European Council as a Crisis Manager and Fusion Driver: Assessing the EU's Fiscal Response to the COVID-19 Pandemic. *Journal of European Integration*, 1–17.

Schwarcz, A. (2023, January 24). Rule of law-related 'Super Milestones' in the Recovery and Resilience Plans of Hungary and Poland, EP Briefing. https://www.europarl.europa.eu/thinktank/en/document/IPOL_BRI(2023)741581. Last Accessed: 22 December 2023.

Sedelmeier, U. (2016). Political Safeguards Against Democratic Backsliding in the EU: The Limits of Material Sanctions and the Scope of Social Pressure. *Journal of European Public Policy, 24*(3), 337–351.

Staudinger, I. (2022). The Rise and Fall of the Rule of Law Conditionality. *European Papers, 7*(2), 721–737.

Tidey, A. (2022, December 13). Hungary Agrees Deal and Lifts Veto on €18bn EU Aid Package for Ukraine, Euronews. https://www.euronews.com/my-europe/2022/12/13/hungary-lifts-vetoes-on-ukraine-aid-and-corporate-tax-to-lower-frozen-eu-funds. Last Accessed: 16 February 2023.

Uitz, R. (2023, December 15). Orbán's Veto Play—The Subsidiarity Card. *Verfassungsblog*. https://verfassungsblog.de/orbans-veto-play-the-subsidiarity-card/. Last Accessed: 21 December 2023.

Vita, V. (2017). Revisiting the Dominant Discourse on Conditionality in the EU: The Case of EU Spending Conditionality. *Cambridge Yearbook of European Legal Studies, 19*, 116–143.

von Bogdandy, A., Kottmann, M., Antpöhler, C., Dickschen, J., Hentrei, S., & Smrkolj, M. (2012). Reverse Solange—Protectign the Essence of Fundamental Rights Against EU Member States. *Common Market Law Review, 49*, 489–520.

von Bogdandy, A., & Łacny, J. (2020, June). Suspension of EU Funda for Breaching the Rule of Law—a Dose fo Tough Love Needed? *SIEPS European Policy Analysis,* (7eps), 1–15.

Zeitlin, J., Nicoli, F., & Laffan, B. (2019). Introduction: The European Union Beyond the Polycrisis? Integration and Politicization in an Age of Shifting Cleavages. *Journal of European Public Policy, 26*(7), 963–976.

CHAPTER 15

The Recovery and Resilience Facility and Its Effects on the Rule of Law Conditionality: A (Potentially) Well-Functioning Connection

Nicola Lupo

1 Introduction

The final steps of the adoption of the "Rule of Law Regulation" (EU, Euratom) 2020/2092 of the Parliament and of the Council of 16 December 2020 (see Hegedus' and Christiansen's chapter, in this volume) occurred concurrently with the approval of the measures aimed at addressing the economic consequences of the COVID-19 pandemic (encompassed in the Next Generation EU package: NGEU). The most important of these measures was the Recovery and Resilience Facility (RRF), established and regulated by the Regulation (EU) 2020/2094 of the Council of 14 December 2020 and the Regulation (EU) 2021/241 of the European Parliament and of the Council of 12 February 2021.

N. Lupo (✉)
LUISS University, Rome, Italy
e-mail: nlupo@luiss.it

C. Fasone et al. (eds.), *EU Rule of Law Procedures at the Test Bench*, Palgrave Studies in European Union Politics,
https://doi.org/10.1007/978-3-031-60008-1_15

As often happens, the temporal overlapping of the negotiation of the two sets of legal instruments was relevant for the Member States reaching an agreement. It was the European Council of 10–11 December 2020 which gave the green light to the Regulation 2020/2092 and also to the new Multiannual Financial Framework (MFF) and the Own Resources Decision, which included the authorization to establish the RRF. Moreover, as will be observed, the compromise reached at that moment included a postponement of the full implementation of that Regulation, in order to overcome the resistance to its approval of Hungary and Poland (who instrumentally opposed the approval of the new MFF, which required unanimity on the basis of Article 312(2) TFEU).

The purpose of this chapter is to highlight how the RRF—viewed as an innovative Euro-national procedure for using financial resources intended to trigger national reforms and investments according to a new "method of government"—interacts with the implementation of the "Rule of Law Regulation". Indeed, compliance with the—then just approved—Rule of Law Regulation (No. 2020/2092), required during the implementation of the National Recovery and Resilience Plans, constitutes a significant and often overlooked element of this new "method of government". This is an element that, as will be discussed, strengthens the conditionality already embedded in this Regulation and is capable of having a meaningful impact in ensuring more effective protection of the Rule of Law in problematic Member States (MS).

2 The Genesis of NGEU and RRF: The Reaction to the Pandemic and Beyond

The RRF constitutes the most significant element of the NGEU. This was the package issued by the European Union, between the second half of 2020 and the first months of 2021, in order to address the economic consequences of the COVID-19 pandemic. After some initial hesitations, the EU decided to not only relax or suspend the financial rules that were previously in force, but also to start a common action comprising new reforms and investments carried out at the national level, using EU funds and framed according to supranational priorities and targets.

As often happens, a crisis offers the opportunity to overcome veto powers. In this case, there was resistance to allowing EU debt issuance to be used as a tool for financing the EU budget and to expanding EU spending conditionality across various sectors (Howard-Schild 2021).

Although conceived as a one-off temporary instrument, the RRF has a time-horizon of more than 5 years (until 31 December 2026). Most significantly, the RRF is the culmination of debates and proposals which had been developed in the European Union during the preceding 10 years.

These features explain why the original "method of government" that the RRF put in place has been deemed, by many, to represent a turning point (Fabbrini, 2022: 36), if not a "Hamiltonian moment", as was argued by the then German Minister of Finance, Olaf Scholz, proposing a parallel with the US construction of a federal public debt at the end of the XVIII century (Lionello, 2020: 22).

Given its encouraging start in the years 2021 and 2022, the same "method of government" has been extended to address new emergencies, such as the energy crisis arising from the war in Ukraine (through the REPowerEU package), and has also inspired, at least in part, the reform of the Stability and Growth Pact underway at the time of writing, intended to be applied during ordinary times.

3 The "New Method of Government", Founded on an Innovative Interpretation of the Legal Bases

As a result of the RRF, the Union has, for the first time, borrowed large quantities of resources from the markets to finance, through grants and loans, a series of reforms and investments in each MS, co-determined with them. The disbursement of these resources to each MS has been made conditional upon the satisfactory achievement of a series of measures, defined through milestones and targets, to be implemented over a five-year period, until 31 December 2026, in accordance with a precise timetable, codified in the individual NRRPs and in the operational arrangements that accompany them.

This "new method of government" has been designed according to mechanisms of spending conditionality, which began to be tested as tools of EU internal governance in the second half of the previous decade (Baraggia, 2015) but which, under NGEU and the RRF, fundamentally depart from the problematic standard of strict conditionality experienced during the Eurocrisis and the rescue programmes (see Fasone and Simoncini, in this Volume). The new method, instead, has considerable potential to ensure the coexistence of and complementarity between EU-wide and domestic priorities (Vita, 2017).

The Union's borrowing of resources to fund investments in individual MS, which had not happened for years, was promoted to address the economic consequences of the COVID-19 pandemic and to foster recovery, making use of a creative interpretation of Treaty provisions. The adoption of NGEU has been described as an exercise in "creative legal engineering", aimed at allowing "a major shift in EU economic policy" (De Witte, 2021: 653 ff.). Due to the substantial impossibility of revising the Treaties, an evolutive interpretation had to be quickly devised to enable the Union to financially support the recovery of its economy.

The European Commission based the draft legislative acts comprising the NGEU on a multi-faceted legal constellation (Fabbrini, 2022: 46). The legal basis for the first two Regulations adopted to deal with the COVID-19 pandemic was identified as being Article 122 TFEU.[1] To this end, an innovative interpretation of Article 122 TFEU was proposed, relying on the joint reading of both its paragraphs (Cannizzaro, 2020). On the one hand, paragraph 1, recalling the "spirit of solidarity between Member States", lacked any concrete effect in the legislative practice until 2020 (Chamon, 2023; Flynn, 2019). On the other hand, paragraph 2 of Article 122 TFEU has been interpreted broadly in so far as it allows the European Union to grant "financial assistance", under certain conditions, to an MS which "is in difficulties or is seriously threatened with severe difficulties caused by natural disasters or exceptional occurrences beyond its control". This last clause, which had already been used as a legal basis for Regulation No 407/2010 of 11 May 2010, establishing the European Financial Stabilization Mechanism (EFSM), has been very extensively reinterpreted and referred not to a single MS, but to all of them, as all were "in difficulties" due to the pandemic (Chamon, 2023).

The legal basis of Regulation (EU) 2021/241, which established the RRF, is provided, instead, by Article 175 (3) TFEU, which allows for specific actions other than those implemented through structural funds, which are also aimed at strengthening economic, social and territorial cohesion. The RRF falls within the scope of Article 175(3): financed in

[1] Article 122 TFEU is referred to by Council Regulation (EU) 2020/672 of 19 May 2020, which, in the very first months following the COVID-19 outbreak, established a European instrument for temporary support to mitigate unemployment risks in the state of emergency (SURE), as well as by Council Regulation (EU) 2020/2094 of 14 December 2020, which established the EU recovery instrument, and determined the amount of resources mobilised for that purpose.

part by resources allocated under cohesion policies, and in part through borrowing. This debt is justified by the exceptional nature of the measure. Moreover, the governance for the design and the implementation of the RRF follows procedural rules which are largely different from those providing for the use of the structural funds, despite having both general and specific objectives in common.

Such an innovative and creative use of the legal bases has evoked criticism by scholars who have questioned the respect of the principles of financial responsibility (art. 125 TFEU) and of balanced budget (art. 310 TFEU). Indeed, it has been argued that, in order to legitimise such a paradigm shift, a Treaty reform is required, so as to transparently strengthen the Union's fiscal integration and to create an autonomous fiscal capacity, in full compliance with the Treaty provisions and their underpinning rationale (Leino-Sandberg & Ruffert, 2022). At the same time, other scholars (Crowe, 2021; De Witte, 2022) have defended the legitimacy and appropriateness of this interpretative effort, which was first carried out by the legal services of the EU institutions, arguing that it does not exceed the significance of the Treaty provisions currently in force.

4 Further Features of the "New Method of Government"

In addition to the common borrowing of resources from financial markets and to the creative use of the Treaty's legal bases, the "new method of government" designed by the RRF is characterised by at least other three features (Fasone & Lupo, 2023).

First, the reforms and investments are specified in performance-based medium-term Plans, so that the flow of the actual payments is not linked to the costs incurred, but to the "satisfactory achievement" of milestones and targets, as assessed by the European Commission. This is a crucial element that has not featured to a significant degree in the (mainly national) discussions regarding the RRF, which is often presented, not much differently from cohesion policies, as "European funds" to be spent. Similarly, there has been inadequate reflection at the EU level on the several critical issues which emerged during the previous experience of performance-based financing (Zeitlin et al., 2023: 14 ff).

Second, the combination between supranational and national elements in drafting and implementing the NRRPs ensures a much more effective coordination of fiscal policy priorities. The Plans are, indeed, dependent upon the respect of macro-objectives of various kinds set by the EU on a general level (cohesion policies, green and digital transitions, rule of law principles, country-specific recommendations, energy autonomy), but detailed and spontaneously submitted by every MS who intends, according to each domestic context, to make use of those resources. This means that the selection of priorities and the design of national Plans helped to shape and actualise the common interest, also considering citizens' perspectives (Bobic, 2023: 202). In doing so, they address the dissociation and close the gap between responsibility and responsiveness, that had emerged in the response to the Eurocrisis in the previous decade (Crespy et al., 2023). Therefore, each MS should clearly take responsibility for and "ownership" of the contents of each Plan, avoiding any possibility to use the EU as a scapegoat. At the same time, the "method of government" of the RRF circumvents the impression (and the potential criticism underlying it) that the reforms in the Plans were merely suggested by obscure bureaucrats in Brussels—or by "an old boring aunt that tells you what to do"—that has often accompanied the Country-Specific Recommendations issued within the European Semester (Bockhorst, 2022: 108).

Third, the framing of the Plans, their modification, and their implementation rely on a constant and continuous bilateral dialogue, at a technical as well at a political level, established between the European Commission and the institutions (especially the Government) of each MS, with the involvement of the Council only for the final adoption and modifications of the Plans (and then, through its Economic and Financial Committee, during the assessment of each request for payment).[2]

It is possibly too early to tell whether this "new method of government" is going to stabilise itself, and thus create a third—and to a certain extent intermediate—decision-making model between the intergovernmental and the community methods. It has some potentialities as it is centred on the European Commission (and other EU institutions) like the community method, but it involves each national Government in a bilateral dialogue with the Commission and, within this dialogue, in defining crucial policy choices regarding the design, submission, and implementation of each national Plan. However, given the very satisfactory initial

[2] See Art. 24 Regulation 2021/241. The Economic and Financial Committee is an advisory body to the Council composed of high-level officials from national finance ministries.

steps of the RRF, this "method of government" has been used—as already observed—without any variation to address the consequences of the war in Ukraine on energy autonomy, but with some adaptations in relation to other policy fields: namely, the management of the European Social Climate Fund[3] and the new Stability and Growth Pact.

5 The Connection with the Rule of Law Conditionality According to the Legal Provisions (Article 8 Regulation 2021/241)

The key legal provision ensuring a point of contact between the RRF and the Rule of Law conditionality is Article 8 of Regulation 2021/241, according to which "The Facility shall be implemented by the Commission in direct management in accordance with the relevant rules adopted pursuant to Article 322 TFEU, in particular the Financial Regulation and the Regulation (EU, Euratom) 2020/2092 of the European Parliament and of the Council".

At first glance, it may look like a second-order provision, just aimed at recalling the existence of the Treaty provision regarding the implementation of the EU budget, and of the (just adopted) "Rule of Law Regulation". On the contrary, it represents a crucial element of the new "method of government": it ensures that compliance with the "Rule of Law Regulation" is a general condition for each MS to obtain from the European Commission the payment of the agreed instalments. As many had hoped (Dermine, 2022: 345), this provision arguably results in the ultimate convergence of the worlds of the Rule of Law and of Economic Governance.

However, as Article 8 refers exclusively to the *implementation* of the RRF, it must be noted that compliance with Regulation 2020/2092 is not intended to be a proper legal pre-requisite for the *approval* of the Recovery and Resilience Plans by the EU institutions. Indeed, formalising such a legal pre-requisite for the approval of the Plan would probably

[3] See Regulation (EU) 2023/955 of the European Parliament and of the Council of 10 May 2023 establishing a Social Climate Fund and amending Regulation (EU) 2021/1060, OJ L 130, 16.5.2023, p. 1–51: The use of the Fund, which will become fully operational in 2025, is tied to a very similar scheme as the RRF, centred on National Social Climate Plans.

have made more sense, in theory. However, it was not feasible in practice, due to the commitment made by the European Commission not to propose any measure according to the new Regulation 2020/2092 until the Court of Justice of the European Union had delivered its judgments on the actions for annulment brought by Hungary and Poland against it (Thu Nguyen, 2020: 4). It is worth remembering that this commitment—harshly criticised especially from a legal perspective (Alemanno & Chamon, 2020; *contra* et al., 2020; Scheppele et al., 2020; Thu Nguyen, 2020)—was ultimately crucial to reaching the compromise, within the European Council, needed to approve the Multiannual Financial Framework 2021–2027, and thus to defining the financial aspect of the Next Generation EU (Baraggia & Bonelli, 2021: 132 f.; Coman, 2022: 232 f.; Hillion, 2021: 272 f.; Pinelli, 2021: 55 f.; Hegedus and Christiansen in this Volume). Consequently, the several intertwinements between RRF and Rule of Law policies, even at the level of highly political decisions, were confirmed.

It is thus solely during the implementation phase that the compliance with the Rule of Law needs to be verified by the Commission, which is responsible for ensuring that the actual payments of the RRF funds are conditional upon a positive assessment of the milestones that are deemed essential from a Rule of Law perspective. As will be remarked, the exclusive focus on the implementation phase has allowed the EU institutions to approve, albeit after long negotiations, the Recovery and Resilience Plans of Poland and Hungary, but has made it very difficult for them to implement the Plans and thus to submit their first requests for payments.

For the sake of completeness, a somewhat reciprocal connection is also indicated by one of the "whereas clauses" of Regulation 2020/2092 (no. 7), which features wording that seems to be entirely compatible with Article 8 Regulation 2021/241 (Scheppele & Morijn, 2022, refer to "nearly identical language"): "Whenever Member States implement the Union budget, including resources allocated through the European Union Recovery Instrument established pursuant to Council Regulation (EU) 2020/2094, and through loans and other instruments guaranteed by the Union budget, and whatever method of implementation they use, respect for the rule of law is an essential precondition for compliance with the principles of sound financial management enshrined in Article 317 of the Treaty on the Functioning of the European Union (TFEU)". However, within the text of Regulation 2020/2092 there is no specific provision confirming this connection, and indeed it could not have been otherwise as the procedure for the RRF was still yet to be regulated in December 2020. That is why, if one looks solely at the legal provisions, the bridge between the two instruments appeared exclusively in Regulation 2021/241 and specifically in the abovementioned Article 8 thereof, which was, at that time, still in the final stages of its approval process.

6 The Connection Between Rule of Law and RRF Conditionality Regimes in the Commission's Rule of Law 2022 and 2023 Annual Reports

The third annual Rule of Law Report was released by the European Commission on 13 July 2022 (on the first two see Pech & Bárd, 2022 and Citino in this Volume). That is, it was published only once the CJEU had rejected the actions for annulment brought by Hungary and Poland through its judgments of 16 February 2022 (cases C-156–2021 and C-157–2021, respectively, on which, see, e.g., Bonelli, 2022; Fisicaro, 2022; and Hegedus and Christiansen in this Volume). Its release also followed the approval, on 14 June 2022, of the Polish NRRP, at the end of a rather controversial process (for a strong critical voice against the Commission see Pech, 2022), which even triggered several lawsuits by the four main European judges' associations to the EU General Court for the annulment of the Council's approval of the Polish NRRP and then of the Financing and Loan Agreements.[4]

The 2022 Rule of Law Report included, for the first time, country-specific recommendations (CSR) (see Capati and Christiansen in this Volume). Through these recommendations, the Commission asked each MS to tackle and solve the problems observed during the Rule of Law assessment. This means that each MS has been the recipient of several recommendations. What needs to be highlighted, in order to verify the connection between the two kinds of conditionality, is primarily the opening clause of each list of country-specific recommendations.

For a first group of MS (Austria, Denmark, Estonia, Finland, France, Germany, Ireland, Lithuania, Luxembourg, the Netherlands, and Sweden), a very general sentence is used: "It is recommended to [*name of the country*] to: (...)".

[4] See cases T-530/22 to T-533/22 (on which Donaire Villa, 2022) and case T-116/23, respectively.

For a second group of MS (Belgium, Bulgaria, Croatia, Cyprus, Czechia, Greece, Italy, Latvia, Malta, Portugal, Romania, Slovakia, Slovenia, and Spain), the clause recalls the need to comply with additional commitments deriving from the NRRPs and other instruments already activated in order to improve the compliance with the Rule of Law Regulation. These CSR are preceded by the following clause: "In addition to recalling the commitments made under the national Recovery and Resilience Plan relating to certain aspects of the justice system [and the anti-corruption framework], it is recommended to [*name of the country*] (…)". In the cases of Bulgaria and Romania, a reference is also made to "the remaining commitments under the Cooperation and Verification Mechanism", to recall the pre-existing obligations assumed by these two countries, following their accessions, to make progress in the fields of judicial reform, corruption and (for Bulgaria) the fight against the organised crime (see Dirri in this Volume).

Finally, in the cases of Hungary and Poland, these opening clauses are even more detailed and stringent. For Poland, the following clause is adopted: "In addition to recalling the need to address the serious concerns relating to judicial independence, in particular those set out in the Article 7 TEU procedure initiated by the Commission, as well as the obligation to comply with the rule of law-related rulings of the CJEU and the rule of law-related infringement procedures referred to in the country chapter, the commitments made under the National Recovery and Resilience Plan relating to certain aspects of the justice system and the checks and balances, and recalling the relevant country-specific recommendations under the European Semester, it is recommended to Poland to (…)".

The formulation adopted for Hungary is rather similar, although the reference to the NRRP is missing, obviously given the fact that, at the time of the publication of the 2022 Rule of Law Report (13 July 2022), the Hungarian Plan had been submitted but not yet approved: "In addition to recalling the obligation to comply with the rule of law-related rulings of the CJEU and the rule of law-related infringement procedures referred to in the country chapter, the concerns raised under the conditionality regulation, the relevant concerns raised in the Article 7 TEU procedure initiated by the European Parliament, and recalling the relevant country-specific recommendations under the European Semester, it is recommended to Hungary to (…)".

The Hungarian Plan, submitted on 12 May 2021, and re-submitted twice following the receipt of comments by the Commission, was indeed the last to be approved, on 15 December 2022.

Also in this case, the decision of the Council evoked criticisms (Scheppele & Morijn, 2022). At the same time, the Council decided to suspend approximately €6.3 billion in budgetary commitments, as a measure for the protection of the Union budget in compliance with Regulation 2020/2092, as a consequence of Hungary's breaches of the principles of the rule of law, concerning public procurement, the effectiveness of prosecutorial action and the fight against corruption. The Commission had in fact requested the suspension of a larger volume of funds, amounting to €7.5 billion (65% of the commitments for three operational programmes under the cohesion policy, while the Council lowered it to 55%).

Not by chance, in the following annual report, the 2023 Rule of Law Report, issued by the European Commission on 5 July 2023, the opening statement regarding Hungary also recalled "the commitments made under the national Recovery and Resilience Plan relating to certain aspects of the justice system, the anti-corruption framework and the checks and balances", in addition to several other recommendations: i.e., the obligation to comply with the rule of law-related rulings of the CJEU and the rule of law-related infringement procedures referred to in the country chapter, the concerns raised under the conditionality regulation, the relevant concerns raised in the Article 7 TEU procedure initiated by the European Parliament [...] the relevant country-specific recommendations under the European Semester".

For the rest, the overall scheme is similar to the previous annual report: the RRF conditionalities are recalled in the opening statements relating to Bulgaria, Croatia, Cyprus, Czechia, Greece, Italy, Malta, Portugal, Romania, Slovenia, Slovakia, and Spain. By contrast with the 2022 report, Belgium and Latvia are not subject to such references. While for the former there is no reason for this omission, the country report for the latter in fact refers to the ongoing preparatory work regarding the establishment of the Academy of Justice, in compliance with a milestone under Latvia's Recovery and Resilience Plan requiring the establishment of a unified training centre for the development of qualifications for judges, prosecutors, and investigators.[5]

[5] See 2023 *Rule of Law Report. Country Chapter on the rule of law situation in Latvia* (SWD(2023) 814 final, Brussels, 5 July 2023, p. 7.

7 The NRRPs of Poland and Hungary and Their First "Super-Milestones" Concerning Rule of Law Reforms

It is still too soon to ascertain whether, and if so how, Poland and Hungary have complied with the reforms promised in their NRRPs. What can be noted is that, as of December 2023, Hungary still has to submit its first payment requests and Poland, as already recalled, has just submitted its first. This means that the implementation is very slow or is not proceeding at all, and that neither of the two countries has yet had access to any (original) funds allocated by the RRF, in addition to the suspension of reimbursement for the structural and investment funds following the violation by the two countries of the Charter enabling condition under the Common Provisions Regulation (see Fasone and Simoncini in this Volume).

It is noteworthy that neither the Polish nor the Hungarian plans have anticipated any pre-financing: this is formally due to an objective reason. The two plans were both approved after December 2021, which was set as the deadline for pre-financing. This means that the actual disbursement of the funds originally allocated to the two MS requires a positive assessment by the Commission of the first group of reforms included in the Plan.

In particular, as the Polish Plan identified among the very first milestones, to be accomplished (in theory) by the second trimester of 2022, both the reform aimed at "strengthening the independence and impartiality of courts" and the reform "to remedy the situation of judges affected by the decisions of the Disciplinary Chamber of the Supreme Court in disciplinary cases and judicial immunity cases", the actual disbursement of funds by the Commission to Poland will necessarily follow a positive assessment of the implementation of these reforms, clearly deemed essential from a Rule of Law perspective.

Hungary's Plan, submitted to the Commission three times, includes, in its final version, 29 reforms related to the rule of law: establishing an integrity authority and an anti-corruption task force; drafting a national anti-corruption strategy and action plan; strengthening judicial review; eradicating healthcare bribery; developing an electronic public procurement system to increase transparency; enhancing the transparency of public spending; drafting an anti-fraud and anti-corruption strategy for the use of EU funds; enhancing cooperation with the European Anti-Fraud Office-OLAF; tax reforms; and justice system reforms. Furthermore, as Hungary failed, by the agreed deadline of 19 November 2022, to adequately implement central aspects of the necessary 17 remedial measures agreed under the general conditionality mechanism (related to the effectiveness of the newly established Integrity Authority and the procedure for the judicial review of prosecutorial decisions), these measures, together with other rule of law reforms related to judicial independence, have been characterised as 27 "super-milestones" (Schwarcz, 2023; see also Hegedus and Christiansen in this Volume). This means that no payment will be forthcoming under the RRF until Hungary has fully and appropriately implemented those "super-milestones".

Both the Polish and Hungarian Recovery and Resilience Plans have been updated and modified according to the Regulation (EU) 2023/435 of the European Parliament and of the Council of 27 February 2023 (REPowerEU). In this way both Poland and Hungarian were able to obtain their quota of pre-financing, calculated having regard to the additional volume of resources assigned to increase the Union's energy security and energy independence, after the war in Ukraine. Concurrently, based on a partially positive report from the Commission regarding its judicial reforms, that addressed some deficiencies in judicial independence (including the removal of the possibility for the Supreme Court to review questions that judges intend to refer to the European Court of Justice),[6] Hungary obtained the unblocking of a portion of the cohesion funds that had been suspended the previous year. This was the doing of the European Commission, probably in exchange for removing the Hungarian veto on the mid-term review of the MFF and on the accession of Ukraine to the EU, which was the subject of several criticisms, also on the part of the European Parliament (Hegedus, 2023; Pavone, 2023).

However, the biggest portion of the funding destined for Poland and Hungary still depends on the receipt of a fully positive assessment by the European Commission of the satisfactory achievement of the "super-milestones" regarding reforms related to the Rule of Law.

[6] See the Commission's press release of 13 December 2023: https://ec.europa.eu/commission/presscorner/detail/en/ip_23_6465.

8 Conclusion: The Good Functioning of the Financial Conditionality in the October 2023 Polish Elections

One of the critical issues regarding the effectiveness of financial conditionality under the RRF—used, as has just been discussed, to also strengthen the CSRs regarding the Rule of Law—relates to the coordination between its timeframe and the national political-electoral cycles (Lupo, 2023). The need for such a temporal coordination is often overlooked, despite being crucial for the success of the "new method of government", based upon a continuous bilateral dialogue between the European Commission and each MS.

To understand the importance of this temporal coordination, it suffices to observe that conditions agreed between the EU institutions and a certain national government, especially if they imply controversial reforms specified within multi-annual performance plans, often need to be implemented by a different national government from the one which committed itself to these reforms, depending on the results of national elections or on a variation of the parliamentary majority which may have occurred in the meantime. In democratic systems, multi-year planning is indispensable for a rational use of financial resources. In order to not fall victim to "short-termism", medium-term plans cannot ignore the preferences expressed by citizens at the time of elections, nor those resulting from the ups and downs of the relationship between Parliaments and Governments.

Examples of this kind have arisen several times since the adoption of the National Recovery and Resilience Plans, which took place between 2021 and 2022. One of the clearest has been the Italian case, because of the transition from the Draghi Government to the Meloni Government, following the elections held on 22 September 2022.

Despite the clear political discontinuity, the management of the transition, as far as the implementation of the NRRP is concerned, has been rather successful. The fact that the Draghi Government maintained its role of "technical government" until the end of its mandate allowed for an intense period of activity of the resigning Government and the Parliament even after its dissolution and pending the elections. The Meloni Government, albeit in the context of a different political direction, as announced since the parliamentary debate on confidence, decided not to repudiate the main commitments made with the Plan, although it aimed to amend the Plan according to the procedure outlined in Regulation 2021/241 (and later expanded by Regulation 2023/435), and to adjust the internal governance for its implementation of the Plan (responding to a new Minister, for EU affairs, cohesion policies and NRRP) (Lupo, 2023).

Even more interesting, especially from a perspective focused on the Rule of Law issues, is the case of Poland, after the outcome of the election held on 15 October 2023. It seems that the delayed payments for the lack of implementation of the RRF have weakened the Morawiecki Government and the PIS (which obtained a relative majority of seats, although not enough to form a coalition supported by a majority of MPs). As has been noted (Wójcik, 2023: 40), electors in Poland (as well as elsewhere, indeed) are generally much more sensible to the actual incoming of financial resources than to criticisms or infringement procedures regarding the "mere" respect for the Rule of Law.

In this context, it is quite likely that the political direction of the new Tusk Government, supported by political forces that were once in opposition to one another, will consist first and foremost in the implementation of a NRRP proposed and negotiated by the previous Government supported by PiS, which consequently should not contrast these reforms too harshly, at least in theory.[7] Should this be the case, we will witness another rather fruitful intersection and coordination between the RRF and the political-electoral cycle.

References

Alemanno, A., & Chamon, M. (2020, December 11).To Save the Rule of Law You Must Apparently Break It. *VerfBlog*.

Baraggia, A., & Bonelli, M. (2021). Linking Money to Values: The New Rule of Law Conditionality Regulation and its Constitutional Challenges. *German Law Journal, 23*(2), 131–156.

Baraggia, A. (2015). Conditionality Measures Within the Euro Area Crisis: A Challenge to the Democratic Principle? *Cambridge International Law Journal, 4*(2), 268–288.

Bobic. (2023). *The Individual in the Economic and Monetary Union*. Cambridge University Press.

[7] Not by chance, on 15 December 2023, the first payment request for the RRF was submitted by the new Polish Government, which had been voted in by the Parliament just 4 days prior (https://ec.europa.eu/commission/presscorner/detail/en/mex_23_6643).

Bockhorst. (2022). The Influence of the European Semester: Case Study Analysis and Lessons for its Post-Pandemic Transformation. *Journal of Common Market Studies, 60*(1), 101–117.

Bonelli, M. (2022). Constitutional Language and Constitutional Limits: The Court of Justice Dismisses the Challenges to the Budgetary Conditionality Regulation. *European Papers, 7*(2), 507–525.

Cannizzaro, E. (2020). Neither Representation nor Taxation? Or, "Europe's Moment"—Part I. 2 *European Papers, 5*(2), 703–706.

Chamon, M. (2023, February 1). The rise of Article 122 TFEU. *VerfBlog.*

Coman, R. (2022). *The Politics of the Rule of Law in the EU Polity: Actors.* Palgrave MacMillan.

Crespy, A., Massart, T., & Schmidt, V. (2023). How the Impossible Became Possible: Evolving Frames and Narratives on Responsibility and Responsiveness from the Eurocrisis to NextGenerationEU. *Journal of European Public Policy.*

Crowe, R. (2021). The EU Recovery Plan: New Dynamics in the Financing of the EU Budget. In Gavin Barrett et al., (Eds.), *The Future of Legal Europe: Will We Trust in It? Liber Amicorum in Honour of Wolfgang Heusel* (pp. 117–139). Cham, Springer.

De Witte, B. (2021). The European Union's Covid-19 Recovery Plan: The Legal Engineering of an Economic Policy Shift. *Common Market Law Review, 58*(3), 635–682.

De Witte, B. (2022). EU Emergency Law and Its Impact on the EU Legal Order. Guest Editorial. *Common Market Law Review*, *59*(3). 3–18.

Dermine, P. (2022). *The New Economic Governance of the Eurozone: A Rule of Law Analysis*. Cambridge University Press.

Donaire Villa, F. D. (2022, October 18). Judicial Associations Sue EU Council for Unblocking MRR Funds to Poland Amidst Rule of Law Crisis: Legal Issues. www.diritticomparati

Fabbrini, F. (2022). Next Generation EU: Legal Structure and Constitutional Consequences. *Cambridge Yearbook of European Legal Studies, 24*, 45–66.

Fasone, C., & Lupo, N. (2023). Learning from the Euro-Crisis. A New Method Of Government for the EU's Economic Policy Coordination After the Pandemic? *STALS Research Paper, 4*, 1–25.

Fisicaro, M. (2022). Protection of the Rule of Law and 'Competence Creep' via the Budget: The Court of Justice on the Legality of the Conditionality Regulation. *European Constitutional Law Review, 18*(2), 334–356.

Flynn, L. (2019). Article 122 TFEU. In M. Kellerbauer., M. Klamert., & J. Tomkin (Eds.), *The EU Treaties and the Charter of Fundamental Rights: A Commentary*, 1275–1297.

Hegedus, D. (2023, December 21). Same, Same but Different?: The Pitfalls in Unfreezing EU Funds. *VerfBlog.*

Hillion, C. (2021). Compromising (On) the General Conditionality Mechanism and the Rule of Law. *Common Market Law Review, 58*(2), 267–284.

Howarth, D., & Schild, J. (2021). Nein to 'Transfer Union': The German Brake on the Construction of a European Union Fiscal Capacity. *Journal of European Integration, 43*(2), 209–226.

Leino-Sandberg, P., & Ruffert, M. (2022). Next Generation EU and its Constitutional Ramifications: A Critical Assessment. *Common Market Law Review, 59*(2), 433–472.

Lindseth, P., & Fasone, C. (2020, December 11). Rule-of-Law Conditionality and Resource Mobilization. The Foundations of a Genuinely 'Constitutional' EU? *VerfBlog*.

Lionello, L. (2020). Next Generation EU: Has the Hamiltonian Moment Come for Europe? *Eurojus, 4*, 22–42.

Lupo, N. (2023). PNRR e Cicli Politico-Elettorali, Tra Unione Europea e Stati Membri. *Federalismi, 28*, iv–xiv.

Nguyen, T. (2020, December). The EU's New Rule of Law Mechanism How it Works and Why the 'Deal' Did Not Weaken it. *Hertie School-Jacque Delors Center Policy Brief, 17*, 1–6.

Pavone, T. (2023, December 17). The EU's Faustian Bargain: The EU Betrays Ukraine and the Rule of Law—And We Will Live to Regret It. *VerfBlog*.

Pech, L., & Bárd, P. (2022). The Commission's Rule of Law Report and the EU Monitoring and Enforcement of Article 2 TEU Values. *EPRS: European Parliamentary Research Service, PE 727.551*.

Pech, L. (2022, June 21). Covering Up and Rewarding the Destruction of the Rule of Law One Milestone at a Time. *VerfBlog*.

Pinelli, C. (2021). Common values, Rule of Law Conditionality and the State of Democracy in Europe. In N. de Boer, B. Michel, A. Nieuwenhuis, J.H. Reestman (Eds.), *Liber Amicorum Besselink* (pp. 51–67). University of Amsterdam.

Schwarcz, A. (2023, January). *Rule of law-related 'super milestones' in the recovery and resilience plans of Hungary and Poland*. European Parliament Briefing. https://www.europarl.europa.eu/RegData/etudes/BRIE/2023/741581/IPOL_BRI(2023)741581_EN.pdf

Scheppele, K. L., & Morijn, J. (2022, November 14). Are Hungary's EU Funds Being Cut (or Not)?: Funding Confusions, Separate Tracks and What May Lie Ahead. *VerfBlog*.

Sheppele, K., Pech, L., & Platon, S. (2020, December 13). Compromising the Rule of Law while Compromising on the Rule of Law. *VerfBlog*.

Vita, V. (2017). Revisiting the Dominant Discourse on Conditionality in the EU: The Case of EU Spending Conditionality. *Cambridge Yearbook of European Legal Studies, 19*, 116–143.

Wójcik, A. (2023, April). *Using Financial Tools to Protect the Rule of Law: the Case of Poland, in The Rule of Law in the EU: Crisis and Solutions* (pp. 36–42). SIEPS-Swedish Institute for European Policy Studies.

Zeitlin, J., Bokhorst, D., & Eihmanis, E. (2023, June). *Governing the RRF. Drafting, Implementing, and Monitoring National Recovery and Resilience Plans as an Interactive Multi-Level Process, Recovery Watch Policy Study*. Foundation for European Progressive Studies (FEPS).

CHAPTER 16

The Role of Competition Law in Defending Rule of Law Values in the EU

Katalin J. Cseres

1 Introduction

The EU's rule of law crisis that unfolded over the past 10 years, has triggered widespread discussions focusing on the drastic re-engineering of certain Member States' constitutional systems and their (non)-compliance with the EU's foundational values. At the same time, how these constitutional transformations impacted economic freedoms of market actors, and EU citizens in local markets have been less often analyzed. Such analysis is, however, crucial as the accumulation of economic power and its dangerous "liaison" with the accumulation of political power harms democracy and entrenches inequality. For example, in Hungary, the rule of law backsliding enabled the government to intentionally use economic regulation to override market mechanisms. By increasing state intervention in certain segments of the economy the room for competition and

K. J. Cseres (✉)
Amsterdam Centre for European Law and Governance, Amsterdam, Netherlands
e-mail: k.j.cseres@uva.nl

C. Fasone et al. (eds.), *EU Rule of Law Procedures at the Test Bench*, Palgrave Studies in European Union Politics,
https://doi.org/10.1007/978-3-031-60008-1_16

equal opportunities for market actors was severely decreased and sometimes eliminated altogether. Competition law instruments, such as merger control, have been systematically set aside for political purposes. The 2018 creation of the media conglomerate, KESMA (CMPF 2019), resulting in the control and operation of nearly 480 publications by a publisher known for his loyalty to the Hungarian prime minister and forming a massive advertising and readership centre, reminds us of how real the harm caused by such arbitrary measures to the economy, consumers and market participants are. Yet, this and similar exemptions for "national strategic interest" from the competition rules, require thorough examination in order to expose how concentrated economic power reinforces political power and impact citizens' economic and non-economic interests related to, for example, media pluralism, access to utilities, reliable information or data protection.

These examples are often considered as "pure" national cases, however, national competition law enforcement is not isolated, but is deeply interconnected with the EU's and 27 Member States' enforcement systems that are to safeguard the system of undistorted competition as a core component of the EU's economic and legal order (Cseres, 2024). Hence, backsliding in one Member State, questions how it influences the competitive process in the internal market, and the relationship between competitive markets and democracy as a central pillar of the EU integration project.

In this chapter, I investigate the question, how EU competition law, with its central constitutional role in the EU's economic and legal order, its exceptionally robust and direct form of enforcement by the European Commission, its interconnectedness with enforcement in the Member States and its intimate relationship with the rule of law and democracy, can defend the rule of law in the EU. I argue that, overall, backsliding in one Member State, weakens or even harms competition across the whole EU and affects enforcement of competition law in Europe. As such, it is a matter of EU law and policy and a responsibility of the European Commission.

2 The Role of Competition Law in the EU

Competition as a specific institutional form of the market is conducive to democracy. Competition law as a key ordering principle of the economy, keeps control over excessive concentration of economic power which risks eroding democratic processes and institutions and leads to rent-seeking, oligarchy, and crony capitalism (Deutscher, 2022). The dispersal of public and private economic power is an important feature of both competition and democracy, as it safeguards individual's economic and political freedoms (Deutscher & Makris, 2016). Competitive markets form vital components of, not only functioning market economies but also of democratic legal and political systems (Cseres, 2023; Deutscher, 2022) Competition defines the boundaries of public power (Prosser, 2005) and by dispersing economic power it ensures the integrity and impartiality of political institutions making interest capture less likely (Deutscher, 2022). By setting bounds to economic power, competition law warrants a free and fair competitive process, which imposes checks and balances on private and public market power and guarantee an inviolable sphere of private activity for individuals (Deutscher & Makris, 2016).

The role of competition as a fundamental institution of a democratic system is a salient concept that influenced the drafting of the Rome Treaty and its central role in creating democratic political systems was re-stated in the 1993 Copenhagen (accession) criteria of the EU (Cseres, 2024). Competition law developed as a quasi-constitutional foundation of liberal democracy and it has been a core part of the EU integration project from its early days. Constitutionalized at the EU level, it developed into the central pillar of the integration project (Joerges, 2015). Over the past seven decades EU competition law became a powerful institution to defend markets across Europe, to safeguard European undertakings' freedom of economic activity and consumers' choice.

The Ordoliberal inspired economic constitution, this law-based order committed to the rule of law and individual economic freedoms helped the Community to acquire legitimacy in the foundational period of the EU and contributed to its "constitutional" character (Joerges, 2002). In this process of supranational constitution building, competition law took centre stage. Accordingly, the protection of the competitive process must be seen in fact as an implementation of Article 2 of the Treaty on the European Union (TEU), which lists, among others, the EU values of democracy, equality, rule of law, and respect for human rights. When states join the EU, they commit to the EU's economic and legal order, which as a "constitutional charter" explicitly includes the system of undistorted competition. Accordingly, by joining, Member States commit to the values of EU law as laid down in Article 2 TEU and make a mutual promise that in the enforcement of competition law, they recognize and respect the EU's values and objectives. In its *Sped-Pro* judgment (Case T-791/19), the General Court confirmed that compliance with the fundamental values of Article 2 TEU applies to the EU's competition law enforcement mechanisms under Articles 101 and 102 TFEU. In this judgment, the General Court for the first time established a direct link between systematic deficiencies in the legal order of a Member State and the ability of its competition authority to take enforcement action under EU law and protect a complainant's rights.

3 Europeanization of Competition Laws and Democracy

Crucially, the fundamental role of competition law has also been transplanted from 1990s into the legal systems of all EU Member States as a key component of their economic policies. By the late 1990s, successful market integration and the process of EU constitutionalization combined with solid supranational enforcement mechanisms transformed competition law into a strong policy field. Coupled with the increasing Europeanisation of national competition norms, competition law became a "common core" of the EU and its Member States (Cseres, 2024; Drahos, 2002). Importantly, by pursuing market integration as a public policy goal, EU competition law has acted as a vehicle for the proliferation of democracy and the rule of law (Ramirez Perez & Van de Scheur, 2013). An explicit restatement of competition law as a building block of market economies and democratic societies was formulated in the governance mechanism of the accession process for the Central and Eastern European countries from the late 1990s to the 2004 enlargement (Copenhagen criteria). Moreover, in contrast with the Article 2 TEU values, which draw on the shared legal and constitutional traditions of the Member States (Scheppele et al., 2020), competition law was centrally established and developed with far-reaching powers unmatched in any other EU legal and policy field (Warlouzet, 2010). Unlike Article 2 TEU values, which are constrained by the EU's limited competences to legislate and enforce, EU competition law is an exclusive EU competence with direct administration and with far-reaching enforcement mechanisms. This means, that EU competition law is a fundamental part of the EU legal order, implemented and enforced by all Member States, and that the protection of competitive markets is a shared value for all Member States. Effective enforcement of this shared value is for the Commission and national competition authorities, which can be undermined by the systematic erosion of the rule of law and democracy by certain Member States. Whether and how EU competition law as a powerful legal and policy instrument should shape responses to the challenges of rising political populism, growing political and corporate concentration, also depends on how the authority of EU competition law is challenged by national economic policies that question neo-liberal ideas of free trade and market competition, as well as by the backsliding of certain Member States on their commitment to the rule of law and democracy in the EU (Cseres, 2024).

4 Substantive EU Competition Rules, Procedures and Enforcement

Through preventing anti-competitive practices resulting from restrictive agreements between undertakings, abuses of dominant position, mergers leading to excessive market power, and state aid that provides economic advantages to selected firms, competition law safeguards the competitive process and ensures they function properly to the benefit of all members of society.

EU competition law consists of specific substantive rules that prohibit (i) anti-competitive agreements (Article 101 TFEU), (ii) the abuse of significant market power (Article 102 TFEU), and (iii) anti-competitive mergers (Regulation 139/2004). It also contains rules that address Member States, such as Article 106 TFEU prohibits them from adopting, with regard to public undertakings or undertakings bearing special or exclusive rights, any measure that would lead to an infringement of another Treaty provision, including Articles 101 and 102 TFEU, and Article 107 TFEU. Article 107 TFEU contains a general prohibition of State aid in order to prevent distortions of competition in the internal market that could result from the granting of selective advantages to certain companies. Hence, these rules impose important checks on private but also public economic power and as such are instrumental in protecting democracy and the rule of law in the EU legal order. EU competition law also contains procedural rules. Regulation 1/2003 lays down the enforcement and procedural framework for Articles 101 and 102 TFEU, Regulation 139/2004 for mergers, and Article 108 TFEU and Regulation 2015/1589 for state aid.

5 Effective Competition Law Enforcement

Competition policy has been extensively delegated to competition authorities with broad enforcement powers (Wilks & Bartle, 2022). Enforcement is by far the most important aspect of competition policy, hence, it is crucial who enforces the rules, on the basis of which mandate, and how enforcement is controlled (Guidi, 2016).

Since the establishment of the Treaties of Rome in 1957, competition law has been for four decades, the main example of direct administration by the Commission affecting "individuals" (legal persons or companies) (Harlow & Rawlings, 2014). The EU competition law procedures form the archetype of administrative procedures in EU law (Mendes, 2011) and its procedural rules formed one of the few areas of EU law that was equipped with a comprehensive set of administrative framework from its very inception in 1962. As the execution of EU law is still largely ensured by national authorities (indirect administration), and thus is defined by the procedural law of the Member States, the direct administration of competition rules by the Commission remains exceptional and relevant for direct enforcement.

The defining characteristic of Directorate-General for Competition (DG COMP) reflects a strong German (Ordoliberal) influence guaranteeing market freedoms and the importance of *Rechtsstaat* values over ad hoc political decision-making (Harlow & Rawling, 2014). German experience was also prominent in drafting Regulation 17/62, and in particular, the institutional design of DG COMP, formally DG IV, as a centralized, independent, quasi-judicial body. From its early days, it stood out among other DGs because of its autonomy, judicial functions, and direct influence on the economy. Yet, it does not function as a fully independent authority: final decisions are adopted through Commissioners' vote, who are political appointments of the Member States.

DG COMP has broad investigative, and sanctioning powers to directly enforce the Treaty competition rules laid down in Regulation 1/2003. The Commission's autonomy in starting investigations and imposing sanctions is exceptionally broad and no other EU institutions or Member State governments have (formal) means to intervene. Historically, competition policy was one of the most centralized and hierarchical EU policies, and most Member States have, "downloaded" it from the EU level (Guidi, 2016). Hence, competition enforcement in the EU is taking place in the shadow of hierarchy, determined by the legal and the historical pre-eminence of the European Commission. The decentralization of enforcement did not eliminate this, in fact, it may have strengthened it (Guidi, 2016).

By the 1990s, a wave of "Europeanisation" was taking place (Bache & Jordan, 2006) and many Member States and candidate countries adopted national competition laws and created competition authorities (Cseres, 2024). As the workload of the Commission enforcing Articles 101 and 102 TFEU became unfeasible, Regulation 1/2003 was adopted in 2004 to delegate enforcement powers to national competition authorities (NCAs) and national courts and relieve the Commission of its increasing administrative burden, and make enforcement more effective. Article 3 (1) of Regulation 1/2003 imposed an obligation on national authorities to apply Articles 101 and 102 TFEU in parallel with their national competition rules when "effect on trade between Member States" can be established. The creation of decentralized enforcement was to give competition policy more democratic support in Europe (White Paper, 1999) but it also carried the risk of renationalizing decision-making within the EU enforcement framework.

Decentralization was a refocus in Europeanization from substantive competition rules towards effective enforcement. Decentralized enforcement came to rely on the enforcement of national administrative authorities embedded (and challenged) in diverse political, institutional, and procedural settings. However, unlike the conditionality mechanism of enlargement that acted as a powerful harmonization instrument for the candidate countries, similar mechanisms are absent in the internal governance of EU competition law enforcement (Cseres 2013). In fact, the decentralized system introduced by Regulation 1/2003 largely left national laws and policies inconsequential in cases when governments did not have the (sufficient) capacity to implement them. It overlooked questions of effective and credible enforcement with capable organizations who can detect problems, set priorities, allocate resources, and penalize non-compliance. A first step in addressing the institutional embeddedness of competition rules that influence effective law enforcement took place with the adoption of the ECN + Directive, (Directive 2019/1), which was to empower NCAs to be more effective enforcers of competition law. The Directive laid down minimum harmonization rules for NCAs' investigative, decision-making, and enforcement powers. Importantly, the Directive (Article 4) sets minimum safeguards for NCAs' independence from market actors and political pressure as well as requires accountability to governments and parliaments.

However, concerning, de facto independence and accountability, the ECN + Directive does not address the broader legal and constitutional context of competition enforcement. The relevance of de facto independence was highlighted by the literature on legal transplants in competition law (Aydin & Buthe, 2016) demonstrating that independence depends on the strength of the rule of law in a given country. Competition authorities need not just "pure" independence but rather "embedded autonomy" (Evans 1992) that enables them to challenge anti-competitive practices of not just private actors, but also the anti-competitive practices of state-owned enterprises, and take on entrenched interests within the government and the state.

Despite diverse institutional settings based on the principle of procedural and institutional autonomy, national competition authorities remain subject to a number of fundamental obligations under EU law. The decentralized system rests on the implicit safeguarding of mutual trust and sincere cooperation, which is manifested in the cooperation mechanism between the Commission and the NCAs, and which demands that they all trust each other in making use of their investigative and fining powers in order to deter uncompetitive conduct (Commission Notice 2004). The principle of mutual trust was confirmed by the General Court in its *Sped-Pro* judgment, which demonstrated that the protection of competitive markets is a *shared value* for all Member States, who are obliged to effectively enforce it. When assessing whether a national competition authority is capable of effectively enforcing competition law and adequately safeguarding a complainant's rights, the General Court addressed rule of law issues. Referring to its own case law developed in the area of the European Arrest Warrant (EAW) (Case C-216/118 *LM v Ireland*) the General Court laid down an important new role for the Commission when enforcing EU competition law. The Commission will have to examine whether an NCA can act de facto independently from the executive in the Member State, and whether there are independent courts that can review the competition authority's decision and adequately protect the rights of complainants. The General Court's judgment shows that the lack of independence of NCAs, analogous with the lack of judicial independence of authorities issuing the EAW, can justify the suspension of cooperation between Member States (Cseres & Hwija, 2023).

Moreover, the principle of effectiveness, which is a central element of Regulation 1/2003 and Directive 2019/01, demands Member States not to render the implementation of EU law impossible in practice or excessively difficult (Case C-453/99 Courage) and they must ensure that the rules which they establish or apply do not jeopardize the effective application of Articles 101 TFEU and 102 TFEU. Competition authorities' power to challenge conduct deemed hostile to competition, particularly when that conduct is by politically powerful actors, is an essential measure of their "embedded autonomy". Consequently, Member States should be barred from adopting legislative or other measures that de facto eliminate the autonomy and independence of its competition authority as the above Hungarian cases show (Cseres, 2019).

The Courts on various occasions emphasized Member States' obligations on the basis of this principle (Case C-439/08 VEBIC), which demand "the availability of sufficiently robust national enforcement structures" (Dunne, 2016). Effective enforcement requires that national sanctioning systems deter undertakings from engaging in anti-competitive conduct fearing prosecution and the obligation to pay a fine. The interdependent nature of decentralized enforcement means that even where most NCAs engage in effective enforcement, the failure of some to apply Articles 101 and 102 TFEU undermines the system. Systemic failure of an NCA to enforce Regulation 1/2003, given the risk this poses to the system of enforcement, should therefore be sufficient to suspend cooperation under Regulation 1/2003 (Borgers 2021). This means that other NCAs no longer mutually recognize the concerned national system as being effective, and cases would be re-allocated from such an NCA to other NCAs to ensure that Article 101 and 102 TFEU are enforced. Alternatively, on the basis of Article 11 (6) of Regulation 1/2003, the Commission can intervene if there is a serious risk of incoherence, by relieving the national competition authority of its competence to act. It has, however, so far not made use of this possibility.

> The European Commission and competition authorities fulfil "court-like" functions (Maher, 2000; Wright, 2009) as they protect the legal position of undertakings as well as citizens' rights to economic activity and free choice in markets. As such, effective enforcement of competition law not only is crucial for safeguarding undistorted competition within the internal market, but also forms part of effective judicial protection as laid down in Article 19 of the Charter of Fundamental Rights.

6 Protecting Media Pluralism Through Competition Law

Recognized as an essential characteristic of well-functioning democracies, free and open societies, media pluralism contributes to the formation of public opinion allowing citizens to make informed choices in their political decisions. In EU law and policy, media pluralism is recognized as a core value on which the European Union is founded (Article 2 TEU), and as a corollary to the right of freedom of expression as enshrined in Article 11(2) of the Charter of Fundamental Rights. A core component of the rule of law, it is an indispensable condition for exercising citizenship and fostering participation in a democratic society by enabling media to fulfil their role in providing complete, balanced, and accurate information, and holding power to account (Brogi et al., 2021). The Commission placed media freedom at the heart of its rule of law reporting. The Rule of Law Mechanism dedicates a key section to media freedom and pluralism, which examines media regulatory authorities and bodies, the transparency of media ownership and government interference, and the framework for the protection of journalists.

Despite its fundamental value in the EU, the EU lacks an explicit competence to regulate media. Media as an EU policy is absent from the Treaties and the EU's legal instruments are limited. The EU has very little "hard law on media pluralism" (Garcia Pires, 2017). However, as an important economic sector of the single market, media markets fall under the EU's internal market and competition law competences. Concerning the internal market, the Commission shares its competence with the Member States, but has direct and exclusive competence with far-reaching supervisory powers concerning competition law.

By preventing excessive concentration in media markets and exclusionary behaviour that forecloses smaller media players and/or impedes market entry, competition law can maintain media pluralism. The application of competition law disperses economic power, and reduces concentration in media markets by focusing on the price dimension of the competitive process, but also by taking account of other consumer interests, such as quality, which can be media diversity (OECD, 2023). Concerning media mergers, it has been argued that merger assessments are complemented with a review prioritizing media pluralism and including a plurality test based on objective and quantifiable criteria (attention share) (OECD, 2021). In this way competition law can be complemented with specific anti-concentration rules to safeguard external pluralism –the offer of a plurality of voices by the market.

With the adoption of the European Media Freedom Act, on the basis of Article 114 TFEU, the Commission included complementary rules to those of competition law, on media concentration and state advertising and allocation of state resources. With this new approach, the Commission is mobilizing its internal market and competition law competences to address abuse of state regulatory and economic powers as drivers of media capture.

6.1 Media Concentration Control

Merger control is a legal instrument, which can decentralize economic power and enable economic opportunities for firms. However, media power, comprising "opinion power" (Helberger, 2020) has a political dimension, and does not necessarily coincide with market power. Still, concentrated economic power can reinforce the political power of capital and impact on citizens' fundamental rights protection related to media pluralism or access to reliable information (Banasiński & Rojszczak, 2022).

Concerning media, the EU shares competence with the Member States, and may only take action to support national initiatives. According to Article 167(5) TFEU, such action may not harmonize national media laws and regulations. Nevertheless, on the basis of the Merger Regulation 139/2004, the Commission is explicitly entrusted with assessing whether a concentration with a Union dimension significantly impedes effective competition. The legal framework is less explicit concerning the Commission's merger assessment in relation with media pluralism, and its competences are limited concerning culture, Articles 167(4) TFEU and 11(2) and 51(1) of the Charter of Fundamental Rights lay down a duty for the Commission to have regard to non-economic goals when implementing the Union's competition policy (Bania, 2013). On the national level, Member States apply merger rules to control the structure of markets. The monitoring of mergers is shared between the Commission and the NCAs by reference to quantitative criteria (Article 1 (2) Regulation 139/2004). However, not all Member States have a merger control regime, and existing merger rules differ concerning media plurality (Study 2022). The Commission has central and exclusive competence over mergers with Union dimension, but, it has no competence in national cases. However, this allocation of jurisdiction is subject to corrective mechanisms and exceptions that enable the Commission to review cases even without a Union dimension: so-called Article 22 referral (Cseres, 2023). Under Article 22 referral mechanism a system of close cooperation exists between the Commission and the NCAs, similar to the cooperation mechanism under Regulation 1/2003 (Cseres, 2023). The close resemblance between the principles of close cooperation between NCAs and the Commission underlying Article 22 referrals and Regulation1/2003, demand the Commission to take account of the additional conditions of effective competition law enforcement and concerns of rule of law backsliding as interpreted by the General Court's judgment in *Sped-Pro*. Accordingly, the lack of independence of NCAs, analogous with the lack of judicial independence of authorities issuing the EAW, can justify the suspension of cooperation between Member States and the Commission and that the case should be dealt with by the Commission.

6.2 The EMFA's **ex ante** *investigation*

The *ex ante* investigation of a media concentrations on the basis of EU or national merger rules often remains limited to the economic aspects of media markets and cannot assess the cultural and fundamental rights perspective of media plurality (Case M.5932, News Corp/BSkyB, para 307). Article 21 of the EMFA introduces a complementary notification obligation for media concentrations that have a significant impact on media pluralism and editorial independence. This includes a requirement on each Member State to establish substantive and procedural rules to assess any concentration involving at least one media service provider.

These criteria focus on the concentrations' impact on the diversity of media players, editorial independence and whether in the absence of the concentration, the acquiring and the acquired entity would remain economically sustainable, and whether there are sustainable alternatives. The proposed assessment has distinctive features compared to existing merger rules, but also contains overlaps. The EMFA's focus on assessing the impact on media plurality and diversity of media players is partly reflected in the competition assessment of whether competition is reduced as a result of the horizontal overlaps between acquiring firm and its target. The EMFA's assessment of the safeguards for editorial independence is reflected in the assessment of efficiencies of the concentration and the possible remedies offered to safeguard effective competition.

The economic sustainability in the absence of the merger, whether the acquiring and the acquired entity would remain economically sustainable is reflected in the assessment of efficiencies and in the doctrine of failing firm (De Meeuse, 2023).

This creates an unclear relationship to decisions taken under the competition law framework, which in some countries includes the possibility for a secondary assessment of the impact on media pluralism already (Cole & Etteldorf, 2023). National rules concerning media mergers vary considerably, less than half of the Member States consider public interest in their merger assessment, and only a few refer specifically to media plurality. Article 21, EMFA aims to change this fragmentation.

However, concerning its enforcement, the effect of the EMFA is disappointing. It requires Member States to designate a national regulatory body to conduct these assessments, and use transparent, objective, proportionate, and non-discriminatory criteria for the notification and assessment of such concentrations. In addition, the European Board would be given the power to issue opinions where media market concentrations may affect the functioning of the internal market, which national authorities would be required to "*take utmost account of*". These provisions fail to address the root causes of why actual enforcement remains ineffective in certain Member States, e.g. Hungary (Bayer & Cseres, 2023).

7 State Aid

Concerning state aid, two areas need mentioning: public broadcasting and state advertising. State aid is prohibited under Article 107 TFEU, but state measures that support public broadcasting services, traditionally seen as Services of General Economic Interest may qualify for an exemption on the basis of Article 106 (2) TFEU. Member States who entrust media organizations with providing quality and varied programming in order to safeguard media pluralism and which, for the performance of this mission, grants aid to these organizations, are entitled to request for a derogation from the general State aid prohibition (Kozak, 2024). The interpretative Protocol on the System of Public Broadcasting in the Member States (Amsterdam Protocol) endorses the role of public broadcasting in fulfilling the democratic, social, and cultural needs of a given society as well as the need to preserve and promote media pluralism. It states that the Member States define and organize the public service in a manner of their choice. However, it lays down that state financing of broadcasting activities may not create distortions of competition that are not necessary for fulfilling the public service mission. Both Article 106 (2) TFEU and the Amsterdam Protocol demand in essence a balance between national interests and the Union interests but do not explain how this balance may be achieved.

State advertising has emerged as a key source of distorting the media landscape and jeopardizing both fair competition and media independence in various EU Member States. For example, complaints were filed concerning state aid for pro-government media outlets in newspaper, online, and television markets in Hungary (Mérték, 2019). State advertising has often been misused by Member States to exercise undue influence over individual media organizations and the media market as a whole (Nenadić, 2022). Criteria for the allocation of advertising by state agencies are usually unclear and only occasionally reveal how the awarding of advertising contracts to the press happened while being used for political influence. State advertising in some countries serves as a significant revenue source for many media service providers, who face economic difficulties and struggle with the sustainability of their business models. The 2022 Media Pluralism Monitor results highlighted the high risk of political influence to editorial independence associated with state advertising in the majority of EU Member States.

Financial support from the state, in any form, is crucial, especially, for less commercial forms of journalism. Fair and transparent rules for distributing state resources are critical. Threat of political capture through opaque and unfair allocation of state advertising may form unlawful state aid posing a risk to the media market by distorting competition (Nenadić, 2022).

8 Transparent and fair allocation of economic resources under the EMFA

Article 24 EMFA addresses these issues of state advertising by complementing the state aid rules. Compared to EU state aid rules, Article 24 addresses the allocation of state advertising in an *ex ante* manner, instead of the EU state rules' *ex post*, case-by-case approach. Focusing on problems created by the unfair allocation of state resources to the media service providers, Article 24 ensures that state advertising is systematically subject to *ex ante* rules on transparency, notably concerning beneficiaries and amounts spent, and on fair allocation of advertising. It aims to prevent the misuse or distorted use of such advertising to influence editorial choices and media content by ensuring transparency, non-discrimination, proportionality, and objectivity in allocation of state advertising to media outlets.

Not all Member States have media-specific measures and general public procurement laws concerning the distribution and transparency of state advertising. Where such rules exist, they diverge significantly and do not cover all state advertising expenditure nor offer sufficient protection against biassed distribution. Opaque and biassed allocation of state advertising is therefore a powerful tool to "capture" media service providers. It is important that Member States make the necessary information related to state advertising publicly accessible in an electronic format that is easy to view, access, and download, in compliance with Union and national rules on commercial confidentiality.

However, according to Article 24(3), the enforcement of Article 24 and monitoring of the allocation of state advertising is left to national regulatory authorities, without an explicit role given to the newly created European Board for Media Services.

Moreover, despite clear definition of what constitutes state advertising the Hungarian case illustrates that states may circumstance such definitions by national law. In Hungary, the state cannot (is not allowed to) pay for advertisement space directly. Instead, state advertising is managed by two media agencies selected via public procurement procedures. How these agencies select advertisement space for state ads and how much they pay for them is unclear. The current Hungarian system of allocating state resources for advertising purposes is designed in a way to escape the reach of the EU state aid rules. Since the recent amendment of Hungary's Fundamental Law, the definition of "public money" in Article 39(3) is narrowed down to the state's direct income and expenditure. The expenditure of the two media outlets is, by law, not categorized as "public expenditure".

9 Conclusions

Competition law is often seen as a distinctive area of law, as it depends on economic theory to define most of its substantive content and it is functional in nature. These characteristics put it at some distance from traditional conceptions of the rule of law. Nevertheless, competition law safeguards the competitive process, which as a specific institutional form of the market is conducive to democracy and the rule of law. A major driving force behind European integration has always been the integration of national economies into a common market. Hence, competition law backsliding in Member States jeopardizes the very essence of European integration. Such backsliding undermines the EU's own legitimacy as an economically powerful state with strong interests in promoting competitiveness, supporting a strong and resilient economy, that encourage international trade and is open to companies to engage in cross-border activities. Its economic power and regulatory strength, however, are only effective and credible to global competitors if European economic policy respects and safeguards the foundations of its own economic constitution: the safeguarding of open markets in which undistorted competition prevails.

References

Aydin, U., & Büthe, T. (2016). Competition Law & Policy in Developing Countries: Explaining Variations in Outcomes; Exploring Possibilities and Limits. *Law and Contemporary Problems, 79*(4), 1–36.

Bache, I., & Jordan, A. (2006). Europeanization and Domestic Change. In I. Bache & A. Jordan (Eds.), *The Europeanization of British Politics*. Palgrave Macmillan.

Banasiński, C., & Rojszczak, M. (2022). The Role of Competition Authorities in Protecting Freedom of Speech: The PKN Orlen/Polska Press Case. *European Competition Journal, 18*(2), 424–457.

Bania, K. (2013). European Merger Control in the Broadcasting Sector: Does Media Pluralism Fit? *Competition Law Review, 9*(1), 49–80.

Bania, K. (2015). *The Role of Media Pluralism in the Enforcement of EU Competition Law* (EUI PhD, Thesis).

Bania, K. (2022). The European Media Freedom Act: A bold Move Raising Bold Questions. *The Platform Law Blog*. https://theplatformlaw.blog/2022/05/02/the-european-media-freedom-act-a-bold-move-raising-bold-questions/

Bayer, J., & Cseres, K. J. (2023). Towards a Better Enforcement of EMFA. *Verfassungsblog*.

Borgers, M. (2021). *Putting the 'Trust' in Antitrust: The Impact of the Rule of Law Crisis on Trust between National Competition Authorities Under Regulation 1/2003*.

Brogi, E., Carlini, R., Nenadić, I., Parcu, P. L., & de Azevedo Cunha, M. V. (2021). EU and Media Policy: Conceptualising Media Pluralism in the Era of Online Platforms: The Experience of the Media Pluralism Monitor. In P. L.

Parcu & E. l. Brogi (Eds.), *Research Handbook on EU Media Law and Policy*. Edward Elgar Publishing.
Centre for Media Pluralism and Media Freedom, The Hungarian Media Conglomerate (KESMA): A Rsk Assessment Based on the Media Pluralism Monitor. https://cmpf.eui.eu/media-pluralism-monitor/mpm-2019-hungary/
Charter of Fundamental Rights of the European Union (2000])OJ C364/1, Art 19.
Cole, M. D., & Etteldorf, C. (2023). Research for CULT Committee—European Media Freedom Act—Background Analysis, European Parliament, Policy Department for Structural and Cohesion Policies, Brussels.
Commission Notice on Cooperation Within the Network of Competition Authorities *OJ C 101, 27.4.2004, p. 43–53.*
Council Regulation (EC) 1/2003 of 16 December 2002 on the Implementation of the Rules on Competition Laid Down in Articles 81 and 82 of the Treaty [2003] OJ L1/1.
Cseres, K. J. (2014). Accession to the EU's Competition Law Regime: A Law and Governance Approach' 7 *Yearbook of Antitrust and Regulatory Studies.*
Cseres, K. J. (2019). Rule of Law Challenges and the Enforcement of EU Competition Law, A Case-Study of Hungary and its Implications for EU law. *Competition Law Review, 14*, 319–339.
Cseres, K. J. (2022). The Commission's missed opportunity to reclaim competition law for the Rechtsstaat. *Verfassungsblog*. https://verfassungsblog.de/the-commissions-missed-opportunity-to-reclaim-competition-law-for-the-rechtsstaat/
Cseres, K. J. (2023). Re-Prioritising Referrals Under Article 22 EUMR: Consequences for Third Parties and Mutual Trust Between Competition Authorities. *Journal of European Competition Law & Practice, 14*(7), 410–422.
Cseres, K. J. (2024). EU Competition Law and Democracy in the Shadow of Rule of Law Backsliding. In C. Colombo, M. Eliantonio & K. Wright (Eds.), *The Changing Governance of EU Competition Law: A Constitutional Challenge*. Hart Publishing.
Cseres, K. J., & Hwija, K. (2023). Sped-Pro: The Impact of Rule of Law Backsliding on the Enforcement of (EU) Competition Law. *Review, Bialystok Legal Studies, 28*(4), 131–144.
De Meeuse, T. (2023). Competition Law in the Media and Audiovisual Sectors. *Crowell*. https://www.crowell.com/a/web/7s5vt9WXj2wNmnJtGbzqRe/era-competition-law-in-the-media-and-audiovisual-sectors.pdf
Deutscher, E. (2022). The Competition-Democracy Nexus Unpacked—Competition Law, Republican Liberty, and Democracy. *Yearbook of European Law, 41*, 197–251.

Deutscher, E., & Makris, S. (2016). Exploring the Ordoliberal Paradigm: The Competition-Democracy Nexus'. *Competition Law Review, 11*(2), 181–214.

Drahos, M. (2002). *Convergence of Competition Laws and Policies in the European Community: Germany, Austria, and Netherlands Hague*. Kluwer.

Dunne, N. (2016). Convergence in Competition Fining Practices in the EU'. *Common Market Law Review, 53*(2), 453–492.

European Commission. (2022). Directorate-General for Communications Networks, Content and Technology. In P. Parcu,E. Brogi, S. Verza, S. et al. (Eds.), *Study on media plurality and diversity online – Final report*. Publications Office of the European Union.

Evans, P. B. (1992). *Embedded Autonomy: States and Industrial Transformation*. Princeton University Press.

Garcia Pires, A. J. (2017). Media Pluralism and Competition. *European Journal of Law and Economics, 43*(2), 255–283.

Guidi, M. (2016). *Competition Policy Enforcement in EU Member States : What Is Independenc For?* Palgrave Macmillan.

Harlow C., & Rawlings, R. (2014). *Process and Procedure in EU Administration*. Hart Publishing.

Helberger, N. (2020). The Political Power of Platforms: How Current Attempts to Regulate Misinformation Amplify Opinion Power. *Digital Journalism, 8*(6), 842–854.

Joerges, C. (2002). *The Law in the Process of Constitutionalizing Europe* (2002/4 EUI Working Paper LAW).

Joerges, C. (2015). *The European Economic Constitution and Its Transformation Through the Financial Crisis'* (47 ZenTra Working Paper in Transnational Studies).

Kozak, M. (2024). The Media Pluralism Principle, The Financing of Public Broadcasters, and EU Law. *German Law Journal*, First View, 1–17.

Maher, I. (2000). Juridification, Codification and Sanction in UK Competition Law. *Modern Law Review, 63*(4), 544–569.

Mendes, J. (2011). EU Administrative Action, Procedural Guarantees, and Participation. *Participation in EU Rule-Making: A Rights-Based Approach*. Oxford Studies in European Law, Oxford University Press.

Mérték, M. M. (2019). *Complaints to the European Commission*. https://mertek.eu/en/2020/09/07/ec-complaints/

Nenadić, I., (2022). What is State Advertising, and Why is it Such a Big Problem for Media Freedom in Europe? EUI Centre for Media Pluralism and Media Freedom. https://cmpf.eui.eu/what-is-state-advertising-and-why-is-it-a-problem-for-media-freedom/

OECD. (2021). *Economic surveys*. https://www.oecd.org/economy/surveys/Hungary-2021-OECD-economic-survey-overview.pdf

OECD. (2023). *The Consumer Welfare Standard—Advantages and Disadvantages Compared to Alternative Standards*. OECD Competition Policy Roundtable Background Note.

Opinion 2/13 of the Court of Justice of the European Union [2014] EU:C:2014:2454.

Patel, K., & Schweitzer, H. (Eds.). (2013). *The Historical Foundations of EU Competition Law*. Oxford University Press.

Prosser, T. (2005). *The Limits of Competition Law*. Oxford University Press.

Ramirez Perez, S. M., & Van de Scheur, S. (2013). The Evolution of the Law on Articles 85 and 86 [Articles 101 and 102 TFEU]: Ordoliberalism and its Keynesian Challenge. In K. Patel & H. Schweitzer (Eds.), *The Historical Foundations of EU Competition Law*.

Scheppele, K. L., Kochenov, D., & Grabowska-Moroz, B. (2020). EU Values Are Law, After All: Enforcing EU Values Through Systemic Infringement Actions by the European Commission and the Member States of the European Union. *Yearbook of European Law, 39*, 3–121.

Van Waarden, F., & Drahos, M. (2002). Courts and (Epistemic) Communities in the Convergence of Competition Policies. *Journal of European Public Policy, 9*(6), 913–934.

Warlouzet, L. (2010). *The Rise of European Competition Policy, 1950–1991: A Cross-Disciplinary Survey of a Contested Policy Sphere'*. (EUI Working Paper RSCAS 2010/80).

White Paper on Modernisation of the Rules Implementing Articles 85 and 86 of the EC Treaty decentralization (1999) Commission Programme No 99/027.

Wilks, S., & Bartle, I. (2022). The Unanticipated Consequences of Creating Independent Competition Agencies. *West European Politics, 25*(1), 148–172.

Wright, K. (2009). The 'Judicial', The 'Administrative' and Consistent Application After the Decentralisation of EC Antitrust Enforcement'. *European Union Studies Association Eleventh Biennial International Conference*.

PART V

Conclusion

CHAPTER 17

Final Remarks on Dissensus Affecting the EU Rule of Law Procedures. Future Research Paths

Cristina Fasone

The analysis conducted in this volume has critically assessed the adoption and use of a wide array of supranational tools and procedures to address the rule of law backsliding in EU Member States, particularly Hungary and Poland. These instruments differ in several ways.

First, as shown in Table 1 below, some instruments were conceived ad hoc to deal with rule of law issues, whereas others—a slight majority—were initially envisaged as general tools of EU law or for other purposes, e.g., the coordination of economic policies, and were subsequently re-adapted to also serve the interest of the rule of law principles.

Similarly, the European Court of Auditors (ECA), in its first assessment of one of the newest instruments within the rule of law toolbox, the Rule of Law Report, vis-à-vis the existing tools has divided them into

C. Fasone (✉)
1Luiss University, Rome, Italy
e-mail: cfasone@luiss.it

C. Fasone et al. (eds.), *EU Rule of Law Procedures at the Test Bench*, Palgrave Studies in European Union Politics,
https://doi.org/10.1007/978-3-031-60008-1_17

Table 1 Old and new instruments for tackling rule of law problems

Existing general instruments	*Ad hoc instruments*
Infringement proceeding	Article 7 TEU
Preliminary ruling procedure	The cooperation and verification mechanism
Technical Support Instrument	Rule of law Framework and Dialogue
OLAF and EPPO	EU Justice Scoreboard
European Semester	Rule of Law Reports
Recovery and Resilience Facility	Rule of Law Conditionality Regulation
Competition law	
Charter enabling condition, CPR	

two categories: those adopted specifically to tackle rule of law problems—e.g., the Rule of Law Report, the Rule of Law Conditionality Regulation, the Art. 7 TEU procedures—and those originally designed for other policies or other areas of law, such as the European Semester, the RRF, the infringement procedures, and the PRP, in addition to the OLAF and the EPPO. Overall, the aim of the ECA was to explicitly focus on the interplay between the Rule of Law Report and the other tools (European Court of Auditors, 2024b; 8).

This book attempts to go one step further to offer a comprehensive analysis of the mutual relations, overlaps, and synergies between the various EU rule of law instruments. It therefore aims to foster further reflection and elaboration at academic and institutional levels on the mix of soft and hard law tools employed by the EU so far as a source of dissensus. The volume provides an informed analysis on the quantitative use of these instruments in addition to a qualitative assessment, evaluating their effectiveness and justifications.

Second, as illustrated in Fig. 1, the EU rule of law instruments range between those which possess a preventive nature, aiming to avoid widespread or systemic rule of law deficiencies (e.g., the EU Justice Scoreboard, the Rule of Law Report, and the European Semester); those designed as rule of law enforcement measures (e.g., the PRP and the Charter combined, competition rules on public procurement, the RRF, and Article 7 (1) TEU); and, finally, corrective or sanctioning measures (e.g., infringement proceedings, the combined activity of OLAF and EPPO, the Rule of Law conditionality regulation, the Charter enabling condition under the CPR, and Article 7 (2–3) TEU).

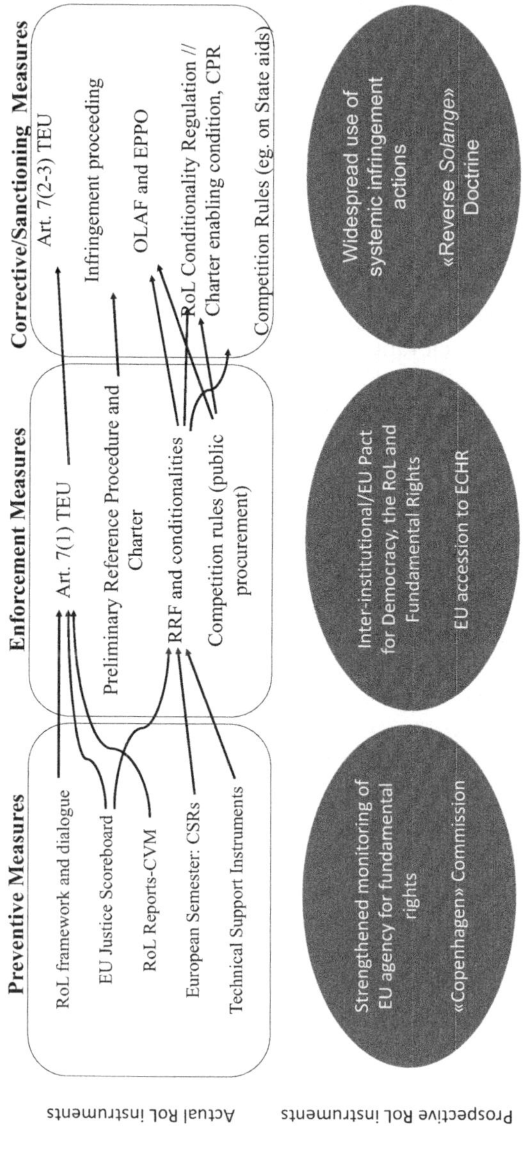

Fig. 1 Rule of Law Tools—Categories of measures "by aim"

The implementation of these various tools, however, highlights that the boundaries between the three categories are blurred. For example, the evidence produced through the EU Justice Scoreboard can provide the grounds to begin infringement proceedings, to activate the rule of law conditionality, or to use the Article 7 procedure; by the same token, the milestones and targets of the NRRPs, in addition to the horizontal enabling conditions under the CPR, can be instrumental to implementing rule of law reforms, but as long as the conditionality is triggered, with the suspension or withdrawal of funds or of their reimbursement, they also serve as corrective and sanctioning measures.

Third, the EU rule of law instruments can be divided—as the structure of this volume indicates—according to the level of cogency and the degree of bindingness of the relevant source of the law. Some are formally soft law tools; others are enshrined in secondary or primary law. However, the concrete use of these instruments suggests a less straightforward categorization. For example, with the inclusion of the RRF governance into the European Semester framework and the new two-way relationship between RRF milestones and targets and the CSRs addressing rule of law problems, the value of those recommendations appears to shift from soft law to binding law as an effect of conditionality. By contrast, the legal force of the CVM, formally enshrined into primary law, has been challenged by both its new channeling through the rule of law reports and by the lack of the CJEU's acknowledgment of its formal legal rank and as a standard for review in the *Asociatia "Forumul Judecătorilor din România" and others v. Inspectia Judiciară and others (AFJR)* preliminary ruling—contrary to the argument that AG Bobek put forward. In addition, the contributions collected in this book underline that it is not necessarily the rank of the EU legal source that dictates the effectiveness of the EU action, as the situation regarding the implementation of Article 7 TEU unfortunately indicates. Indeed, the introduction of legally binding instruments on paper does not necessarily remedy rule of law deficiencies in practice (Priebus & Anders, 2024: 236). One of the main findings highlighted in this volume refers to the intertwinement between the various EU tools and procedures to counter the degradation of the rule of law. They build on one another, and there are many more mutual connections between them than may initially appear. As Fig. 2 illustrates, no instrument can be considered in isolation.

In fact, the rule of law toolbox is "a set of complementary tools that can be used in parallel rather than hierarchically," which also permits the

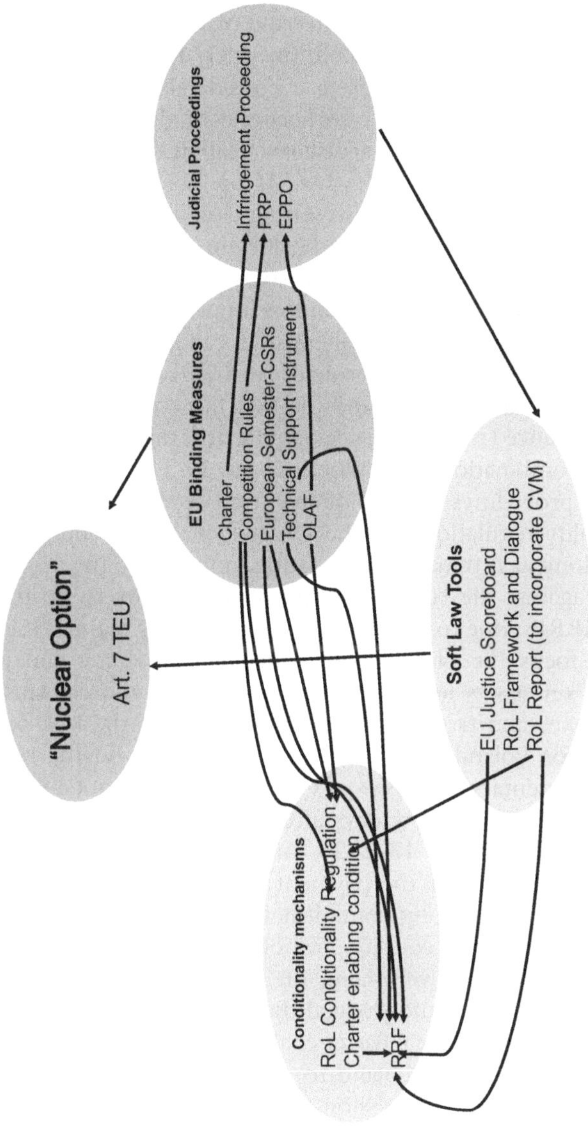

Fig. 2 Procedural linkages between EU RoL instruments

best-tailored choice to face multiple threats to the rule of law (European Court of Auditors, 2024b: 42). An example is the reciprocal influence between competition law and the rule of law "policy" in the EU. Although it is clear that EU competition rules, for instance on public procurement and state aid, can have a considerable impact on media pluralism at the national level—a cornerstone of the rule law—by the same token, the CJEU's rule of law case law dealing with the execution of the European Arrest Warrant since the *LM* preliminary ruling (C-216/18 PPU) has now contributed to also setting clear standards for the independence of national competition authorities in order to ensure mutual trust and sincere cooperation (*Sped Pro* judgment, T-791/19).

To give further examples, in relation to Hungary and Poland, multiple instruments have been used simultaneously to address corruption problems affecting EU funds (from the rule of law framework and dialogue to CSRs, competition rules, OLAF, and the RRF) or concerning the lack of judicial independence (the EU Justice Scoreboard, the rule of law report, the Charter in combination with Articles 2 and 19 TEU through preliminary reference procedures and infringement proceedings, and the rule of law conditionality regulation and the Charter enabling condition under the CPR). As long as it remains in operation, until 2026, the main procedural catalyst against the rule of law problems appears to be the RRF through the NRRPs, due to the multiple conditionality regimes it embeds and the clear focus the plans have on strong democratic and judicial institutions as key assets for promoting investments and reforms, foreseen as milestones and targets. Indeed, the impact of the lack of access to RRF funds for Poland under the PiS Government on the results of the Polish parliamentary elections of October 2023 cannot be underestimated. Conversely, just a few days after the appointment of the Tusk Government, on December 13 2023, one of the first priorities of the new Cabinet was to ask for the payment of the first installment of the Polish NRRP, with the strong commitment to adopt a series of judicial reforms. Furthermore, as a consequence of the introduction of a judicial reform bill by the Tusk Government, on February 29, 2024 the European Commission finally acknowledged the satisfactory fulfillment of two "super-milestones" and of the Charter enabling condition under the CPR, thereby "paving the way for Poland to access up to 137 billion euro in EU funding" (European Commission, 2024a).

It is clear that over the last decade, the EU rule of law instruments have grown exponentially, within and outside the official toolbox, and many of them have built de facto or *de iure* increasing synergies. However, the proliferation of the tools has taken place to a large extent in an uncoordinated manner given the urgency to respond to the weakness of some of the instruments or to their delayed implementation. The status quo demonstrates the need to rationalize and streamline the governance of the rule of law inside the EU to avoid duplications and confusion, particularly for the average citizen who should be the final beneficiary of the Union's rule of law policy. At the same time, EU institutions should seriously reflect on the many academic proposals put forward to strengthen European action in this field and how the new initiatives can be combined with the plethora of existing tools (listed in Fig. 1). The former range from preventive measures, such as the enhanced role of the EU Agency for Fundamental Rights and the setting up of the "Copenhagen" Commission (Tuori, 2016); to enforcement measures, for example, those stemming from a revamped EU Pact-Interinstitutional agreement for democracy, the rule of law and fundamental rights, and from the EU accession to the ECHR, whose new attempt is currently ongoing; and to corrective measures, such as systemic infringement actions (Scheppele, 2016) and the reverse *Solange* doctrine to be put into practice by the CJEU (von Bogdandy et al., 2012). Ideas on how to fruitfully integrate these old and new instruments have already circulated and any future institutional and academic investigation should begin from here (von Bogdandy et al., 2017; Södersten and Hercock, 2023).

The growth in the number of rule of law instruments devised and deployed, often unsuccessfully, has led to increasing dissensus. On the one hand, the use of a strategy combining different tools together increases the probability of achieving the targeted objectives—this is what the EU has attempted against the controversial Disciplinary Chamber of the Polish Supreme Court, although it does not help in understanding which of the instruments have been decisive. On the other hand, pursuing an incremental strategy may delay the achievement of the desired aim and can lead to concerns about the discretion left to EU institutions. The adoption and implementation of the rule of law conditionality regulation next to the RRF is telling in that respect. The European Council's political compromise on the former to seal the deal on the MMF 2021–2027 and on the RRF has been widely criticized in addition to the subsequent inaction of the Commission (Alemanno & Chamon, 2020, among others). The Commission has questionably applied a double standard to Hungary and to Poland on the activation of the rule of law conditionality mechanism for eminently geopolitical considerations, notably due to the different stances of the two countries vis-à-vis the war in Ukraine (Bárd & Kochenov, 2021: 49). As scholars have effectively pointed out, the double-standard critique of the EU rule of law strategy has even led to the endorsement of a manipulative interpretation of legal values and institutions in other rule-of-law-backsliding Member States, which has paved the way for "abusive comparativism" (see, among many, Grabowska-Moroz 2022: 340).

Several scholars have noted this diverse approach of the Commission toward Hungary and Poland since the Russian invasion of Ukraine, which has led to a more assertive role toward Hungary compared with far more forbearance to Poland, given the latter's active support for Ukraine. Hence, it has been argued that this is the result of Poland's alignment to the prioritization of the "EU's response to the war over RoL enforcement policies" (Hernández & Closa, 2024: 968; Kelemen & Pavone, 2023). In addition, the Commission has also tried to confront Hungary on different negotiating tables: that of the rule of law conditionality, of the approval of the NRRP until the decision was taken in December 2022, and of the freezing and then partial unblocking of cohesion funds following the activation of the Charter enabling condition under the CPR.

Here, two views can be compared: some may argue that this strategy of threatening the use of various "conditionality" instruments is welcome and strongly necessary insofar as it is effective as a deterrent against the further worsening of the rule of law degradation; others may argue that the strategy leaves too much political discretion to the EU institutions and is unpredictable, undemocratic, and controversial from the perspective of legal certainty and of the legitimate expectations of the citizens. To some extent, the latter concern has been advanced in the special report of the ECA, published on February 21, 2024. In that regard, the ECA clarified that "a possible short-term consequence of such budgetary measures is that national authorities may not have the financial or legal capacity to implement programs in the same way as they would with EU support. Failure by the Member States to fulfill their obligations may impact the achievement of the EU's objectives, such as social and territorial cohesion and the professional and personal development of people in education, with potential negative effects on EU citizens in the short term. For example, students may not be able to participate in the Erasmus + exchange programme" (European Court of Auditors, 2024a: 22).

For these reasons, the rise of dissensus on the EU rule of law instruments is unsurprising. The EU institutions themselves tend to disagree on how to counter rule of law issues, with the Council and the European Council being much more reluctant than the other EU bodies to adopt corrective measures and the Commission frequently being caught between intergovernmental institutions and the European Parliament. This divergent approach also emerges when examining the growing tension between the ECA, which is very much focused on protecting the EU's financial interests, and the Commission, which instead tends to consider a broader picture, which also includes political and contextual constraints at the expense of the predictability and accountability of its decisions. For example, for the ECA, the Rule of Law Conditionality Regulation, together with the specific provisions of the Recovery and Resilience Facility and the Common Provisions Regulation, have improved and contributed to the rule of law toolbox; by contrast, the Commission does not consider them rule of law instruments as their main tasks are different (European Court of Auditors, 2024a: 20; European Commission 2024b: 3–4). Despite this, it is worth recalling that, as long as it does not turn into destructive conflicts, a certain degree of dissensus on the rule of law policy is also inherent to any democratic system and is an outcome of complex deliberative processes that feature potentially multiple veto players.

The dissensus also stems from the unclear scope of the EU action on the rule of law problems: for some too narrow; for others too broad. There is most likely a competence issue to be addressed concerning EU values, including the rule of law. Indeed, formally the EU lacks a general competence to address rule of law issues, even more so in purely domestic situations (except for the enforcement of Article 7 TEU), unless the enforcement of EU policies and norms is directly affected. The CJEU has attempted to expand the role of the EU and, hence, its "mandate" on the protection of the rule of law at the national level (Spieker, 2023), in particular since the landmark ruling in *Associação Sindical dos Juízes Portugueses* (C-64/16), in 2018, in response to the largely silent and ineffective role of EU (and domestic) politics. If it is evident that we now have a clear and well-defined notion of the rule of law in the Union (Pech, 2022), also thanks to the numerous CJEU rulings and the codification in EU Regulation 2092/2020 (Article 2), then the reach and scope of the EU action on the rule of law itself are less clear. The CJEU has been accused of failing to elaborate standards consistent with the ECtHR case law on a key dimension of the rule of law, judicial independence (Bárd and Kochenov), and, most importantly, of not applying them in a coherent manner to the Member States and to itself (Kochenov & Butler, 2021). At the same time, although the CJEU has come as far as to acknowledge that the rule of law, under Article 2 TEU, can be a self-standing standard for judicial review at the EU level (cases C-156 and C-157/21), it has not yet clarified if and to what extent a violation of fundamental EU values by a Member State trumps concerns regarding EU competence constraints and whether those fundamental values amount to supreme principles of EU constitutional law.

These considerations acquire new significance in light of the direction the EU is taking in countering rule of law problems by predominantly relying on economic leverage. In particular, conditionality can increase the confrontation on the Union's rule of law policy and is indeed a "trojan horse" for the expansion of EU competences if applied decisively. For example, through self-commitments and self-constraints, conditionality mechanisms can allow the EU to intervene in domestic areas, such as the organization of the judiciary and the civil service, where the EU is not formally the competent authority to act. Once these commitments have been made, the difference between nudging and coercion on the EU side, to use the US Supreme Court terminology, becomes questionable—as also revealed by the experience of the Eurozone crisis—if there are no clear boundaries to ascertain the legality of the EU's intervention (Baraggia & Bonelli, 2022). Further reflections on the wider democratic implications (and backlash) of the EU rule of law conditionality, also concerning accountability, responsiveness, and rate of dissensus, should inform future academic work on the topic. However, for the time being most scholars argue that the Union's institutions could and should have been using spending conditionality, for example through structural funds (Halmai, 2019; Kelemen & Scheppele, 2018), against illiberal regimes for a long time already and with more transparent procedures (Pech et al., 2023), and that their refusal to do so has undermined the EU's credibility.

References

Alemanno, A., & Chamon, M. (2020). To Save the Rule of Law you Must Apparently Break It. *VerfBlog*. https://verfassungsblog.de/to-save-the-rule-of-law-you-must-apparently-break-it/.

Baraggia, A., & Bonelli, M. (2022). Linking Money to Values: The New Rule of Law Conditionality Regulation and its Constitutional Challenges. *German Law Journal, 23*(2), 131–156.

Bárd, P., & Kochenov, D. (2021). War as a Pretext to Wave the Rule of Law Goodbye? The Case for an EU Constitutional Awakening. *European Law Journal, 27*(1–3), 39–49.

European Commission. (2024a, February 29). Poland's Efforts to Restore Rule of Law Pave the Way for Accessing up to €137 Billion in EU Funds (Press Release).

European Commission. (2024b). Replies to the European Court of Auditors' Special Report. Bruxelles.

European Court of Auditors. (2024a). Special Report n. 3/2024 on the Rule of Law in the EU An Improved Framework to Protect the EU's Financial Interests, but Risks Remain. Luxembourg.

European Court of Auditors. (2024b). The Commission's Rule of Law Reporting, Review 02. Luxembourg.

Grabowska-Moroz, B. (2022). The Systemic Implications of the Supranational Legal Order for the Practice of the Rule of Law. *Hague Journal of Rule of Law, 14*(2–3), 331–347.

Halmai, G. (2019). The Possibility and Desirability of Economic Sanction: Rule of Law Conditionality Requirements Against Illiberal EU Member States. *Hague Journal on the Rule of Law, 11*, 171–188.

Hernández, G., & Closa, C. (2024). Turning Assertive? EU Rule of Law Enforcement in the Aftermath of the War in Ukraine. *West European Politics, 47*(4), 967–995.

Kelemen, R. D., & Scheppele, K. L., (2018). How to Stop Funding Autocracy in the EU. *VerfBlog*. https://verfassungsblog.de/how-to-stop-funding-autocracy-in-the-eu/

Kelemen, R. D., & Pavone, T. (2023). Where have the Guardians Gone? Law Enforcement and the Politics of Supranational Forbearance in the European Union. *World Politics, 74*(4), 779–825.

Kochenov, D., & Butler, G. (2021). Independence of the Court of Justice of the European Union: Unchecked Member States Power After the Sharpston Affair. *European Law Journal, 27*(1–3), 262–296.

Pech, P. (2022). The Rule of Law as a Well-Established and Well-Defined Principle of EU Law. *Hague Journal on the Rule of Law, 14*, 107–138.

Pech, L., Wójcik, A., & Wachowiec, P. (2023). The Case for Activating The Rule of Law Conditionality Regulation in Respect of Poland, Study for the Greens/EFA Group, European Parliament.

Priebus, S., & Anders, L. H. (2024). Fundamental Change Beneath the Surface: The Supranationalisation of Rule of Law Protection in the European Union.

Journal of Cutaneous Medicine and Surgery: Incorporating Medical and Surgical Dermatology, 62(1), 224–241.

Scheppele, K. L. (2016). Enforcing the Basic Principles of EU Law through Systemic Infringement Actions. In C. Closa & D. Kochenov (Eds.), *Reinforcing Rule of Law Oversight in the European Union*. Cambridge University Press.

Södersten, A., & Hercock, E. (Eds.). (2023). *The Rule of Law in the EU: Crisis and Solutions*. Report No. 1, SIEPS, Stockholm.

Spieker, L. D. (2023). *EU Values Before the Court of Justice. Foundations: Potential, Risks*. Oxford University Press.

Tuori, K. (2016). From Copenhagen to Venice. In C. Closa & D. Kochenov (Eds.), *Reinforcing Rule of Law Oversight in the European Union*. Cambridge University Press.

von Bogdandy, A. (2012). Reverse Solange—Protecting the Essence of Fundamental Rights Against EU Member States. *Common Market Law Review, 49*(2), 489–520.

von Bogdandy, A., Von Antpöhler, A., & Ioannidis, M. (2017). Protecting EU values: Reverse Solange and the Rule of Law Framework. In A. Jakab & D. Kochenov (Eds.), *The Enforcement of EU Law and Values: Ensuring Member States' Compliance*. Oxford University Press.

Index

C. Fasone et al. (eds.), *EU Rule of Law Procedures at the Test Bench*, Palgrave Studies in European Union Politics, https://doi.org/10.1007/978-3-031-60008-1

SPRINGER NATURE

GPSR Compliance

The European Union's (EU) General Product Safety Regulation (GPSR) is a set of rules that requires consumer products to be safe and our obligations to ensure this.

If you have any concerns about our products, you can contact us on ProductSafety@springernature.com

In case Publisher is established outside the EU, the EU authorized representative is:

Springer Nature Customer Service Center GmbH
Europaplatz 3
69115 Heidelberg, Germany

The manufacturer's authorised representative in the EU is Springer Nature Customer Service Centre GmbH, Europaplatz 3, 69115 Heidelberg, Germany. If you have any concerns regarding our products, please contact ProductSafety@springernature.com

Printed and bound by CPI Group (UK) Ltd, Croydon, CR0 4YY

30/09/2026

02225583-0012